The Branding of America

The Branding of America

From Levi Strauss to Chrysler, from Westinghouse to Gillette, the forgotten fathers of America's best-known brand names

by Ronald Hambleton

A division of Yankee Publishing Incorporated, Dublin, New Hampshire

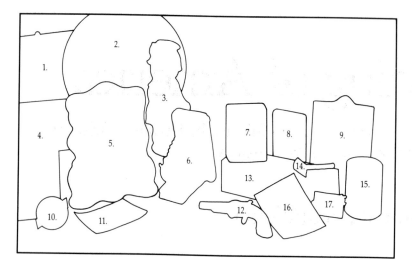

Cover Photo Credits

1. Anna Bissell. Courtesy Bissell, Inc.
2. Pabst Blue Ribbon serving tray. Courtesy Dream World Antiques, Milford, New Hampshire.
3. Campbell's Kid doll. Courtesy The Campbell Soup Company.
4. Remington Noiseless Typewriter. Courtesy Lorna Trowbridge.
5. F. A. Seiberling. Courtesy The Goodyear Tire and Rubber Company.
6. Eastman Kodak camera. Courtesy Dream World Antiques, Milford, New Hampshire.
7. Baker's Chocolate tin. Courtesy Dream World Antiques, Milford, New Hampshire.
8. Prince Albert tobacco can. Courtesy R. J. Reynolds Tobacco Company, Inc.
9. Elisha Graves Otis. Courtesy Otis Elevator Company.
10. Studebaker emblem. Courtesy the collection of Walter Sanborn.
11. Baker's Chocolate label for vanilla extract. Courtesy Dream World Antiques, Milford, New Hampshire.
12. Smith & Wesson pistol. Courtesy the collection of Roy Jinks.
13. Kraft two-pound cheese box. Courtesy Kraft, Inc.
14. Gold razor. Courtesy The Gillette Company.
15. Can of Franco-American Cream Sauce. Courtesy The Campbell Soup Company.
16. King Gillette. Courtesy The Gillette Company.
17. Buick emblem. Courtesy the collection of Walter Sanborn.

Designed by Eugenie Seidenberg
Photo research by Jamie Kageleiry

Yankee Publishing Incorporated
Dublin, New Hampshire 03444
First Edition
Copyright © 1987 by Ronald Hambleton

Library of Congress Catalog Card Number 86-80335
ISBN 0-89909-101-6

Contents

Acknowledgments and a Note on Sources

These brief anecdotal stories about well-known brand names and their beginnings first appeared as part of a weekly series of magazine articles, each one dealing with a company still carrying on business in the world market under the name of the original founder.

The stories have been around for a long time, but the material would have been much harder, and in some cases impossible, to assemble without the pioneering work of researchers and writers, most of them anonymous, of an earlier day. There are some published company histories, a few biographies of founders who have excited public attention, and a wealth of meticulously detailed research on important families like the Fords. A handful of originals, such as carmaker Walter Percy Chrysler, have written their own stories, while a romantic incident in the life of a well-known maker of blue jeans became the central theme of *Die Levi-Strauss-Saga*, a fictionalized history by Irmalotte Masson and Ursula von Wiese published in Germany.

Fortunately for the journalist meeting a weekly deadline, the work of the American inventor and entrepreneur has also been recorded in both popular and specialist journals and in newspapers and preserved in company records. With only a few exceptions, much has been permanently recorded (though many details have been corrected by later research) in the reference books that first began to appear before the turn of the century.

The three great biographical dictionaries — *Appleton's Cyclopedia of American Biography* (1888), the *National Cyclopedia of American Biography* (from 1892) with its supplements, and the continuing *Dictionary of American Biography* (from 1927) — offer a wonderful sweep of American history over the centuries.

There are many well-rounded portraits of inventors and innovators in the three-volume *A History of American Manufactures*, published in 1886, while *Scientific American* began keeping its readers abreast of the latest in industrial innovation from its first issue in 1845.

The *Obituaries Index* of the *New York Times* has been a valuable lead to contemporary appreciations of newsworthy people, and it was often possible, given a death date, to find similar memorials in other newspapers. *Current Biography*, which began its annual publications in 1940, is both newsy and full of circumstantial detail.

Not all companies keep archives, but those that I approached responded promptly and generously to my requests for information about the origins of their companies and the early struggles of their founders. Others helped enormously to confirm or correct factual material while the book was in production.

My indebtedness to all these diligent conservators of American industrial accomplishment both past and present is here gratefully acknowledged.

Special thanks are due to Colin Muncie, who gave continuous encouragement and support as editor of the Canadian trade magazine *Marketing*, where these historical profiles first appeared in a somewhat different format (beginning in February 1981) in the weekly series titled "What Was That Name Again?" and to Andrea Chesman for her meticulous editorial scrutiny of the text.

Introduction

If that product or service you buy is a household name, chances are it was an actual person who thought it up, improved on it, or put it on the market under his own name.

In the beginning, before multinational corporations, before boards of directors and proxy fights, before mergers and franchises and takeovers, there were family businesses founded on individual enterprise or invention.

Before the corporate image or the company logo, there was the individual name stamped on a product, a service, a laborsaving device, or a form of entertainment, usually because it was the proud handiwork of one individual.

Many of these names are still attached to the tools or appliances we use in the workplace. They stare at us in the home and follow us around no matter how we travel.

If your name is on the door, you probably have a Bigelow on the floor. If you lunch on Kraft's and go to bed with Horlick's; if you shave with a Gillette or a Schick; if you drive a Ford, a Buick, or an Oldsmobile; if you run up a quick seam on a Singer or turn out an essay on a Remington portable; if you shoot with a Winchester or an Eastman Kodak; if you eat at a Woolworth lunch counter; if you ride in an Otis elevator or fly high on a Ferris wheel; if you buy your wife a week at the Elizabeth Arden health spa and she gives you a subscription to *Harper's;* if you enjoy a Pabst cooled in your Westinghouse before you curl up in your slacks from Saks; then you know the names even if you never paused for a moment to wonder who all these people are.

Every day these names crop up on billboards, in newspaper ads, in television or radio commercials. We hear them from stand-up comics, in popular songs, in old wives' tales, in everyday conversation. The names are so familiar we tend to pay them only lip service; but we cannot go through a single day without dropping some of them at least once.

Suppose a jump in the Dow Jones lets you sell your Dow Chemical shares at a profit and you splurge on a trip to Florida in somebody's private Pullman car. You pick up a rental Chevrolet and ride out to the beach on Seiberling tires.

Who are all these people? You never met Smith or Wesson, Ferris or Pullman, Chevrolet, or Schick. They are just names, just a few of the faceless but not nameless people who contribute to your comfort, fill in your idle hours, get you from one place to another, and satisfy some of your appetites.

Company formation goes on around us all the time, but today's fashion has moved away from the personal or family name so common in the past. Today, companies are apt to be given descriptive titles, such as Jolly Jumper, Snowmobile, Apple, or Silkience. Some great historic names — Maxim, Ferris, Studebaker, Packard, Collier — have disappeared forever, while others, like McCormick and Mack, have become part of multinational corporations with names like Navistar and International Motors.

In the old days, most new products, whether radical inventions or ingenious developments, had the inventor's name stamped on them from the beginning, simply because he, like as not, was a machinist or a mechanic, or a dabbler in one of the sciences. The cant hook used by lumbermen to control logs in the water is known as a peavey from its inventor Joseph Peavey, though he never formed a company. Nor did Charles Goodyear, the discoverer of the vulcanization process. But his name survives in industry because of Frank Seiberling, another dabbler in rubber, who named his first tire company after Goodyear.

One of the tantalizing company names is Chesebrough-Pond, formed by a merger in 1955, but the name is more a historical monument than a record of a partnership between two living people. Chesebrough, born in 1837, was a child of the scientific age of petroleum, while Pond, interested in natural substances, died years before the first drilled well struck oil in August 1859.

Robert Augustus Chesebrough's monument is the indispensable Vaseline®, which he formulated in 1871, while the famous Pond's Extract of Witch Hazel, Theron Tilden Pond's first and only product, dating from 1841, has not been manufactured for years. Both names, however, live on in the marketing of cosmetics and beauty preparations.

There has also been substitution. No one today buys a Buick bathtub or a Winchester shirt, but the names of the bathtub inventor and the shirtmaker are found on world-famous cars and guns.

The automobile was no one man's invention, but until the efflorescence of image-making names — Thunderbird, Toronado, Maverick, Impala — that began after World War II, almost every car (Locomobile, Silver Ghost, and Fiat are three exceptions) bore the maker's own name on the hood, a practice that has continued right down to De Lorean.

The brand name consumer society was born more than 130 years ago, and this book is an introduction to some of those who assisted at the birth. Invention and scientific discovery went on with ever-quickening momentum between 1800 and 1925, which is the richest period of name-giving, but this is not so much a history as a celebration of those whose names have lived on in their companies. The great family names, most of which have become internationally known, are woven into the fabric of American history, though they are rarely linked with great political or economic events. It may, however, be thought an accurate, if ironic, reflection of American society that three of the oldest brand names still surviving are Baker's chocolate, Du Pont chemicals, and Colgate soap.

There are household names among financiers and tycoons, but Carnegie, Frick, Rockefeller, and Morgan can scarcely be called brand names. Neither can Vanderbilt, one of the oldest of American names, though the name of the founder's descendant, Gloria Vanderbilt, has recently become as marketable as the name of Levi Strauss, the German immigrant who turned a simple pair of pants into a legend.

Levi Strauss, simply because he is a man, is more typical than Gloria Vanderbilt of the magnificent innovators of the past 150 years. The reader will be quick to note that in this survey of brand name founders, there is only one woman, Elizabeth Arden. Like Helena Rubinstein and Gloria Vanderbilt, she is of this century, when women more and more are generating new activity in the consumer market and in industry.

It could scarcely be otherwise. In that earlier society, no one questioned the obvious division of labor into provider and housewife. Yet some companies could not have survived, and some might not even have been established, without women like Mrs. Ellen Augusta Butterick, Mrs. Anna Sutherland Bissell, and Mrs. Anna Rorex Stokely, mother of the five Stokely brothers, pioneers in the canning industry.

If women bore only a supporting role in nineteenth-century America, it was surely the youngsters of America who made the astonishing advances in science and mechanics. There are many important developments credited to and still being marketed under the names of mature men, such as Borden and Otis and Singer, but it is remarkable how many inventors were still in their teens at the time they intuitively grasped the essential of some vexing technical problem.

Many of these youngsters were orphaned or stranded; many were sole support of a widowed mother and other dependent children; some were crowded out of a home because there were too many children to feed; others left home to seek a fortune out west; and not a few were put out to work, usually on a neighbor's farm, as young as nine or ten, and in at least one instance, as young as five.

Yet they seized the moment when they saw it.

No wonder the phrase "it's just like a Horatio Alger story" is so often used to marvel at some poor boy who has become a rich businessman. For Horatio Alger, more than any other writer, dedicated himself to telling stories based on the lives of youngsters he knew personally, who were adrift in New York, and who pulled themselves out of that sordid life by their enterprise.

There were also, of course, a happy number who grew up surrounded by skills of all kinds, which they absorbed as naturally as they breathed, and — what is perhaps just as essential — with access to tools and raw materials and with time to think and dream.

We are the beneficiaries of those inquisitive minds, that luxuriant imagination, and the tireless energy found in such abundance in youngsters of an earlier day and in many of their elders.

In this collection of brief profiles, the message can be seen repeatedly that neither poverty nor the lack of book learning nor, for that matter, the cold shoulder of a self-centered society need be a hindrance to the exercise of a creative intelligence.

The branding of America was not only an economic exercise and an aspect of an industrial revolution, it was also a flowering of native invention.

The legacy can be seen in the profusion of brand name goods and services we pick and choose from every day, of which a surprisingly large number still carry the names of clever people from the past.

Here are a few dozen you might like to meet. ♦

BRANDING THE AMERICAN HOME

BAKER

M any believe that *Bubbles* by Sir John Millais, dated 1886, was the first painting ever selected for advertising purposes when it was used in the 1890s as artwork for Pears Soap.

Yet some fourteen years before *Bubbles* was even painted, Baker's, the American chocolate manufacturer, chose *La Belle Chocolatière* to adorn their packages of breakfast cocoa in 1872, and it was formally adopted as the company's trademark in 1883.

The company was not only the first to marry fine art to merchandising, it could also claim that Baker's is the oldest American brand name still being marketed. It has proved to be as durable as the painting that became their trademark.

La Belle Chocolatière was Anna Baltauf, daughter of an impoverished knight and bride of an Austrian prince who fell in love with her when he met her serving as a waitress in a Viennese chocolate shop. He commissioned the painting in 1745 as his wedding gift to her.

It is a romantic story, but there is a different kind of romance in the story of the Baker's chocolate company and how it passed from one hand to another, from Baker to Pierce to Gallagher, the last being a Canadian-born immigrant to the United States.

But the Baker story really begins in 1765, when an immigrant Irishman named John Hannon converted an old powder mill for chocolate manufacture in Dorchester, Massachusetts, now part of Boston. Dorchester can boast of being the first town in the British Provinces of North America to have a chocolate mill.

Hannon was described in an old history of Milton as "a wayfarer, encountered at the Lower Mills, who seemed to be in distress, and to require the attention and sympathy of those disposed to help the suffering. He was a stranger in a strange land, penniless and friendless, and exhausted by hunger and fatigue."

A company brochure tells how Dr. Baker found him "dangling his legs disconsolately in the Neponset River" and struck up a friendship. With the help of James Boies, who owned a mill on the banks of the Neponset, and who "became convinced of the sincerity and capacity of the man," Dr. Baker persuaded Wentworth and Stone, who were at that time building a new powder mill in nearby Milton, to make provision in their plans for the manufacture of chocolate. That is how John Hannon came to make the first chocolate in the New World.

Dr. James Baker

♦

Baker's Chocolate is the oldest American brand name still being marketed.

♦

"La Belle Chocolatière" was adopted as the company's trademark in 1872.

"La Belle Chocolatière" was still on the package in 1955. Over the years, the company's packaging has changed very little.

Opposite page: *This magazine advertisement for Baker's Chocolate ran in the 1930s.*

The business passed through several hands until in 1771 it was acquired as an investment by the same Dr. James Baker, who put it in the charge of a local resident named Edward Preston and "by his business energy soon gained the advantage over his competitors." Chocolate under the Baker name dates from that time.

According to a *History of Dorchester*, "Mr. Preston could not make chocolate fast enough to meet Mr. [sic] Baker's demands."

Hannon wasn't around for these changes. He stayed for only three years, moved away to Boston, later came back, but finally in 1780 left the country, perhaps to return to his native Ireland.

By 1789, demand for Baker's chocolate brought about expansion into a new mill especially built for chocolate. When sales increased still further, James Baker found it too exhausting to commute between his home and the factory just outside town. In 1791, he fitted up yet another stone mill in Dorchester, and there set up his son Edmund as his partner and manager.

James Baker, the founder of the business, retired in 1804, which makes him an authentic pioneer. It was his son Edmund who brought the business full circle when he acquired the powder mill/chocolate factory in Milton where John Hannon started it all.

Even so, the fact remains that the Baker of the company name does not refer to Dr. James Baker nor to his son Edmund. The business began with James Baker in 1772, but the company had its formal beginning with the founder's grandson, Colonel Walter Baker, probably in 1824. In that year, says the *National Cyclopedia of American Biography*, the business "took the name of Walter Baker & Company."

He had been taken in as a partner by his father in 1818 and took charge six years later when Edmund Baker retired. He became a respected manufacturer with a fine stone building on the banks of the Neponset River.

Earlier he had begun mixing chocolate with cloth. "The war," says the Dorchester history, "had created a great demand for broadcloths and satinets, and to meet this, Walter Baker erected a stone building for the combined purposes of a woolen and chocolate mill." He continued manufacturing "broadcloths and satinets" until peace came in 1815.

Colonel Walter Baker — he was not a chocolate soldier but a real wartime colonel — was such an important Dorchester resident that when the Lyceum Hall was built in 1840, the idea was to name it Baker Hall, but the Colonel himself scuttled that. He died in 1852, and the chocolate Bakers came to an end, but not the company, not by any means.

Cut now to Sackville, New Brunswick, Canada, where at about that time, the Gallaghers were rejoicing over the birth of their first son, Hugh Clifford.

Orphaned while still in his early teens, young Gallagher got work at sixteen as a skilled mechanic in a Boston organ factory. In 1877, he moved up in the world as bookkeeper for Josiah Webb & Company, chocolate manufacturers of Dorchester, a Baker's competitor.

NOW MY MOM'S CHOCOLATE CAKE IS BETTER'N ANYBODY'S, I BET!

THERE'S A STORY BEHIND THOSE WORDS...

BOBBY'S FUNNY! At dinner one night he said: "Gee, Mom— Buster Blair's mother makes swell chocolate cake!" "Better than mine?" I teased. "Well—gee, Mom!" he stammered. "Never mind, son," I laughed, "it's all right to like hers better"

NEVERTHELESS—"I'M JEALOUS!" I told Mrs. Blair. "How do you make such grand-tasting chocolate cakes?" "My dear," she exclaimed, "I'm using Baker's Chocolate now. It's so much richer it makes my cakes taste far more moist and chocolaty!"

"WORTH A TRIAL!" I thought. And believe me, it was! Now my son thinks nobody can beat me making chocolate cake! Indeed, everything I make with Baker's Chocolate is so extra rich and delicious, I just can't imagine ever again using anything else!

CHOCOLATE MINT ROLL
(4 eggs)

6 tablespoons sifted Swans Down Cake Flour
½ teaspoon Calumet Baking Powder*
¼ teaspoon salt
¾ cup sifted sugar
2 squares Baker's Unsweetened Chocolate, melted
4 egg whites, stiffly beaten
4 egg yolks, beaten until thick and lemon-colored
1 teaspoon vanilla

Sift flour once, measure, add baking powder and salt, and sift together three times. Fold sugar gradually into egg whites. Fold in egg yolks and vanilla. Fold in flour gradually. Then beat in chocolate, gently but thoroughly. Turn into 15 x 10-inch pan which has been greased, lined with paper to within ½ inch of edge, and again greased. Bake in hot oven (400° F.) 13 minutes, or until done. Quickly cut off crisp edges of cake and turn out on cloth covered with powdered sugar; remove paper. Spread half of Mint Frosting over cake and roll as for jelly roll. Wrap in cloth and cool about 5 minutes. Cover with remaining frosting. When frosting is set, cover with bittersweet coating, made by melting 2 additional squares Baker's Unsweetened Chocolate with 2 teaspoons butter.

*This recipe has been developed with Calumet Baking Powder. If another baking powder is used, adjust the proportions as recommended by the manufacturers.

MINT FROSTING

Combine 2 egg whites, unbeaten, 1½ cups sugar, 5 tablespoons water, and 1½ teaspoons light corn syrup in top of double boiler, beating with rotary egg beater until thoroughly mixed. Place over rapidly boiling water, beat constantly with rotary egg beater, and cook 7 minutes, or until frosting will stand in peaks. Add green coloring gradually to hot frosting to give a delicate tint. Remove from boiling water; add ¼ teaspoon peppermint extract and beat until thick enough to spread.

(All measurements are level)

Look for the "Baker Chocolate Girl" on the package to get America's finest, *richest* chocolate — the quality famous since 1780. Baker's Chocolate is a product of General Foods.

Copyright, General Foods Corp., 1936

BAKER'S CHOCOLATE
HALF POUND NET WEIGHT
PREMIUM NO. 1 *Unsweetened*

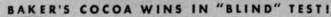

BAKER'S COCOA WINS IN "BLIND" TEST!

IT HAS FINER FLAVOR—MUCH RICHER AND SMOOTHER!

BAKER'S COCOA WAS THE WINNER by a wide margin in a recent blindfold test taken by hundreds of women on cocoa. Fifty per cent more women voted for Baker's because of its "finer flavor," its "richness and smoothness." For generations, women have agreed that Baker's is America's finest cocoa — so much richer than any other.

BAKER'S COCOA

NEW, DIFFERENT CHOCOLATE CAKE AND DESSERT RECIPES!

Free! Chocolate Peppermint Cake! Chocolate Cream Pie! A new kind of Devil's Food! These and eleven other gorgeous cake, pudding, candy and beverage recipes (illustrated in full color) sent free! Just mail this coupon — today! — to GENERAL FOODS, BATTLE CREEK, MICHIGAN.

Your name _____
Street _____
City _____ State _____
(If you live in Canada, address General Foods, Ltd., Cobourg, Ont.) Offer expires Oct. 5, 1936.

Above: *A magazine advertisement, circa 1930, for Baker's Chocolate.*
Right: *Women packing tins of Baker's Chocolate into boxes for shipping.*

With Walter Baker dead, his chocolate business was inherited by his son-in-law Sydney Williams; but in fact, it was managed and later owned by Henry Lillie Pierce, a twenty-seven-year-old relative who had joined the company as a clerk only two years earlier, in 1850. (The company reports that it was Pierce who saw the original painting of *La Belle Chocolatière* while on a trip to Europe in 1862.)

Young Pierce was greatly interested in politics and involved himself in Republican matters for the rest of his life, but he was also a good businessman. Single-handedly, he built Walter Baker & Company into the largest chocolate manufactory in the country and, in 1881, bought out Josiah Webb — lock, stock, and Hugh Clifford Gallagher.

Pierce took a shine to Gallagher, who was twenty years his junior, and brought him along, from bookkeeper to superintendent of the plant, paving the way for him to assume the presidency of the company in 1901, a post he held until his retirement in 1928.

That was the year after the company was acquired by General Foods, three years before Pierce's death at the age of seventy-five, and 148 years after the first of the chocolate Bakers took over what John Hannon had started with the help of a Baker. ◆

COLGATE

A s John Wesley, the great English preacher, put it in a sermon in 1740, "Cleanliness is next to Godliness."
He would have got no argument from William Colgate, who made converts to Baptist Christianity with no less zeal than he made soap for the unwashed millions in his factories, first in New York and then in Jersey City, New Jersey.

Born in Kent, England, in 1783, Colgate was the son of a political refugee. His father, Robert Colgate, one of the most vociferous enthusiasts of the new democracy as it was being practiced in the United States, would have been arrested as a traitor to the British Crown if his friend William Pitt, then prime minister, had not warned him in time. Leaving behind most of their personal possessions, he and his wife and their young son William, then only twelve, fled across the Atlantic to take up homesteading on a farm in Delaware County, New York.

Once past the age of twenty-one, William Colgate left the farm forever to begin work as an ordinary laborer for a tallow chandler at 50 Broadway, New York City. In those days, a chandler was a specialist in candlemaking, using as raw material rendered fat from animals, including dogs and cats. One by-product was yellow, mottled, or curd soap.

Two years later, in 1806, Colgate was out of a job when the tallow chandlery went bankrupt. Without hesitation, he moved into a house on Dutch Street, just off Broadway at the Battery end, lived in one furnished room, and went into business for himself.

At that time, soapmaking was a primitive craft, even though soap had been in use since before the days of Pompeii, where a complete soapmaking plant has been unearthed. In early America, most farms could turn out pot-ash-based utility soap, using a recipe or formula dating back more than a thousand years.

In Colgate's youth, soap was still a mysterious substance. It lathered and cleansed, but not even scientists understood how. As a soapmaker in the early part of the last century, Colgate routinely carried out the obscure traditional chemical processes, turning out soap and tallow candles.

In the meantime, a French chemist named Michel Eugène Chevreul, who lived to the incredible age of 103, was so precocious that at the age of 20 in 1806 (the same year Colgate went into business for himself), he took over the laboratory of the College of Paris. After studying the composition of oils and fats, he separated for the first time the three components of fats: oleine,

William Colgate

He made converts to Baptist Christianity with no less zeal than he made soap for the unwashed millions.

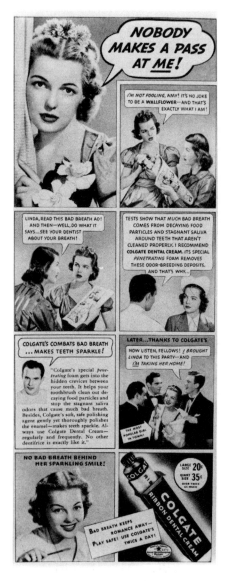

margarine, and stearin. When combined under heat with either soda or pot-
ash, they yield a fatty acid, which combines with an alkali to produce soap,
and the by-product glycerin.

These new developments in an ancient craft reached North America just
in time to awaken the interest of Colgate's son Samuel. By the time the family
of three sons was growing up, they had moved out of the Dutch Street place
into their own house, and Colgate, who wanted his sons to go into the
professions, had money enough coming in to pay for his sons' education at
private schools.

Only the eldest, James Boorman Colgate, actually made it into a profession by founding the Wall Street banking firm of J. B. Colgate & Co. The
second son, Robert, became a manufacturer of white lead, one of the earliest
known pigments, used in paints and putty. Samuel, the youngest, left school
at sixteen on his own initiative to work in the family company beside his
father, who at once changed the firm name to Colgate & Co.

Samuel Colgate was young enough to see the possibilities in Chevreul's
new chemistry. He persuaded his father to buy French perfumes and add
toilet soap to their products. He brought in new vegetable and animal oils;
installed machinery to separate, purify, and deodorize Chevreul's three components; and most revolutionary of all, began using steam as a heat source,
making it possible to control the chemical process scientifically and to cut
down on labor costs.

By 1850, the company was making a hundred different kinds of soap,
from the hardest of laundry soap to the rarest of fancy soap, as well as a
variety of candles using a new candle-molding machine. They also had a
factory that could turn out a thousand soapboxes a day with a newly devised
dovetailing machine. "The department of Fancy Soaps," as noted in *A History
of American Manufactures*, "was added to the business in 1850, and their

Above: *In advertisements circa 1939,
Colgate Dental Cream promised to
fight bad breath and make teeth
sparkle.* Right: *In 1806, Colgate moved
into a house on Dutch Street, just off
Broadway, in New York City, and
began to manufacture soap.*

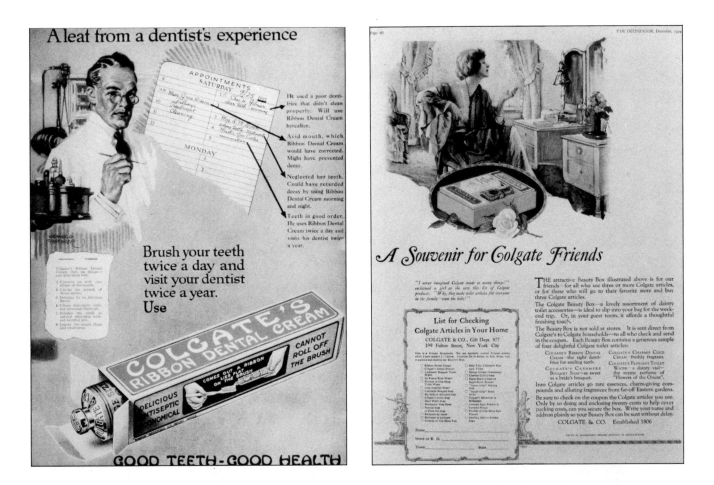

success in this branch has materially diminished the importation of Foreign Soaps."

By the time William Colgate died in 1857, the house on Dutch Street had expanded to a building with four hundred feet of frontage, covering two-thirds of a city block. Under Samuel Colgate's empire-building drive, they had opened another plant in Jersey City.

There was not much godliness in that drive to expand the business, perhaps, but Colgate and all his sons led double lives as leaders in the Baptist congregation.

William Colgate joined the church the year he became a soapmaker and poured money into its missionary organizations and Bible societies. For the last eight years of his life, he was treasurer of the American Bible Union, which he helped to organize.

As early as 1820, he provided some of the start-up funds for a theological seminary in Hamilton, New York, and by the time it became Madison University, nearly three-quarters of the entire establishment had been paid for by the Colgate family, in whose honor the name was changed in 1890 to Colgate University. ◆

Left: *One of Colgate's key marketing pitches: the dental cream cannot roll off the brush.* Right: *This advertisement appeared in* The Delineator, *December 1924. At the time, Colgate was manufacturing many products in addition to toothpaste, including toilet water and perfume, soaps, talcum powder, shaving cream, brilliantine (hair cream), smelling salts, and vanishing cream.*

HARPER

John Harper

James Harper

In the century and a half of our modern brand name society, most cars have been named for the people who made them, and most magazines haven't.

Among periodicals, the names offer a variety almost as wide as the dictionary itself, from *Archery* through *MAD* to *Zoology*. There used to be magazines called *Collier's, Scribner's, McClure's, Munsey's,* and *Lippincott's,* but they have all folded and are as little remembered as their founders.

Peter Fenelon Collier's magazine lasted from 1888 to 1957; Charles Scribner's from 1877 to 1942; Samuel Sidney McClure's from 1893 to 1929; Frank Andrew Munsey's from 1889 to 1929; and Craige Lippincott's from 1868 to 1914. They were all topical magazines of general interest, featuring the best and highest paid writers of the day.

Among today's existing publications, *Barron's,* a business tabloid, dates from 1921, and *Forbes',* a finance journal, dates from 1917. But only *Harper's* has its roots far back in American history.

Harper's New Monthly Magazine was originally planned to start publication in January 1850, but the first issue did not roll off the presses until June of that year, with a run — astonishing for those days — of seventy-five hundred copies. Within six months they were printing fifty thousand and the future looked rosy.

Less than three years later, however, on the morning of December 10, 1853, just as the staff were preparing to run off the January 1854 issue, disaster struck.

In the Camphine Room (camphine is an old term for rectified oil of turpentine), a workman who wanted to douse a lighted taper threw it into a bucket he thought contained water. Instead, it contained highly flammable camphine.

"By nightfall," reported *Publishers Weekly,* looking back on the evening twenty-five years later, "the work of a generation had been laid waste by fire."

It was not just a fledgling magazine that had gone up in smoke, but the entire establishment, which occupied nine interconnected buildings on Cliff Street, New York, of Harper & Brothers, Publishers. The property alone was worth more than a million, but the greatest loss lay in the papers and records, the autographed manuscripts, the engravings, and the hundreds of copies of bound books representing the stock in trade built up over the previous thirty-three years.

In the mid-1850s, they used to ask, "Which is the Mr. Harper, and which are the brothers?" for the brothers included James, John, Wesley, and Fletcher.

The answer was always the same: "Either one is Mr. Harper, and all the rest are the brothers."

Strictly speaking, the Harpers were John and James, the oldest of the six children (two of whom died in infancy) of Joseph and Elizabeth Harper, strongly religious Methodist farmers of Newton, Long Island. James was born in April 1795 and John about twenty months later in January 1797. As each turned sixteen, he was apprenticed to a different New York printer. James became a skilled pressman and John a first-class compositor. By the time they had learned the trade, they had also saved enough money to think of opening up a small printing shop of their own, which they did with the help of a loan from their father.

They were both in their early twenties when in March 1817 they founded J. and J. Harper, Printers, located on the second floor of a frame house at Front and Dover Streets, New York City. For the first three months, they did only job printing; but in July, they brought out an English translation of *Seneca's Morals*, the first book to carry the name of Harper as publishers.

Harper & Brothers published books, calendars, and various magazines in their long history.

"Before you went to bed"
From "The Morning Glow of Childhood Calendar"

"A Debutante"
From "The American Artists' Calendar"

From "Hunting Calendar"

"Waiting for the Second Table"
From "The Tragedies of Childhood Calendar"

HARPER & BROTHERS' ART CALENDARS FOR 1904 *See opposite page*

HARPER'S WEEKLY.
JOURNAL OF CIVILIZATION.
VOL. XXIX.—No. 1495.
NEW YORK, SATURDAY, AUGUST 15, 1885.
TEN CENTS A COPY.
WITH A SUPPLEMENT.

GENERAL GRANT'S FUNERAL—MAJOR-GENERAL HANCOCK AND STAFF AT THE HEAD OF THE PROCESSION.—DRAWN BY T. DE THULSTRUP.—[SEE PAGE 656.]

THE HOUSE OF HARPER

NEW YORK
*One Door West of
Mr. Vanderbilt's Inn*

**Publishers of BOOKS and of
HARPER'S MAGAZINE**

Established 1817

Above: *Joseph Wesley Harper.*
Center: *The Harper imprint.*
Right: *Fletcher Harper.*

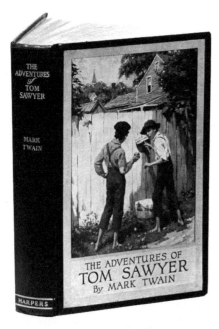

The Adventures of Tom Sawyer *by Mark Twain was originally published by the American Publishing Company in 1876. In November 1895, Harper signed a contract with Samuel Clemens to publish new editions of old works, of which this edition of* Tom Sawyer *was one.*

In the meantime, younger brother Wesley came along and signed on as apprentice in the new family firm as proofreader. When Fletcher, born in 1806, joined them in 1825 to take over the mechanical operations, the four joined together in partnership as Harper & Brothers.

In the twenty-eight years preceding the disastrous fire, the Harpers, according to a newspaper contemporary, "printed an average of twenty-five volumes a minute, ten hours a day" by all the leading authors of the day, as well as the Harper Family Library, the Franklin Square Library, books for young people, and the *New Monthly Magazine;* not to mention ancient classics, topographical maps, biographical dictionaries, cookbooks and domestic economy guides, illuminated Bibles, and a lavishly illustrated Shakespeare.

These were some of the volumes that were almost totally destroyed on that terrible December day. "The brothers were no longer young," wrote *Publishers Weekly,* "and could retire wealthy if they so wished, but John Harper refused to give up."

John Harper was quoted as saying, "We all have sons, and they will soon take our places. We will carry on, and show the boys that we are not old fogies yet."

That evening, they met to plan a new "perfect printing plant," which was to be the first fireproof shop and the first to use modern I-beams of cast iron.

The January issue of the *Monthly* came out on schedule, though every word had to be rewritten. By mid-1854, the Harper brothers were in business again in their new home covering half an acre.

The brothers died within a few years of each other: James in 1869, Wesley in 1870, and John in 1875. Fletcher, the youngest — who in 1867 originated *Harper's Bazar,* as it was then spelled — died in 1877.   ◆

LEVI STRAUSS

You could stock a clothing store with articles named after people — Wellingtons, Bluchers, Derbies, Macintoshes, Stetsons, Cardigans, even Sam Brownes — but if you wanted the world to beat a path to your door, you would have to stock Levi's, the universal garment for men, women, and children of all ages, and from the richest to the poorest. Even if you just called them blue jeans.

And it all started with a single pair of pants carved out of a piece of tent canvas in the days of the California gold rush by an industrious young immigrant named Levi Strauss.

Over the years, the business founded on that pair of pants has generated more wealth than any prospector ever took out of the gold fields, and the story of Levi Strauss has become a part of the folklore of mercantile America.

"Everyone knows his first name," says the company as they recount the legend of the world's first pair of Levi's:

Levi Strauss

> In 1850, Levi Strauss, a 20-year-old Bavarian immigrant to the U.S., boarded a New York sailing ship bound for the California gold rush. He arrived in San Francisco with a small stock of dry goods, including some rough canvas he intended to sell to miners for tents and wagon cover.
>
> Once ashore, he met a prospector who asked Levi what he'd brought with him on the boat. Levi Strauss pointed to his roll of canvas.
>
> "You should have brought pants," said the miner.
>
> "Pants? Why pants?" asked the surprised newcomer.
>
> "Pants don't wear worth a hoot up in the diggins," came the reply. "Can't get a pair strong enough to last."
>
> That's when Levi got his great idea. He took a roll of canvas and had a tailor make it into a pair of pants for his new friend.

Not everybody agrees on the exact date of this historic event, but then Levi Strauss's early years have never been documented in great detail.

According to the long obituary of Levi Strauss published in the *Call* of San Francisco on Sunday, September 28, 1902 — headlined "Levi Strauss, Merchant and Philanthropist, Dies Peacefully at his Home" — Levi Strauss "was born in the Kingdom of Bavaria in 1829, and before he attained his majority came to America to seek the fortune that awaited brains and energy such as he possessed."

Whether a man found gold or not, he still had to buy clothes to wear and a canvas tent to sleep in.

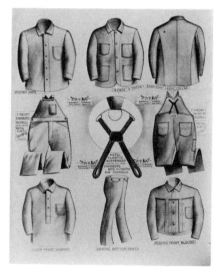

These advertisements for Levi Strauss's garments, including the famous copper-riveted pants and overalls, were directed to retailers.

There has been speculation surrounding his origins, and uncertainty over his birthplace, but in March, 1984, an article in the *Fränkischer Tag* by Dr. Karl H. Mistele of Bamburg confirmed the place as Buttenheim, in Bavaria. Levi's father, Hirsch Strauss, was a dry goods salesman, who had four children by his first wife and two children — Fanny and Levi — by his second wife, Rebecca Haas. When father Hirsch Strauss died of consumption in 1845, his widow petitioned the courts for emigration papers to go to North America. "In 1847," writes Mistele, "the family, together with their 18 years [sic] old son, emigrated to New York."

Levi's step-brothers Jonas and Louis were already established in New York City as Strauss & Brother, dry goods, but Levi soon headed west, and though his travels have not been documented with accuracy, the obituary says that he spent five years in Louisville, Kentucky, "and other parts of the South" before coming "with the swelling tide of gold seekers to California," where "he did not, however, turn his attention to the gold fields, except in an indirect way."

Ed Cray in *Levi's*, the story of the company, says that Strauss "was seventeen [that would be in 1846] when he first set out from Lexington [not Louisville?] Kentucky;" while *The Encyclopedia Judaica* dates Strauss's arrival on American shores at 1848, when he "followed his two brothers [Jonas and Louis] to New York." The company, however, fixes the date firmly at 1847, which would make him a young man of eighteen, well old enough to face the world.

An article in the fall 1952 issue of *American Heritage* adds that "in 1849 he sailed around Cape Horn, arriving in San Francisco early the following year. In order to make a grubstake before heading to the Mother Lode country, he carried with him rolls of fabric, all of which he succeeded in selling to fellow passengers, all that is except a roll of tent canvas."

Ed Cray with a graphic flashback sets Levi Strauss firmly in the picture as an itinerant peddler. "These young [salesmen] didn't appreciate how much better off they were than he had been when he first came to America. They carried no eighty-, no hundred-pound packs. They *schlepped* no rutted tracks to weatherworn farmhouses in mountain hollows, hoping for a twenty-five-cent sale of needles or duck cloth or handkerchiefs. They didn't tramp ten miles in a day to sell three dollars' worth of goods — and there had been days when he counted himself lucky to sell a dollar's worth."

But "once shouldered, the peddler's pack was never forgotten." In his duffel bag Levi Strauss carried samples of canvas and cloths from the storeroom of Strauss Brothers, for he intended to set up as a merchant. San Francisco had been settled for less than twenty years, and it had been ceded to the United States only a few months before gold was found. Within a year, the population of five or six hundred multiplied ten times; and when Levi Strauss got there, he found a turbulent lawless camp of gold-hungry men.

There he made his first pair of pants for one nameless but now famous

Left: *Another advertisement for Levi's directed at retailers.* Right: *Two miners pose in their Levi's at the Last Chance Mine, Placer County, California, 1882.*

prospector, who was so pleased he talked up these "pants of Levi's," and the name stuck.

"With small capital," says the obituary, "but with a clear head, a willing and hopeful heart, he opened up the house of Levi Strauss & Company, dry goods and general merchandise, as the head and principal owner of which he remained until his death — nearly forty-nine years."

"Strauss," writes Art Roth in *American Heritage*, "had more garments made and sent back East to his brothers' clothing firm for all the heavy duck and denim they could possibly secure." When Levi Strauss began specializing in pants, he decided to use a famous twilled cotton cloth called *serge de Nîmes*, shortened to denim, which he had specially shipped in by the bale from France. And they're now called jeans from the cloth named for the city of Genoa.

Not liking the look of it, Levi had the cloth colored with the indigo dye that had been used for centuries, even before the Christian era, for ritual coloring. The early Britons called it woad and dyed their bodies with this same blue. That could have heightened its symbolism for the mystical teenagers of the 1960s. Today it is the standard coloring for a universal garment.

As for the famous rivets, they were the brain child of a widely traveled merchant named Jacob Davis, with whom Levi Strauss formed a business partnership in the 1870s. According to Ed Cray, Davis was born Jacob Youphes

near Riga, Latvia, in 1831, arrived in San Francisco in 1856, and then turned up in Virginia City with other fortune-hunters around the time of the Comstock silver strike.

Whether it was for Alkali Ike, a silver prospector who overburdened his pants pockets with chunks of silver ore, or for a railwayman of Reno, Nevada, who wore out his pockets too fast, it was certainly Davis who improved somebody's pants pockets by hammering rivets into the corners for added strength. That date is given clearly enough by Ed Cray as December 1870.

At the time, Davis was buying yard goods from Levi Strauss & Company, turning out dozens of pants with his patented rivets, and after some correspondence, the two entrepreneurs pooled their resources in a mutually profitable arrangement dated May 20, 1873.

Within two years, a merchant in Wadsworth, Nevada, became the first

All over the West, prospectors (above) and cowboys (right) took to wearing the sturdy rivet-reinforced pants.

merchant to stock Levi's riveted jeans, and a year later, the first of what was to become a long and continuing list of imitations came on the market.

The copper rivets were protected by patents, but Levi Strauss also created their pictorial trademark of two horses trying to pull a pair of pants limb from limb. When *Time Magazine* marked the company's 100th anniversary on February 27, 1950, they recorded an anecdote by Walter A. Haas, husband of one of Levi Strauss's grand-nieces. He became president in 1928, and pushed for expansion. "Now and then," he said, "some waggish farmer actually hitches up two horses and pulls a pair apart. Whenever that happens, I always send the farmer another pair."

Considering the world-wide currency of the name, it is ironic that this *Time* article, published at the end of Levi's first century, appears to be the first national recognition in print of Levi's jeans. By then, the company had turned out 95 million pairs. "When dude ranches became popular in 1930," *Time* wrote, "Haas pushed Levi's for Ladies, but the big time came when they became virtually a campus uniform." In 1953, *Business Week* claimed that "the Eastern yen for western togs has spurred Levi Strauss to open a new plant in Knoxville, Tennessee, the first in the east."

As Art Roth said, "Levi's are worn constantly not only by the Texas cowboy on the range and in the rodeo arena, but by the Vassar co-ed, the big city sandhog, the African safari hunter, the Northwood lumberman, and the weekend gardener."

The *San Francisco Chronicle* had already boasted, "We are unable to think of any influence that radiated outward from San Francisco to be compared with Levi's." The name of Levi Strauss also entered romantic fiction, when in 1978 a pair of German novelists built a sentimental love story, full of longing and despair, into the real events of a life already packed with incident.

Levi Strauss never married, but he was, as the obituary says, "a man of very pronounced domestic tastes." He opened his first shop at the foot of Sacramento Street with his brother-in-law David Stern, described by Cray as "a one-time peddler from St. Louis." Stern had married Levi's sister Fanny, who joined them in 1856 with her children.

Over the years, the company that Levi Strauss founded became a family partnership of brothers and brothers-in-law, but Levi himself remained a bachelor. Ed Cray quotes him saying that on that account, "I need to work more, for my entire life is my business. My happiness lies in my routine work."

In 1890 he incorporated the business, taking into partnership his four nephews — Jacob, Sigmund, Louis, and Abraham — sons of his sister Fanny Stern. And when he died, he left large sums to charities — including Protestant and Catholic as well as Jewish orphanages — but the bulk of his $6 million estate, including the business, went to his nephews. ◆

The famous Levi Strauss & Co. trademark.

An artist's rendering shows women sewing pants at Levi Strauss & Co.'s overall factory. The original caption read "This factory gives employment to over five hundred girls."

SINGER

Isaac Merritt Singer

◆

"You want me to do away with the only thing that keeps women quiet: their sewing!"

◆

It would make quite a bumper sticker: *Singer Despises Women!* But date it the middle of the last century.

What an ironic statement to make about the man whose name practically means sewing machine, the wonderful laborsaving tool not only of the housewife, but also of the millions who worked in the clothing sweatshops before the turn of the century.

Yet Isaac Merritt Singer, as Ruth Brandon makes clear in her "capitalist romance," *Isaac M. Singer and the Sewing Machine,* was a womanizer, a faithless husband, and a bigamist, as well as a bully in business matters, a disloyal friend to those who helped him in difficult days, and a loudmouth with a gift for profanity.

He didn't think much of the sewing machine either, when he was first asked to bring to bear on it his genius as a machinist and an inventor. Indeed, he is quoted as saying to Orson Phelps, the machine shop owner who became — until he was booted out — Singer's partner, "You want me to do away with the only thing that keeps women quiet: their sewing!"

What Singer really wanted to be was a Shakespearean actor. He was a six-foot blond giant and played several seasons in small theater companies in New York State, though he earned his living as a machinist. He even founded his own theater company, the Merritt Players, which lasted several years.

The family name originally was Reisinger. Isaac's father, born in Saxony, settled in Troy, New York, at the age of sixteen, married a Dutch-American woman, and worked as a cooper and millwright. When Isaac, born in 1811, was a child, the family was living in Iroquois country near Oswego. By the time he was ten, his parents were divorced. Two years later, without money, friends, or much education, he was out in the world on his own, living in Rochester, which was then booming because of the new Erie Canal.

The *New York Atlas* in 1853 ran a "Portrait of Isaac Singer," just after his sewing machine began to be popular. The article described his home life, how he went to school in winter and worked in summer, and how he became a master mechanic in four months though the apprenticeship was supposed to last four years. It also recorded how he had restless feet and went discontented from one job to another, and from one grand idea to another.

When he was nineteen, he married a fifteen-year-old girl, but within a year he was promising marriage to another, while his young bride was pregnant with her second child. At thirty, stranded penniless because a company of players he was in failed in a small Ohio town, he got a job carving wooden

type in a print shop, tedious handwork that he thought should be done by machine.

It was just his bad luck that he invented and built a workable prototype for a type-carving machine just when cast-lead type was coming into use.

In the meantime, Elias Howe had invented the sewing machine, which could do everything except sew a continuous seam and sew round corners. Orson Phelps was trying to adapt Howe's machine in the front room of his machine shop while Singer was working on his type-carving machine in the back.

Phelps tried to pick Singer's brain, and that is when Singer made his crack about keeping women quiet; but he did become interested. Within days Singer devised the two features that distinguished his machine from Howe's: a presser foot to keep the cloth flat on the sewing table and a cam to vary the direction of the sewing. He also mocked up a packing case that could double as a trestle base.

Typically, Singer wanted to share the patent (dated August 12, 1851) with nobody, so he secretly carted the invention from Boston (where he had been employed in a machine shop) to New York, where Smith & Conant's Clothing Store bought the first two Singers ever made, at $125 each.

The story of Singer's legal shenanigans to drive out Orson Phelps and George Zieber, another man who worked with him, would fill a book, and in fact has filled several books.

Singer diverted money to his own use, then pleaded lack of cash flow to his partners. He even tried to coerce Zieber to sell out while the man was feverishly ill and delirious in bed.

He was sued in 1853 for infringement of Howe's patent, threatened to kick Howe downstairs, and launched himself into the Sewing Machine War, as the papers called it, which he lost after three years. He had to pay Howe forty-five thousand dollars in damages.

The publicity helped Singer's product, however, as did his own barn-

These advertisements for the Singer Sewing Machine, dated 1900, show the sewing machine neatly stored in a cabinet-table. By this device, "the machine is thoroughly protected from dust, and the stand forms an ornamental and useful table that is fitting and appropriate to any home."

Between the
Dress Material
And the
Finished Dress

the woman who owns a Singer
Sewing Machine often saves half
on the cost of her gowns.

SINGER
Sewing Machines

enable many thousands of
women to dress stylishly and
comfortably on a limited allow-
ance. These machines do every
possible kind of sewing so easily,
so perfectly and economically,
that they put the most elaborate
and otherwise costly dresses
within the reach of every woman.

By This   Will Find
Sign   Singer
You May   Stores
Know And   Everywhere

A late 1800s advertisement from The
Delineator, *for Singer Sewing
Machines.* The Delineator *was
published by Butterick, publisher of
clothing patterns.*

storming around the country, drawing on his theatrical experience to give free
demonstrations at fairs and carnivals. He even sang "The Song of the Shirt," a
popular tear-jerker of the day.

Sales grew from the original 2 in 1850 to about 130,000 in only twenty
years.

In 1863 Singer, still holding 40 percent of the common stock, moved to
Paris. "But the Communists," to quote his obituary in *The New York Times*,
"made it unpleasant for him." So he went from there to England, where he
built a crazily extravagant house in Torquay, "a well-known watering place in
Devon, England." ◆

BORDEN

I f it's Borden's, it's got to be milk. But if it is Gail Borden, it's got to be incredible.

The best way to tell this story is to start with his most famous invention, condensed milk, which made Gail Borden's name a household word throughout the world. On August 19, 1856, he was granted U.S. Patent No. 15,553 for a device for the "concentration of sweet milk and extracts."

Borden was not the first man to try, as he put it, "to keep milk sweet for a very long time." Attempts go back to the beginning of the nineteenth century, and there are even legends of a milk paste being produced in fourteenth-century Russia. Powdered milk was patented in 1855, when Borden had already been trying for ten years to get his condensed milk process approved.

His idea was first written up in *Scientific American* on July 2, 1853, but his patent was held up for more than three years because the authorities would not believe that the process could work. And anyway, they said he had stolen other men's ideas.

Gail Borden

Borden's unique contribution to the search for condensed milk lay in his use of a vacuum. In the Borden method, the entire evaporation process takes place with air excluded "to prevent incipient decomposition of the milk and render it preservative and soluble."

The inventor, born in 1801, was then in his fifties, but he looked seventy, as Joe Frantz writes in one of several vivid word-portraits in his 1951 biography *Gail Borden, Dietitian to a Nation*. "Sunken temples, greyhound nose, thin, underfed body, terribly stooped. The trenchant eye of a kindly fanatic. Arms like willow switches and hands that waved like Texas windmills during a blue norther."

Borden's destiny was to nourish the world, but he himself looked ready to drop from starvation. He was so poor that in trying to finance his invention, he used to call on businessmen or merchants ("wearing patched clothes that did not fit," says Frantz) without notice or introduction to beg for money. It seems ridiculous, when his total estimate of start-up costs was only six hundred dollars, but all he got was the cold shoulder.

At last, he got backing from Jeremiah Millbank, described in *Harper's Weekly* as a "farseeing, conservative, enterprising financier," who helped him to launch his new business in 1858.

Borden's condensed milk was described as "the only milk ever concentrated without the admixture of sugar or some other substance . . . . It is simply Fresh Country Milk, from which the water is nearly all evaporated, and

---

The misery of hungry children prompted him to invent a process to keep milk sweet.

"Men are still a great big puzzle to me!"
SIGHED ELSIE, THE BORDEN COW

"**W**HAT IN thunderation is so puzzling?" hedged Elmer, the bull, guiltily. "Just ask the old master anything you want to know, woman. I have *all* the answers."

"I don't doubt it," said Elsie tartly. "What puzzles me is how anyone, *even you*, would want to eat a meal of cake alone. It's baffling, that's what it is!"

"It is *NOT!*" contradicted Elmer. "It's the doggondest best cake you ever baked. This frosting's sure on the beam. I'll bet you make it with velvety-smooth *Borden's Eagle Brand Condensed Milk!*"

"Don't try that blarney on me," laughed Elsie. "Everybody knows frostings made with Eagle Brand *are* gloriously smooth and creamy. *BUT* cake alone doesn't make

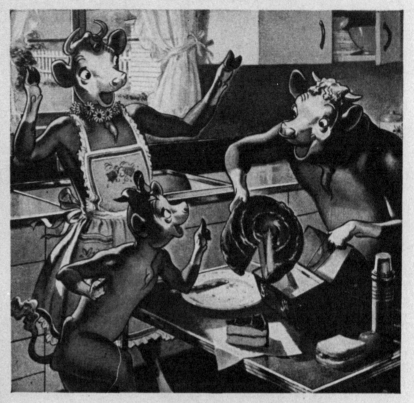

a balanced meal."

"I don't *want* to balance my meals," complained Elmer. "I want to *eat* 'em!"

"Who *wouldn't* want to eat all those grand desserts Eagle Brand makes?" asked Elsie. "And without a grain of extra sugar, either! But you can't keep healthy if you don't eat a variety of foods, such as Borden's—"

"I knew it!" roared Elmer. "You'd ruin my fun just to get buzzing on Borden's!"

"Not at all, dear," answered Elsie. "I mention Borden's only because they bring folks so *many* wonderful foods. Milk, for example. Children should have a quart of the precious stuff every day, grownups a pint. *Borden's Homogenized Milk* is milk in its most delicious form. So—"

"So I'll take cake," said Elmer. "Cake with Eagle Brand frosting."

"A very fine food—in its place," smiled Elsie. "And awfully good with rich Borden's Homogenized Milk. There's cream and Vitamin D in every sip."

"Roll out the milk bottle, Beulah!" roared Elmer. "Your mother's campaigning for Borden's again!"

"*Again?*" laughed Elsie. "Why I'll *always* go on telling folks about the wholesome

nourishment in Borden's delicious foods. *I'm* proud of Borden's big family of fine foods!"

"Boy, is *that* news!" guffawed Elmer. "*Next* you'll be telling me how good *every* doggoned product is!"

"But, of course, dear," giggled Elsie, "each and every one *is* good—*if it's Borden's, it's GOT to be good!*"

—if it's Borden's, it's got to be good!

nothing added."

In the years it took to make dairymen, merchants, and consumers trust this new "long-life" milk, competitors sprang up all around, one who marketed a product under the name of Borden, forcing the original maker to coin the name Eagle Brand, which became just as famous as the name Borden itself.

Borden showed the world how to condense milk but left no clues about how to condense the story of his amazing life.

The January 14, 1875, issue of the *New York Tribune* ran nearly two-thirds of a column on "the checkered and interesting career" of the late Gail Borden in a day when obituaries tended to be twenty-five words or less. The Frantz biography fills more than two hundred pages before he even gets to condensed milk.

Gail Borden was the eldest of seven children, the son and namesake of a sixth-generation American farmer who had bought a 250-acre farm near Norwich, New York, just two months before Gail's birth in November 1801. Gail Junior grew up on the farm, picking up many practical skills, including surveying.

When he was thirteen, the family moved to Kentucky, then on to the territory of Indiana, where Gail got eighteen months of schooling, which was all the formal education he ever had. But he also farmed, surveyed, joined the local volunteer militia, and became an expert shot. At that, he was more learned than most in the territory, so in his late teens he taught school for nearly two years. In 1822, suffering from a persistent dry cough, he struck out on his own for Mississippi, where again he taught school part-time, while working as county surveyor in Amite County.

Just after Borden turned twenty-eight, newly married and with a child on the way, he made the great decision to follow his brother Tom, one of the original settlers of the state of Texas. He took up land and went into farming and surveying. With an associate, he started a newspaper, the *Telegraph and Texas Register*.

This was in the troubled year just before the fall of the Alamo, the wooden building known as "the cradle of Texas liberty," and the Texans' victory over the Mexicans later that year at San Jacinto.

Gail Borden took an active political part in all those events. After the Republic of Texas was established, he moved with his family to the future site of Galveston on the Gulf of Mexico, where he was appointed collector by Sam Houston, president of the Texas Republic.

As agent for the Galveston City Company, property developers — a post he held for the next twelve years — Borden proceeded to survey and lay out the city, which at that time did not exist even on paper. He also drew the first topographical map of Texas. Borden was not just a real estate salesman, though he did turn over several hundred city lots to new immigrants at a value of nearly $1.5 million, on which he drew a salesman's commission.

He also had an active, inquiring, and inventive mind. At a time when

A Borden's Condensed Milk can, circa 1863, found at a Civil War battle site.

Opposite page: *An advertisement for Borden's from the 1940s shows the range of products Borden's manufactured.*

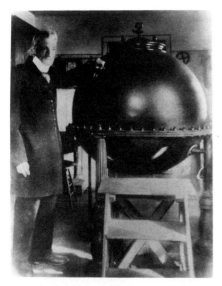

The vacuum pan made it possible for Gail Borden to condense his milk. Beside the pan is Alonzo Holister, who was present when Borden made his first successful experiment with it.

Borden's invention of the meat biscuit won him a gold medal at the Great Exhibition in London in 1851.

fresh water was scarce (his paper reported that the rats in Houston played it safe by drinking gin), he discovered a fount of fresh water for Galveston. He invented a portable bathhouse to permit female swimmers to change in privacy. He made his wife a dining table with a revolving center so that dishes could be passed more easily. He invented a new vehicle and called it "terraqueus" because it could travel on both land and water, which it did the only time it was tested. He sketched out a steamboat to be driven by mechanical oars, which never saw the light of day. He devised a plan to convert Catholics to Protestants, which went nowhere. And he invented the meat biscuit.

This "useful preparation of concentrated extract of beef, baked in flour" could be looked on as a dress rehearsal for Borden's condensed milk. It arose out of his concern for the people who flocked into western Texas and had to endure the agonies of illness brought on by putrid food.

Borden set out to formulate a concentrated nonperishable food. Pemmican, or dried pulverized meat mixed with fat and berries, had been used by the Northwest Indians for generations, and some white explorers also used it. But Borden's idea, though he was not a scientist, was based on the science of nutrition. He filtered the broth of boiled meat, evaporated it to a fluid consistency, mixed it with flour, kneaded it, and baked it. The result was a hard, portable biscuit that could be reconstituted with the addition of water to be used as a filler in pot roasts. Or made into puddings or custard. Or added to fruit pies. And when not in use, it was kept in a closed container.

That was about 1850. Borden was so elated with his meat biscuit, especially when the U.S. Army expressed an interest in it and when people started lining up to buy a license to manufacture it, that he entered it in the Great Exhibition of London in 1851 and walked off with a gold medal, one of only five awarded to U.S. entries.

But Borden's meat biscuit never survived. Ingenious and novel it may have been, but people just did not like the taste. Borden dropped it like a hot potato, losing thousands of dollars. But as he said, "I never drop an idea except for a better one."

The better idea was condensed milk. They say that on his way back from London, he was so distressed by the misery of the immigrants in steerage, especially the children, that he first thought of the idea of "milk that would stay sweet." The result was a name that has stayed fresh for more than 130 years.

Borden's other monument, by the way, is a county in Texas named Borden, where the county seat is named Gail. ◆

STEINWAY

I f Heinrich Engelhard Steinweg had ever written his life story, he could have made it read like a historical novel, with hairbreadth escapes, bloody revolution in turbulent Europe, family tragedy, and finally exile when he was past fifty.

How different from the serene, even conventional life of Henry Steinway, who handed on to his children and grandchildren when he died in New York at the age of seventy-four a growing business and a renowned product.

Yet it is all one life, broken into its two contrasting parts. Steinweg in Europe, Steinway in America, he was head of the family that created the modern American concert piano.

From the company's point of view, their history begins in 1853, when Steinway & Sons was established, though the family name was not legally changed from Steinweg until 1864.

The father, his four sons, and three daughters — one son, Theodore, remained in Europe — began piano making in New York in a building not far from the present Holland Tunnel. Within a year they had to move to larger premises —three houses knocked together on Walker Street — then they pressed on with patent after patent, refining, developing, and experimenting with both mechanical innovation and marketing.

Expansion into still larger premises began in 1860, when Steinway built a plant at Park Avenue and 42nd Street, with 150,000 square feet of space. In 1866 they opened Steinway Hall, which stimulated artistic and cultural activities. Four years later, they bought a property in Astoria to make iron frames and cut piano legs from timber. In 1910 came the move to Long Island, where the family literally put the name Steinway on the map, just west of La Guardia airport, on their four-hundred acre tract of land.

The Steinway revolution was a radical new way of stringing the piano.

But that is a long remove from Heinrich Steinweg's first half century of life.

Born in Germany in 1797, when Napoleon was beginning to chalk up one brilliant victory after another, young Steinweg was orphaned before he was fifteen. His mother died when she and her children fled into a mountain refuge from Napoleon's armies driving into Germany. Then, some years later, while he and his father and some others were hiding in a hut, a bolt of lightning struck, killing everyone inside except Heinrich Steinweg.

There is a story, which may be true, that at eighteen Steinweg was a bugler at Waterloo; but when peace came, since he was more mechanically inclined than musical, he established himself as a cabinet builder and instru-

Above: *A 1905 advertisement for Steinway pianos.* Bottom right: *The Steinway factory.*

Opposite page: *With paintings and even operas commissioned expressly for Steinway pianos, Steinway promotions appealed to buyers' aesthetic longings as well as to their pocketbooks.*

ment maker in the Harz Mountains of Germany, renowned for the singing birds and as the source of many German legends.

One legend says that Steinweg made his first piano in 1836 as a gift to his young wife, who was in time to present him with five sons and three daughters. But the first instrument in the long line of Steinways must have been the instrument jointly built by Heinrich and his son Theodore, then fifteen, in 1839. It was exhibited at a fair in Brunswick and awarded a gold medal.

Another legend, preserved by American writer Elbert Hubbard, once hired to write the company's story, says that the father immediately placed the medal around Theodore's neck, who was so embarrassed that he burst into tears in front of the illustrious guests.

This award-winning instrument, bought for one thousand talers for a noble family, brought the name Steinweg to public notice for the first time, even though that public was more local than national.

The family business might well have gone its quiet way in Seesen for a generation if post-Napoleonic problems had not begun to affect politics in every part of Europe. Theodore's brother Charles, involved in the political movements of 1848, emigrated to the United States the following year, got work as a cabinetmaker, and began a correspondence to persuade the other family members to join him, which they did in 1851.

Only Theodore Steinweg stayed behind, to run his own piano-making business. The others made the long sea crossing, moved into a New York tenement, and after a period of work in separate jobs, finally joined forces on that historic day in 1853.

It must have seemed like the end of a fifty-six-year journey for Heinrich Steinweg, but in fact, it was merely the beginning of another lifework, which was to involve neither more nor less than a revolution in the piano through a

STEINWAY
THE INSTRUMENT OF THE IMMORTALS

THE KING'S HENCHMAN, *painted for the* STEINWAY COLLECTION *by* N. C. WYETH

The première of "The King's Henchman"—an opera composed by Deems Taylor to the libretto by Edna St. Vincent Millay—took place at the Metropolitan Opera House in New York on February 17, 1927. Its reception was enthusiastic. It is the first successful work in this field by an American composer and librettist.

THE reasons for owning a good piano are so varied and conclusive that no thinking person can afford to disregard them. For its influence in moulding musical traditions . . . for its undoubted decorative effect . . . for the joy of personal creation which it gives . . . cultivated people everywhere regard it as indispensable.

That such people should choose the Steinway is both natural and inevitable. Their taste will not tolerate anything short of the best. Their homes are graced and brightened by its presence. And their ear delights in that marvelous, singing tone which has won the praise of virtually every musician of note, from Franz Liszt to Deems Taylor.

Yet for all its unquestioned superiority, the Steinway is among *the least expensive of pianos.* The durability which is built into it—carefully, step by step—extends the limits of its service over 30, 40 and even 50 years or more. And no

matter which size you select, it will yield that rich return of pride and pleasure which only a Steinway can give—to you, and your children, and your children's children. You need never buy another piano.

There is a Steinway dealer in your community, or near you, through whom you may purchase a new Steinway piano with a small cash deposit, and the balance will be extended over a period of two years. Used pianos accepted in partial exchange.

Prices: $875 *and up*
Plus transportation
Steinway & Sons, Steinway Hall
109 West 57th Street, New York

radical new way of stringing and new uses of metal in the frames.

When Henry Steinway died in 1871, his obituary in the *New York Daily Tribune* recorded that his success in the manufacture of pianos "may be dated from the year 1855, when they exhibited at the New York Industrial Exhibition of the American Institute, held in the Crystal Palace, a piano that was constructed after a new system, and was awarded a gold medal."

Described in the company history as "brilliant, irascible, and meticulous," Theodore Steinweg, distant in Germany, took part in these changes by letter. He was a brilliant engineer, chemist, and experimenter in sound physics who brought science to bear on the old craft of piano making. Later, when two of the Steinway brothers — Charles and Henry, Jr. — died in the same year, 1865, Theodore moved to New York for five years to make a new working partnership with his brother William — the father being less active in the business — and on that partnership the twentieth-century reputation of the Steinway piano has been built.

All the Steinways shared Theodore's personal motto:

Who knows his trade is a journeyman;
A master is he that invents the plan;
An apprentice is each and every man.

♦

BUTTERICK

arly in 1860, the Italian patriot Giuseppe Garibaldi led his army of a thousand Red Shirts to victory in Sicily and Naples against the political enemies of King Victor Emmanuel II.

So what has that to do with the price of women's dresses? More than you would think.

First backtrack ten years or so to the year 1850, to the town of Sterling, Massachusetts, where Ellen Augusta Pollard has just been joined in matrimony to a young tailor and shirtmaker named Ebenezer Butterick.

Her young man, recently turned twenty-four, was the son of a local farmer and carpenter who had founded an intellectual discussion group known as the Universalist Society.

Ebenezer had begun earning his own livelihood as a clerk in his brother's general store before working through an apprenticeship with a tailor in nearby Worcester to become a specialist cutter in men's clothing. At the time of his wedding, he owned a business in Fitchburg, a few miles north of Sterling.

His wife, like most women married to small businessmen, helped in the shop, especially in small neat work on children's clothing. It was all handwork, since Isaac Singer's magical new sewing machine was not produced in quantity until the mid-1850s.

In Ebenezer Butterick's own field of men's tailoring, he found it boring and time-consuming to cut almost identical patterns for custom-made shirts, going through the same motions time and again. Almost from the day he set himself up in business, he looked for some way to standardize pattern-cutting.

The original idea to use standard-sized patterns may well have been his wife's, since the first experiments in sized patterns — a form of mass production beginning in 1863 — were made in children's dresses. Once the method was seen to work, it was easily adapted to men's shirts.

Instead of drawing each individual pattern directly on the cloth with wax chalk, a standard pattern was cut out of stiff paper, which could then be used as a template for one garment after another. It seems so obvious today, but consider the times.

Learned essays have been written on what is called "the democratization of fashion" to show how the clothes we wear reflect deep political currents. In *The Journal of American History*, Margaret Walsh points out that in Ebenezer Butterick's day, only the wealthy wore specially designed clothes. Although there were dress designs on the market, mostly copied from the latest Euro-

Ebenezer Butterick

The mothers of America lined up the moment the Garibaldi suit pattern hit the market.

BUTTERICK'S PATTERNS FOR BOYS.

In this 1867 brochure, patterns #60 and #155 are two versions of the famous Garibaldi jacket.

From The Delineator, *an illustration of Ebenezer Butterick and his wife at home.*

pean styles and offered for sale in exclusive shops such as Madame Demorest's emporium in New York or published in magazines such as *Godey's* or *Peterson's,* they were meant for professional dressmakers. And they were not patterns but designs, which still had to be interpreted by the individual seamstress. Most women made their own clothes by a sort of recycling process: picking apart one worn-out dress to use as a pattern for a new one. The Buttericks changed all that by packaging fashion in a way that made it available to any woman, though it was not an instantaneous revolution. "Madame Demorest," Walsh writes, "plays the role of the autocrat, while Butterick is cast as the manufacturer of democratic fashion."

For years, the Buttericks used their stiff paper patterns for their own tailoring, sharing the idea with a few agents in western Massachusetts. Even by 1868, after they had switched to tissue paper and begun marketing patterns complete with printed instructions, the patterns were not bestsellers.

The trigger, oddly enough, is directly traceable to the political turmoil in faraway Italy. Overnight, by his individual heroism, Garibaldi became a popular idol to American youth, and his uniform, the "Garibaldi suit," became almost the T-shirt and jeans of the 1860s. Every kid on the block wanted one.

Butterick met this demand by creating a paper pattern of the Garibaldi suit and launching it on a market ready and waiting for it.

By 1863, Butterick had already made the decision to leave tailoring for pattern making, but it was his marketing of the Garibaldi suit pattern (price fifty cents) that brought his name into every household. The mothers of America, nagged by their youngsters, lined up by the thousands the moment the Garibaldi suit pattern hit the market. The date, oddly enough, is very exact: June 16, 1863.

The first patterns were cut and folded by members of the Butterick family, but within a short while, extra rooms were taken in an adjoining house, and five women were employed full-time. Soon, Butterick had to move to a larger building in Fitchburg, where he launched his first "fashion plate" of the latest in children's garments. Within a year, he had opened a shop at 192 Broadway in New York City, specializing almost entirely in patterns for boys' and men's clothing for the first three years.

It was not until 1866 that he packaged his first women's dress patterns. Within months his range expanded to include not only dresses, but sacks and capes in thirteen different sizes, as well as skirts in five sizes, all pictured in the first Butterick quarterly magazine, published in 1868.

Butterick and his wife were real workers. They put in such long hours that Butterick brought to New York his own invention, a bedstead designed to be folded up against a wall. Could this have been the first "Murphy bed"?

With the publication of his first quarterly magazine, however, Butterick began slowing down. He had gone into partnership in 1867 with Jonas Warren Wilder, also born in Sterling, who had sold his sawmill in 1864 to help his friend Ebenezer develop the Butterick patterns. By 1881, Butterick, a widower

Beginning—TWO SPLENDID SERIALS—In This Number

THE DELINEATOR

October 1918

THE BUTTERICK PUBLISHING COMPANY, NEW YORK

In 1882, the Butterick Publishing Company moved to larger quarters at 555 Broadway in New York (below). By then the company had launched into a period of wide-ranging publishing activity, mostly within the field of home economics. In addition to The Delineator *(left), a general-interest ladies' magazine, there were books and pamphlets on such topics as amateur photography, pet care, nursing, party games, masquerade costumes, pastimes for children, and education.*

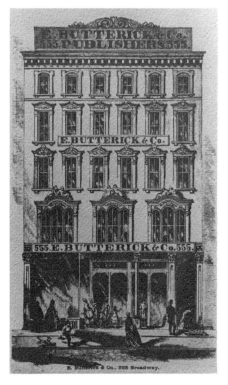

for ten years, virtually retired, keeping a one-third interest, while Wilder and the company secretary, Abner Pollard, took control.

They established the Butterick Publishing Company, started the *Metropolitan Magazine*, which was restyled as *The Delineator* in 1874, and between them pushed sales to nearly 50 million patterns a year by the time Ebenezer Butterick died in 1903 at the age of seventy-six. *The New York Times* memorialized him as "the originator of the tissue paper dress pattern."

In 1961, Butterick entered into a licensing agreement with Condé-Nast Publications, by which Butterick took over the production of Vogue patterns.

And Garibaldi? He had been dead for twenty years by the turn of the century, and American boys found a new hero. They all wanted to be Rough Riders and dress just like Teddy Roosevelt. ◆

CAMPBELL

Joseph Campbell

Campbell's Condensed Soups, "a marvel of excellence and cheapness."

Would you believe a tomato so big it took two strong men to carry it, slung from a thick pole supported on their shoulders?

Yet there it was, pictured on the label of a bottle containing the famous Beefsteak Tomato Ketchup made by the Joseph Campbell Preserve Company of Camden, New Jersey. The two men seem tiny compared with the monster fruit.

The truth, of course, is that the "Celebrated Beefsteak Tomato" grew only in the rich imagination of some early marketing manager back in the mid-1860s — probably Abraham Anderson, owner and proprietor of the Anderson Preserving Company, the seed from which grew the Campbell Soup Company of today.

Anderson himself is not pictured, but on an early label of Anderson's Concentrated Soups ("Each can makes 6 plates"), the trademark shows a plump and smiling friar holding a can of soup over a bowl. He is obviously just about to add water and stir.

Abraham Anderson was not only a soupmaker (seventeen varieties), he also packed poultry and vegetables, including the New Jersey sweet potato and the "Celebrated Beefsteak Tomato," which was described in the advertising copy as being so large "that only one can be packed in the can."

About this time — the early 1860s — a well-established purchasing agent for a wholesale fruit and vegetable concern was seriously thinking of buying into the canning business, which was extremely active, as Mary B. Sim shows in her *History of Canning in New Jersey*. His name was Joseph Campbell, and he had grown up surrounded by fruits and vegetables.

When Joseph Campbell was born in the spring of 1817, his father was a successful fruit farmer just outside Bridgeton, in the southern part of New Jersey. The town developed canneries and over the years became the shipping center for that large agricultural region.

Joseph Campbell grew up on the family farm, but when he became a young adult, he moved to Philadelphia, where for about the next twenty-five years he worked at various jobs in the fruit and vegetable industry, coming into contact with pioneers of the American canning industry, many of whom were located in New Jersey.

Campbell must have had good business dealings with Abraham Anderson, one of the earliest canners, with his line in jams, jellies, apple butter, mincemeat, soups, tomatoes, and poultry; but there is no record of the negotiations that made them partners early in 1869.

The Campbell Soup Company dates its company history from that year, and with complete justification, for there is evidence that Joseph Campbell soon became the dominant influence in the Anderson and Campbell partnership. He kept his home in Philadelphia for a while, commuting to the business in Camden.

Among their strongest lines were the Celebrated Beefsteak Tomato (the ketchup by-product came later), as well as Anderson's Mincemeat (more than twenty-five ingredients). The firm also claimed to be the first in the United States to pack "strictly fancy small peas."

Unfortunately, the temperaments of these two men did not blend as smoothly as their mincemeat. By the time their preserves had won a medal at the Centennial Exposition of 1876 in Philadelphia — the medal was immediately printed on Campbell Soup labels — Anderson was showing some uneasiness about Campbell's ideas for the future.

Anderson's age in 1876 is not known, but Campbell, age fifty-nine, had a young man's outlook. Anderson was content to let the business grow slowly like a garden, while Campbell had the idea that the business could be forced into faster growth.

Anderson could not agree, so according to one of his grandsons, he "proposed that Mr. Campbell make the choice as to whether he wished to buy or sell." Mr. Anderson assumed that since Campbell had bought into the partnership in the first place, he would be the one to sell out. He assumed wrong.

"To my grandfather's surprise," records Frank B. Anderson, "Mr. Campbell elected to buy."

On August 12, 1876, perhaps even to Mr. Campbell's surprise, he found himself the sole owner of a canning and preserving factory in the block between Second and Union Streets in Camden. With it came the stock, machinery, and equipment, plus all the recipes.

"My grandfather," said Frank B. Anderson, "found himself in an excellent cash position, but with no buildings and no business." In fact, Abraham Anderson started all over again in an old carriage factory, which he converted to his own use.

Meanwhile, the Joseph Campbell Preserve Company, just as Campbell had planned, started its expansion into new buildings with better equipment and got up such a head of steam that he took his son-in-law, Walter Spackman, into the business in 1880. Two years later, Spackman brought him together with a wealthy businessman of Bristol, Pennsylvania, named Arthur Dorrance, who was looking for a profitable investment.

There is nothing like money to make dreams come true. Within months, says George R. Prowell's 1886 *History of Camden County*, Campbell had "a new manufactory with new and improved appliances for conducting a more extensive business, in a large brick building on Second Street and extending the entire depth to Front Street."

In 1914, some seventeen years after the introduction of Campbell's Tomato Soup, Campbell's published a small booklet describing just how the tomato soup is made, beginning with tomato breeding experiments in greenhouses and laboratories, continuing in the field, where only red-ripe tomatoes are harvested, and concluding at the Campbell Plant, where French chefs supervise the blending of the eighteen ingredients that go into the soup. It also included handy recipes for using the soup — in such concoctions as spaghetti with bacon, a sauce for fish, a salad dressing, and Welsh rarebit.

Above left: *Sealed cans of Campbell's soups are lowered into sterilizing units and processed at temperatures of at least 245 degrees.* Above right: *The labeling machine was capable of labeling 17,500 cans of soups in one hour.* Below: *One of the famous Campbell Soup Kids, taken from a 1945 advertisement. The Campbell Soup Kids were first drawn in 1904 by Grace Weiderseim Drayton and were used to promote Campbell's soups, especially on advertisements posted in trolley cars in New York City.*

The new Campbell letterhead listed "preserved fruits, jellies, fruit butters, mincemeat, ketchup and canned goods."

What, no soup? It was certainly not mentioned by name. As for marketing ideas, they went after nostalgia, with labels specially printed to imitate the pen and ink labels of homemade preserves.

But by 1899, nostalgia was out and merchandising was in. In the February 15 issue of *American Grocer*, there is a display ad for Campbell's Condensed Soups, "a marvel of excellence and cheapness." Gone were the housewife's imitation labels, replaced by the now familiar red and white labels of Campbell's Soups.

This was probably the work of Arthur Dorrance, who lit a fire under aging Joseph Campbell the way Campbell had tried to light a fire under Abraham Anderson. Dorrance had bought a controlling interest in 1887, and this was confirmed at incorporation of the Campbell Soup Company in 1892. Though Joseph Campbell still turned up at eleven o'clock every morning for the tasting ceremony in the kitchens, the business came more and more under the influence of the new owners.

On March 28, 1900, while walking to the train on his way to the factory, Joseph Campbell collapsed. He died later that day, at the age of eighty-three.

He never lived to see the Campbell Kids, which hit the ads in 1904; nor the purchase of Franco-American Products; nor the establishment of the first foreign subsidiary in Canada in 1930; nor the diversification through V-8, frozen foods, Godiva chocolates, pet foods, Pepperidge Farm, Groko, Nobo, Kia-Ora, and EfficienC.

It is a long way back to the Celebrated Beefsteak Tomato. ♦

HORLICK

There is a story that when Robert E. Peary finally reached the North Pole on April 6, 1909, he found a bottle of Pabst Blue Ribbon beer already chilled in the polar ice.

He also had a hot drink in his luggage for those long arctic evenings. According to one obituary biography, he could curl up in his furs with his hands wrapped around a steaming mug of Horlick's Malted Milk, the same hot drink that went to the South Pole in 1911 with Roald Amundsen. It also went with Dr. Carl Lumholz on his research ships before World War I and with Rear Admiral Richard E. Byrd to Little America in Antarctica in the early 1930s. In June 1986, Reuter's announced that "a priceless collection" of 240 hand-colored glass slides recording Amundsen's race to the South Pole in 1911 had been found in an Oslo attic, "stored in an old yellow crate stencilled Horlick's Malted Milk in Tablet Form."

It is worth pointing out, however, that you would never learn about these intrepid explorers' drinking Horlick's by reading their own accounts. Take Peary, for example. The foods listed in his diaries and other writings include dry cereal, pemmican, ham and eggs, corned beef, bread and butter, musk ox steak, and beverages such as condensed milk, coffee, and compressed tea. He was also carrying thirty gallons of alcohol, but that was for fuel.

The day he reached the pole, he wrote, "The Pole at last! I wish Jo [his wife] could be here with me to share my feelings. I have drunk her health and that of the kids, from the Benedictine flask she sent me."

Not a word about either Pabst beer or Horlick's Malted Milk.

Yet William Horlick, the manufacturer of this traveling drink, must have contributed in no small way to all the expeditions, for his obituary in *The New York Times* recalled that he was knighted by King Haakon of Norway for the support he had given to explorers and scientists. Furthermore, his son and heir, William Horlick, Jr., supplied provisions to both Amelia Earhart and Roald Amundsen and even donated an entire ship, the *Bear of Oakland*, for the Richard E. Byrd expedition.

Horlick's was a natural for those early explorers. In their day, Horlick's Malted Milk Powder was as modern an instant food as you could get. It was the pre-World War I equivalent of today's long-life milk, freeze-dried coffee, or powdered soups. And it was a merchandising oddity. Though it was developed in the United States, it was manufactured and marketed simultaneously on both sides of the Atlantic by the two Horlick brothers, William, an engineer, and James, a pharmacist.

William Horlick

Horlick's Malted Milk: "the Ideal Drink for All Ages."

The inventor was probably James Horlick, though it depends on whether you read English or American source material. It is clear that both brothers, born in the farming country near Gloucestershire, England, came to the United States in about 1869 and settled in Racine, Wisconsin.

The story is that James Horlick, dissatisfied with life in England, came to the States to study dietetics, especially the problems of infants who have trouble digesting whole milk. In Racine, he worked out a combination of liquid extracts of wheat and barley as a milk modifier. It reduced the formation of hard curds, making the milk easier to digest.

Although the medical profession did not fall all over itself hailing this as a great breakthrough, the Horlick brothers set themselves up, not in Racine to start with, but in Chicago in 1873 to manufacture their new preparation for babies and invalids. Just add milk and stir.

The drink was in such demand that the two moved back to Racine in 1876 to set up their first factory, which turned out a product at first called Horlick's Food. But they had a problem: They could not be sure that the local milk their customers added to their powder was pure enough.

In the 1870s and 1880s, the dairy industry in Wisconsin was having growing pains. In 1870, the French chemist Mège Mouriès invented a butter substitute, using first ox fat and then vegetable fats. He called the product margarine, from margaric acid.

When Mouriès's invention was patented in the United States in 1873, the fat was in the fire because it came up against Wisconsin laws that prohibited anyone from adulterating or counterfeiting dairy products.

Against this background, William and James Horlick were turning out a food product that required the addition of milk. When they learned that all too often the drink was ruined by being mixed with impure milk, they made their great decision to establish their own pure milk supply and include milk as part of the product recipe.

That is the American version of the story. English sources simply say that the Horlick brothers took the advice of the medical profession and blended in the milk to add to the other nutrients.

It took them more than three years of laboratory experiments to find the best way to combine milk and the extract of wheat and malted barley and how to evaporate it to reduce it to powder form.

In fact, it was not until 1882 that they hit on their formula. They began production the following year, but did not use the name Horlick's Malted Milk until 1886. By then, incidentally, Robert E. Peary was just beginning his earliest explorations across Greenland's icy mountains.

From that time on, it was all expansion and development for Horlick's. From their Racine plant, which was designed as a replica of an old English manor covered with ivy and surrounded by lawns cut through by curving driveways, they turned out many different varieties.

First came malted milk in tablet form, even more portable and easy to

Horlick's Racine plant was designed as a replica of an old English manor.

Opposite page: *Horlick's stressed nutrition in its early ads.*

Left: *As advertised in a 1923 issue of Ladies' Home Journal, Horlick's was sold in both natural and chocolate flavors, in powder or tablet form.* Center: *Infant nutrition was an important sales point in early advertisements. This piece ran in Munsey's Magazine in December 1900.* Right: *Later, as infant mortality became less of a concern, the good flavor of the beverage was stressed, as shown in this advertisement from 1950.*

use; then a pure extract in powder form. Eventually the business grew into one of Racine's largest industries. The company's donations to the city included Horlick Park and Athletic Field, the two Alice Horlick Hospitals, William Horlick High School, and other memorial buildings.

William Horlick remained head of the American company until his death at ninety in 1936. His son and namesake, who was born in Chicago the year his father and uncle James moved back to Racine, was involved in the business all his working life.

The family's domestic affairs did not, however, go down quite as smoothly as the famous drink. In 1927 young William brought to Racine the Toronto, Ontario, lawyer W. Perkins Bull as his guest. Bull's name popped up a dozen years later as a $300,000 beneficiary in the will of the elder William Horlick's only daughter, Mabelle. Her son fought back and forced Bull to settle for a mere $175,000.

There was an even bigger court battle over the father's will, when the State of Wisconsin failed, after a long suit, to lay claim to inheritance taxes on the $7.4 million he had given to members of his family before his death.

James Horlick, on the other hand, missed all the excitement. He moved back to England in 1890 (the English version says 1906) and imported the product until sales made it possible to open a plant west of London in Slough, where he produced his own malted milk.

He called it "the Ideal Drink for All Ages," and it became widely adopted as a British nightcap. But it never made it to the North Pole.

Five years after his death in 1921, the business split in two, with James Horlick's two sons running the British half, and William Horlick heading the Horlick Milk Corporation until his death in Racine on September 26, 1936.

The final turnabout came in 1945, when the British company took over the American business to protect the name and patent. ◆

SWIFT

"Pssst! Wanna buy a lake?"

If you had been in the meat-packing business about a hundred years ago, you would have pricked up your ears at a come-on like that. In the 1870s, one of the strangest new businesses to surface in that growing industrial society was the brisk trade in lakes, not for their beautiful shorelines, their swimming, or their stock of trout, but for the ice that could be harvested from them.

Refrigeration was the coming thing, and if you either bought or sold meat, you had to strike while the ice was cold. The man who turned ice into cold hard cash was Gustavus Franklin Swift, when he made the refrigerated railway car a commercial reality.

The drama began when one tiny railroad, ancestor of the Chicago & North Western, began operation in 1848, spawning a network of lines that within a dozen years was to connect points in Illinois, Wisconsin, Indiana, and Ohio. By 1860, there were already three routes between the eastern seaboard and Chicago, soon to become "hog butcher to the world." At first the cars carried live cattle, but when they began carrying meat, something had to be done about spoilage.

The first cold cars were simply freight cars with bins of ice at each end. But by the 1860s, the first patents for refrigerated freight cars were coming out, some calling for complicated vanes to blow cold air through the car, others with V-shaped hoppers, and one that used the principle of slowly evaporating air, as with porous pottery.

It was experimental and primitive, but it was the modern way of looking at the industry. With the boom in the sale of ice-covered lakes, others developed new ice-cutting tools and built way stations on the right of way where trains could replenish their ice bins.

Gustavus Swift sniffed the air in 1875 and smelled profit in Chicago, so that is where he headed.

He was then thirty-six years old and had been in the meat business practically all his life. Born in 1839, ninth of the twelve children of a farmer near Sandwich on Cape Cod whose land was neither big enough nor productive enough to feed so many, Gustavus Swift made up his own mind when he was not quite sixteen to leave home and fend for himself.

Luckily, he got a job with his older brother, the town butcher. He picked up the business so fast that within a few months he had bought a heifer with his own money, slaughtered it, and peddled the dressed meat from door to

Gustavus Franklin Swift

"A prodigious worker, who talked and thought the meat business most of the time."

Swift's Little Cook promoted Swift products in the early 1900s. These ads both appeared in 1906.

door. Surprisingly, his brother tolerated this competitive moonlighting, and they rubbed along together pretty well, since Gustavus's customers were mostly out of town.

Once a week for nearly four years he turned up at Brighton, site of the main New England livestock market, bought a steer, and peddled the meat to his customers before the next market day.

By the time he was twenty, he had opened his own butcher shop, turned a profit, sold it to his more conservative brother, and begun building up distribution centers in nearby communities, which he linked together by his meat wagons on regular daily routes.

This attracted the attention of James A. Hathaway, a big Boston meat dealer, who hired him as chief buyer and later took him into partnership as Hathaway & Swift. By the time he turned up as the firm's representative in Chicago in 1875, Swift had behind him nearly twenty years' experience in the meat trade and direct personal experience in shipping dressed meat as well as cattle.

Long after his death in 1903, one of his sons recalled that his father was "a prodigious worker, who talked and thought the meat business most of the time. I think he was a genius."

Hathaway & Swift were meat packers serving local markets, not wholesale shippers of cattle. But in 1877, Swift began slaughtering cattle in Chicago's Union Stock Yards, first established in 1866. It was then he first realized that refrigeration had to be scientifically controlled, not so much to avoid meat spoilage as to increase profits. Said his son, "He was always hell-bent on economy of operation, conscious of the wastage in freight. After all, 1,000 pounds of steer was only 60 percent meat."

The business of shipping cattle back east was a rich market for the railways, and they went after it no holds barred. Cornelius Vanderbilt and Jay Gould were only two of the giants battling for those profits. No wonder they turned a cold shoulder to refrigeration, since nearly half their freight rate income came from hauling the dead weight of those parts of the live steer that were then thought unusable and thrown out as garbage.

Swift was a pioneer in the use of by-products made from discarded animal parts and developed ways of producing oleomargarine, glue, soaps, fertilizer, and, much later, pharmaceutical preparations, though it was his competitor Philip Armour who first boasted that he "sold everything but the squeal."

The railroads refused to build refrigerator cars; it was not in their interest. Indeed, as soon as Swift began shipping dressed meats in 1877, they promptly raised their rates.

The Swift version of the refrigerator car was a simple application of the old principle that hot air rises and cold air falls. While others had tried packing the ice down the sides of the car, Swift and his engineers stored ice in the roof of the car, which forced cold air down and expelled warmer air through

ventilators near the floor.

That was in 1879, and it may be no more than coincidence instead of a crafty business ploy that Swift did not come up with his great idea — his version of a refrigerated car — until just after he had dissolved his partnership with Hathaway to form his own company with his brother Edwin, under the name Swift Bros & Company in 1878.

That was the beginning of the Swift rise to million-dollar status. A mere seven years later, the business had increased so enormously through the United States and even Europe (with modern refrigerated cargo holds built to the Swift pattern), that they recapitalized as Swift & Company, with more than sixteen hundred employees. After another twenty years, the work force had leaped to twenty-six thousand.

Gustavus Swift, however, had died in 1903, but the business moved swiftly ahead under the direction of four of his sons, George, Harold, Charles, and his namesake, Gustavus F. Swift, who lived to see the company his father had started with $25 rack up annual net sales of more than $1 billion.

But it was not all clear sailing. On at least one occasion, during the panic of 1893, Swift was so close to bankruptcy that bankers threatened to close him down. Swift pounded his fist on the table and shouted, "Swift cannot fail!" and walked out of the bank with a new note and an extension for new funds.

He never did have any trouble making both ends meet.   ◆

The workers at the Swift Stockyards pause to take a group photograph, circa 1902.

HEINZ

Henry John Heinz

He produced more than "57 varieties."

If you are looking for truth in advertising, you will not find it in the Heinz catch phrase "57 Varieties."

Even when Henry John Heinz coined the phrase in 1892, he was perfectly aware that his company did not produce fifty-seven varieties of canned, pickled, preserved, bottled, or barreled eatables. In fact, they produced far more, but how many more not even H. J. Heinz himself could tally.

According to his long-time private secretary, E.D. McCafferty, Heinz was riding the elevated in New York one day when he noticed an ad for shoes in "21 different styles." Heinz said to himself, "We don't have different styles, but we do have varieties of products."

As he rode along, he began jotting down every Heinz product he could think of. He went way past fifty-seven, but that number stuck in his mind. It sounded magical, and it seemed to have psychological meaning. Fifty-seven varieties *sounded* right.

He got off the train, went straight to a lithographer, and designed a streetcar card to be distributed immediately throughout the United States. "I myself," said Heinz later, "did not realize how successful a slogan it was going to be."

Heinz was full of ideas. He thought up what must have been the grandest advertising idea ever: a complete pier in Atlantic City, jutting out into the ocean, festooned with flags by day and illuminated by night, and furnished with rest rooms, a lecture hall, and an art and antique collection.

They say that Heinz saved the World's Columbian Exposition of 1893 in Chicago by a simple giveaway gimmick. Attendance was so poor that the exposition might have closed down, until Heinz scattered thousands of small oval brass checks throughout the grounds, each one representing a souvenir gift at the Heinz booth. The rush of freeloaders to the food products exhibit became so great that they had to build supports under the floor.

At the time, Henry John Heinz was going on fifty, and he had started merchandising more than forty years earlier.

Born in 1844, he was the eldest of the nine children of Henry and Anna Margaretha Heinz. Both came from Germany, but they met and married in Birmingham, now a part of Pittsburgh, Pennsylvania. The father was a builder and contractor who also made his own bricks, and though his son Henry as a teen-ager helped him with the bookkeeping, the boy actually got his start in business as his mother's helper.

At eight, he was working with her, cultivating her four-acre vegetable patch behind their house in Sharpsburg, six miles east of Pittsburgh, where they had moved shortly after he was born. At nine, he was selling her surplus vegetables from a basket door to door. He did so well at this that by the time he was ten, he was carrying the produce around in a wheelbarrow; and at twelve, he had expanded to a horse and cart. Then, by persuading his mother to use hot beds and intensive cultivation, Henry John Heinz tripled both the acreage and the output within three years. Before he turned sixteen, he was employing three women in the garden and was making three deliveries a week to the Pittsburgh markets.

In his spare time, he took courses at business college to become his father's bookkeeper in the brickyard, and this he put on a year-round basis by installing heating flues and drying apparatus. For that ingenuity, he was made a partner when he reached twenty-one. Indeed, for the rest of his life, Heinz was a connoisseur of bricks and often found relaxation in laying a few courses whenever one of his company's buildings was under construction.

It was when he was nearly thirty that he made a slightly disastrous blunder in a partnership with two brothers of a leading Sharpsburg family. Formed to market bottled horseradish, celery sauce, and pickles, the business grew fast. But in 1874, right after they had contracted to buy cucumbers and cabbage at a fixed price, a bumper crop flooded the market with bargain-priced vegetables. Then came the business panic, and Heinz & Noble went bankrupt.

Heinz, who had signed all the purchase orders, took personal responsibility. In his 1874 diary he noted, "No Christmas gifts this year," and he opened a special accounts book labeled "The Moral Obligations Book of Henry J. Heinz, 1875." As a bankrupt, he had no legal obligations, but over the next years, he discharged his moral obligations in full.

This ad appeared in Harper's Magazine *in May 1905.*

Above: *The house in which the company began.* Left: *An artist's rendering of the Heinz plant in the early 1900s.*

HEINZ
OVEN BAKED BEANS

THE GREETING OF SMILES—pleasant smiles of appreciation—is to be expected when Heinz Baked Beans are
served. They are welcomed by the whole family because of
their unusual, delicious taste.

The products of H. J. Heinz Company are known as the 57
Varieties. Some are foods,—hearty, delicious foods such as
Beans or Spaghetti. Some are condiments that add flavor to
other foods, such as Ketchup or Vinegar. Everywhere, they
are recognized as the highest attainment of purity, cleanliness
and deliciousness.

The great group of buildings at Pittsburgh is the Home of the
57, but all over the map are dotted branch factories, warehouses and salting stations. And all of this complete organization is maintained so that each Heinz product shall be
made as perfect as if the entire Heinz reputation rested on
it alone.

All Heinz goods sold in Canada are packed in Canada

CREAM SOUPS   TOMATO KETCHUP
VINEGARS   SPAGHETTI

SOME OF THE   **57**   VARIETIES

Left: Heinz Ketchup as advertised in 1934. Right: Peanut butter as advertised in 1926.

He fought back. He was thirty-one, had a wife and two children, and was flat broke. With sixteen hundred dollars borrowed from his brother John and a cousin Frederick and another thousand dollars from a friend, he launched a new food-processing business on February 14, 1876, under the name F. & J. Heinz. The initials refer to the brother and the cousin, since Henry himself, as an undischarged bankrupt, could not hold shares.

Frederick was a German-trained florist and gardener; John was manufacturing superintendent; and Henry was on salary as manager.

Twelve years later, in 1888, when John Heinz decided to move out west, his brother Henry, now free of debt and moral obligations, bought out his interest and reorganized the company under his own name: H. J. Heinz.

Outside the business, Henry John Heinz was an expert on ivory carvings, antique watches, and brickmaking. He promoted interracial harmony in his travels from Europe to Japan. He belonged in turn to Lutheran, Methodist, and Presbyterian churches, serving twenty-five years as a Sunday school superintendent. And he led the fight for flood control of the Allegheny River.

As a private citizen, he could easily have counted fifty-seven varieties of personal interests. ◆

An advertisement for Heinz Worcestershire Sauce.

Opposite page: *Heinz Baked Beans as advertised in* Pictorial Review, *June 1920.*

BISSELL

Melville Reuben Bissell

"*I have invented certain new and useful improvements in Carpet Sweepers.*"

T o whom it may concern," wrote Melville Reuben Bissell in his application to the U.S. Patent Office, filed June 6, 1876, "I have invented certain new and useful improvements in Carpet Sweepers . . . . The object of my invention is to adapt it to sweeping carpets and floors with uneven surfaces more readily than the ordinary sweeper."

It was about time, as far as the Bissell family was concerned. For too many years, Bissell and his wife Anna — not to mention his parents, both of whom were getting on toward seventy — had had to put up with the dust swept up from the cracked floors of their crockery store in Grand Rapids, Michigan. Worst of all, Bissell, who was still only in his thirties, suffered from an allergy, which they blamed on the straw the crockery came packed in.

So he took a good long look at the Welcome carpet sweeper, then the most popular make on the market and the one his store carried in stock, and vowed he could do better than that.

Bissell cannot have been the only man in the United States dissatisfied with carpet sweepers. The U.S. Patent Office records in the two preceding years show several applications from hopeful inventors with radical improvements. But names such as Frank Palmer, Albert A. Spencer, William G. Morry, Conrad Pulis, and Hartwell A. Palmer got swept into oblivion, leaving the field, and the world's carpets, to Bissell.

Though Melville Reuben Bissell had the idea and was the fabricator of the new machine, it emerged by a pretty roundabout route out of a business established originally by his father.

Alpheus Bissell was born in 1801 to a New England family, one of whose ancestors was the dispatch rider of Massachusetts Bay Colony who helped Paul Revere in the galloping relay that carried news of the British landing to Concord and on to Philadelphia where the Continental Congress was in session. Young Alpheus grew up helping to work his father's farm in Otsego County, New York. He branched out at twenty-five into the selling of produce and later dairy products, switched to dry goods for a while, then moved to a brokerage business in wheat, lumber, and real estate. That route took him, over some forty years, from Otsego through Earlsville, New York, to Racine and Berlin, Wisconsin, and Kalamazoo, Michigan. When he moved for the last time in 1869 to Grand Rapids (population then about sixteen thousand) as a dealer in the curious mix of real estate and crockery, his son Melville Reuben, who was born in 1843, was already old enough to go into business with him.

At twenty-six, young Bissell had already been married for four years to

Anna Sutherland, the daughter of a Scottish sea captain of Pictou, Nova Scotia, where she was born. She, as it turned out, was to have far more to do with the company than just sweeping up the dust from packing straw.

The *Dictionary of American Biography*, published around 1897, says that it was the commercial panic of 1875 that made Bissell decide to put out an improved carpet sweeper as a sideline, in case the crockery business went smash; but the company traces the decision to a sudden brain wave early in 1874.

"In a crockery and house furnishing store at 27 Canal Street, Grand Rapids," says their history, "a carpet sweeper called 'The Welcome' of more or less crude construction was being shown to a customer. It was a new-fangled contraption, claiming to take the place of the dirty broom. In reality, it was a crude affair, and Mr. Bissell noted that there was a defect in its construction."

He "immediately conceived the idea of a new principle" and sent out at once "for some walnut lumber to make a case."

The first machines were made laboriously by hand, with Melville and Anna assembling the brushes — tufts of hog bristles dipped in hot pitch — in a room above the store, with Bissell himself making the walnut cases, "all corners dovetailed, finished in natural color, and hand-decorated with floral designs." Said the company's fiftieth Anniversary Report, "It sounded like a threshing machine, but it effectively accomplished the work."

It was the cogwheel drive that made the noise, but this was soon replaced by an iron friction wheel and later by one with rubber tires.

Once the patent was granted, the Bissells ordered one thousand cases from a local woodworking shop. The brushes were made by "widows and other poor but respectable women" working in their homes, using material Anna Bissell delivered to them from the factory, which for the first two years was housed in the loft above the crockery store.

The business grew so fast that within four years the machine, improved with patented "broom action" and ball bearings, was being marketed over a large area, including an exclusive shop in New York City. In February 1883, the Bissell Carpet Sweeper Company was incorporated with capital of $150,000 and housed in a new five-story brick building with ninety employees and the capacity to make twenty-five dozen sweepers a day.

A year and a month later, a fire broke out in a carding mill two doors away. Within two hours, the entire block had been burned to the ground, including the new Bissell factory. Without insurance, they might well have folded then and there, but there were orders on hand, so salvaging began at once. Within nineteen days, they were shipping carpet sweepers again from temporary quarters while rebuilding went on.

From that fire rose what is now known as Bissell Inc., which makes or markets through subsidiaries a vast range of products from Bio-shield bath safety mats to snow shovels to disposable toothbrushes, not to mention carpet cleaning machines and other vacuum cleaners, and of course "the ultimate

Anna Sutherland Bissell carried on as company president after her husband's death in 1899.

From a 1902 advertisement, which claimed that Bissell was the "Largest Sweeper Makers in the World."

Left: *A 1906 advertisement which appeared in* Harper's Magazine. Right: *The first Bissell carpet sweeper was handmade of solid walnut with hog-bristle brushes. It promised "a lifetime of hard usage."*

carpet sweeper," a descendant of the handmade prototype of 1876.

For one long period of thirty-four years, the company was directed by Anna Sutherland Bissell herself after her husband died at the age of forty-five of the "black grippe" (or influenza) in March 1889, only five years after the great fire.

At forty-two, the mother of three sons and a daughter, Anna Bissell found herself suddenly in charge of a growing business. She weathered the depression of 1893 by bringing out a toy carpet sweeper, The Little Helper. As company president, she was the first woman elected to the National Hardwaremen's Association. From 1923 until she died in 1934, she remained chairman of the board.

Her eldest son, M.R. Bissell, became president in 1923. ◆

HIRES

If Charles Elmer Hires had ever thought of writing his autobiography, at least one chapter could have been titled "How I Made $7,000 as a Sidewalk Superintendent."

It must have looked as if he was just goofing off, that fine spring day in the late 1860s. He was eighteen years old and had recently opened his own pharmacy in Philadelphia, and there he was wasting time watching some workmen digging the foundation for a new building.

All of a sudden, he perked up and offered to slip the guy with the wheelbarrow a few dollars if he would dump his loads into the cellar of the pharmacy, just in the next block.

Was he plumb loco? Was he just another country kid out of his depth in the big city?

Charles Hires, born in August 1851, was the sixth of the ten children of a Roadstown, New Jersey, farmer of English, German, and Welsh ancestry. As the second son, with no hope of inheriting the farm, he got work with a chemist in a nearby town. At sixteen, Hires moved on to Philadelphia with only fifty cents in his pocket.

He had no trouble finding work. He headed for the nearest pharmacy, where he worked for a year. Then he picked up more about the business in a wholesale house, studying pharmacy at night school. After trying out a partnership with two other young fellows in a drugstore, he borrowed enough money to open his own on December 1, 1869. The company records note that "one of his cherished possessions was an ornate soda fountain of Tennessee marble."

So who was minding the store while he was buying wheelbarrow loads of dirt? Hires was crazy like a fox. Trained in chemistry, he recognized the clay as a hydrous bisilicate of alumina, also known as fuller's earth, a substance so prized in the woolen industry that in Britain people could be fined for sending it out of the country. The stuff absorbs grease so readily that it is used for cleaning raw wool and for taking spots out of clothes.

Hires happily retreated to his mud-filled cellar, rolled out the clay in sheets, and cut it into cookie-shaped discs, which he then wrapped in tissue paper and sold as "Hires Fuller's Earth." That cellarful of clay netted him seven thousand dollars. It not only put his pharmacy on its feet financially, but gave him the capital for his next brain wave, which hit him at yet another unexpected time and place.

In January 1870, Hires married the daughter of a neighbor who was also a

Charles Elmer Hires

"They'll never drink it if you call it tea. Better call it root beer."

Philadelphia merchant. Later that summer he took his bride for a brief holiday, stopping for the night in a boarding house where the landlady served them a drink she had compounded of a blend of roots, herbs, and spices, including sassafras bark. Though such teas were common drinks of the day, Hires had never before tasted one. He found it delicious.

Ever since his successful experiment with fuller's earth, he had wanted to create a business for himself to free him from the daily round of a pharmacy. Why not a new beverage based on this familiar and homely drink? Besides, as a Quaker, he had been concerned with the drunkenness found among the laboring classes, which was more public and therefore looked upon as more of a social problem than the drunkenness found among the wealthy.

Back in his pharmacy, Hires carried on various experiments to find a seductively palatable taste for his new concoction.

Sassafras is a tree that grows to a height of fifty feet in warm climates and yields an aromatic wood smelling something like fennel. Pharmacists for centuries have used it as the basis for a stimulant and a diuretic medicine in treatments for rheumatic diseases.

Though the Hires recipe is a trade secret, it is known that one of the key flavors in his drink was not sassafras but the root of the sarsaparilla, related to the lily and the onion. It grows in Central America, where the swampy land can shoot it rapidly into growth at elevations of more than four thousand feet. When the sarsaparilla root was introduced into Europe in the sixteenth century, it was considered a mind-altering drug, but modern science calls it "pharmacologically inert and therapeutically useless." An inert and useless extract with a pleasant taste sounded like the ideal base for a popular soft drink, and Hires seized on it, adding other ingredients, probably to mystify the competition.

But what to call it? He talked the matter over with a friend, the Reverend Dr. Russell H. Conwell, later the founder of Temple University, who agreed with Hires that it might be offered for sale, in the interests of temperance, to Pennsylvania coal miners, a notoriously drunken lot. When Hires suggested that it be called "root tea," Conwell disagreed. "They'll never drink it if you call it tea. Better call it root beer."

The new beverage was sold through Hires's pharmacy and introduced to the public at the Centennial Exposition at Philadelphia in 1876, gaining national attention when Hires began to market it through drugstore soda fountains. Within months he began to broaden his marketing methods, with packaged ingredients (just add water, sugar, and yeast), then liquid concentrate in the 1880s, bottled root beer in 1893, and soda fountain syrup in 1905.

As early as 1877, Hires, acting on a suggestion from the publisher of the *Philadelphia Public Ledger*, became an advertising pioneer. One early ad claimed that the product would yield "health for the baby, pleasure for the parents, and new life for the old folks." Another offered *Happy Hours in Fairy Land*, a free book for the kiddies, with every twenty-five-cent package.

These advertisements for Hires ran in the 1890s.

Opposite page: *An advertisement for Hires from the 1920s.*

Left: *In 1933, Hires was promoting its original root beer against competition from imitators. This advertisement ran in* Collier's. *Right: In 1937, Hires was selling for 5 cents for a small bottle, 10 cents for the family size. This advertisement ran in* The Saturday Evening Post.

It was a one-man business for nearly fifteen years, operated as part of a wholesale botanical drug business, which Hires established in 1877. In 1890 he incorporated as the Charles E. Hires Company with capital of three hundred thousand dollars.

Hires also pioneered in condensed milk. In the twenty years between 1896 and 1916, he organized a chain of factories processing condensed milk in eastern states and in Canada, while in private he rebuilt an old Quaker meeting house, where William Penn had once attended services, and indulged his love of deep-sea fishing.

In 1917 he sold off the condensed milk business but hung on to his root beer, which he continued to supervise until his death in 1937 at the age of eighty-five, almost exactly sixty-seven years after sampling that holiday landlady's sassafras tea. ◆

GILLETTE

If you had been an American investor just before the turn of the century, you could have put your money into the Twentieth Century Company, incorporated to set up a business designed to run the entire world on efficient administrative lines. And you would have lost every cent. The company folded in 1899, before the twentieth century even started.

The "crackpot" who thought up that idea was King Camp Gillette, who had another crazy idea. He actually thought that he could invent a razor blade sharp enough on both sides to give a good shave but cheap enough to be thrown away when it got dull.

The idea was insane. Everybody knew that razors, even the new-style safety razors, like Star and Gem and Yankee, had to have blades of high-quality steel like a hollow-ground straight razor so they would last a lifetime.

Russell B. Adams, Jr., who wrote the story of King C. Gillette "and his wonderful shaving device," quotes Gillette's own description of the morning he made his discovery. When he started to shave he found his razor not only dull "but beyond the point of successful stropping and it needed honing, for which it must be taken to a barber or a cutler. As I stood there with the razor in my hand, my eyes resting on it as lightly as a bird settling down on its nest — the Gillette razor was born."

Conceived is a better word, for he struggled with the idea for more than ten years. It was so far-out for those days that not only did he have trouble finding investors, he could not at first find a mechanic to work on a prototype. It took four years before he at last gave himself a shave with the world's first throwaway blade, and another six to get the product on the market.

Success, however, was instantaneous. The sales of razor sets for the first year, at five dollars each: 51. The sales for the second year: 90,844 — an increase of more than 180,000 percent! In the third year, sales were up a mere 304 percent, but by then the revolution in shaving had arrived.

In 1904 the U.S. Patent Office granted Gillette a seventeen-year patent. Although there sprang up more than three hundred competitors, only Gillette had the patent on the double-edge blade, which accounts for the large number of single-edge blades that came on the market. Foreign counterfeits flooded the market with names such as Agillette, Billette, and Gillotin.

Over the next few years, throwaway-blade merchandising flourished in many forms. The blades were used as giveaways in the sale of tea and coffee, overalls, shaving cream, pocket knives, celluloid collars, and chewing gum; even new bank accounts carried them as premiums.

King Camp Gillette

"If I had been a technically trained engineer, I would have quit."

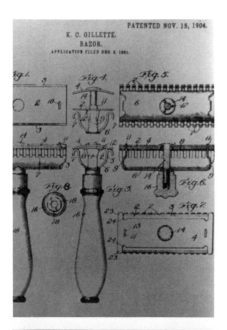

Top: *Drawings from Gillette's 1904 patent application.* Bottom: *Engineer Brown with the company's first grinding machine, 1902.* Right: *An ad from 1910. Gillette pioneered in sports advertising, sponsoring the World Series in 1939.*

When the United States entered the war in 1917, the government bought four million Gillettes, Everreadys, and Gems, and gave one to each soldier, sailor, and marine.

Oddly enough, Gillette had not intended to change the world with a strip of steel. He was only a visionary dreamer who saw the world as a gigantic machine and himself as the inspired tinkerer who could set it running smoothly. In the practical world, however, Gillette was a struggling salesman, the son of a Chicago postmaster who loved taking things apart. The boy, born in 1855 the youngest of three sons, was named King for a judge friend of his father, and Camp, which was his mother's maiden name.

The Gillettes were a close-knit, self-reliant family. When the Chicago fire of 1871 destroyed everything they owned, they moved to New York, where the father opened a hardware supply business and King drifted. He was a clerk in Chicago and a drummer in Kansas, but always a tinkerer. He invented a new bushing, a new valve for industrial taps, and an electric cable conduit.

He traveled through Britain selling Sapolio, a scouring powder. On his return to the States, he married an oilman's daughter, then wrote *The Human Drift*, a non–best seller outlining his scheme to incorporate the entire world. He published it himself in 1894, and it sank into oblivion. His mother, however, was a best-selling author. In 1887 she published a cookbook, which was revised and reprinted several times in the next fifty years.

Gillette's disposable razor blade was a nothing idea in his mind compared

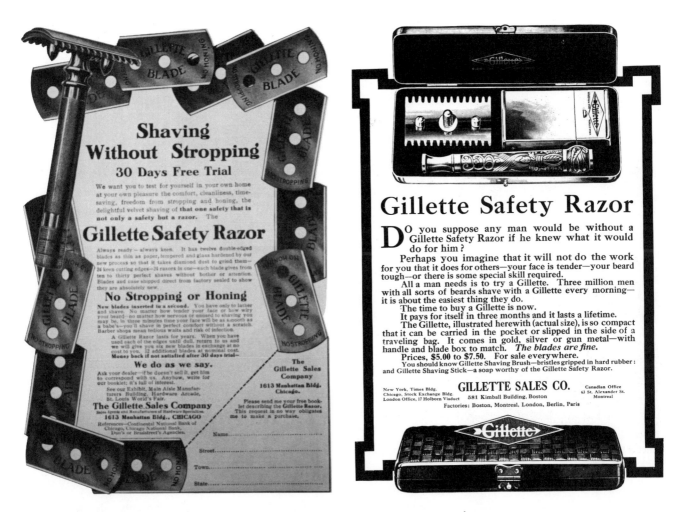

Early ads for Gillette Safety Razors.

with his great cosmic plans. After all, the blade was only one of many attempts he made to come up with some commercial product that everybody would buy, discard, and buy again. Though he probably never heard the phrase, Gillette, in his thinking, was the patron saint of planned obsolescence.

So he tinkered away, bored his family and relations and friends with his strange notion, and finally succeeded, mainly because he did not believe that a blade made to his specifications was technically impossible, despite what he had been told by cutlers and metalworkers and even by the experts at the Massachusetts Institute of Technology, all of whom he consulted.

"If I had been a technically trained engineer," he was quoted as saying in 1948 by *Advertising & Selling*, "I would have quit." ◆

KRAFT

James Lewis Kraft

He was "destined" to be the maker of "cheese that would perish not."

"Many's the long night," said old Ben Gunn, the marooned sailor in *Treasure Island*, "I've dreamed of cheese."

Mr. Gunn, meet Mr. James Lewis Kraft, who dreamed of cheese both night and day and became the big cheese of American business by creating process cheese as the market knows it today.

Perhaps in Ben Gunn's day, cheese was just cheese, the traditional way of preserving milk and its nutrients. Cheesemaking has always been one of the old home industries, with regional cheeses emerging over the centuries from farms and cottages, from Cheddar to Roquefort to Brie. There was no such thing as a cheese factory until George and Jesse Williams, farmers in New York State, set one up in the early 1850s, and the idea did not spread to Britain and Europe until ten years later.

Even in these new factories, cheese was still made by traditional methods, with sour curd as the starter for the process. This commercial cheese was so perishable that in the last years of the nineteenth century the average consumption was only about a pound a year. It just didn't keep.

That was the world of cheese that James Lewis Kraft knew as a boy growing up in Fort Erie, Ontario. Born in 1874, James was the second of the eleven children of Mennonite farmer George Kraft and his wife Minerva. One of James Kraft's earliest jobs was clerking in Ferguson's General Store, where he later remembered watching the local women suspiciously sniffing the cheese before they bought it.

A Fort Erie journalist quoted a passage from an interview with James Kraft in the *Christian Herald* early in the 1940s, which read, "Mr. Kraft noticed that no housewife with half her wits would buy cheese without first sampling it, for no matter how wholesome it was when it left the manufacturer, it often reached the market in a state of extinct virtue. Young Kraft took stock of his inward hankerings and felt that destiny had marked him a maker of cheese that would perish not."

The idea, however, matured slowly. He went from Ferguson's store to a Buffalo food distributing company, then went back to Ferguson's, then started the Shefford Cheese Company, and moved to Chicago in 1903 to start a wholesale cheese business.

He picked a good time, for it was in those early years of this century that scientists began to introduce radical changes in cheesemaking, such as accurate measurement of acidity, use of a pure culture called lactic streptococci as a starter instead of sour curd, mild heating or pasteurization to destroy harmful

In 1903 Kraft peddled his cheese to Chicago grocers, traveling store to store in a cart pulled by his horse, Paddy. He paid sixty-five dollars for the horse and cart.

microorganisms, and refrigerated ripening.

James Lewis Kraft did not pioneer in pasteurization, as some claim, but he was one of the first commercially minded producers to seize on these new developments, in his own rough and pioneering way.

In the autumn of 1903, he invested sixty-five dollars in a cart and a horse named Paddy and went from one small grocery to the next trying to persuade retailers that they could trust the cheese he had bought on credit from an obliging wholesaler. Even then, Kraft was a persistent salesman.

According to legend, when he was not out peddling somebody else's cheese, he was experimenting at home in an old copper kettle over a wood stove, trying out various mixes in search of a cheese that would not spoil so fast. It was not cheese pasteurization he was working on but cheese processing.

After constant experimentation throughout the years to give cheese long-lasting qualities, Kraft's major contributions came as a result of his success in grinding and blending cheeses, as well as pasteurizing them, to make the product that quickly became a nationally accepted food. Pasteurization was possible after he discovered that he could heat cheese and prevent its separation into oils and solids by high-speed stirring. The result of his experimentation, process cheese, a bland-tasting, uniform product, was granted a patent in 1916.

By then Kraft had been selling his cheese for ten years, and his brothers Fred, Norman, John, and Charles, who took over the production department in 1906, had joined him. In every sense it was a closely knit family enterprise.

Ferguson's General Store in Fort Erie, Ontario, where Kraft worked as a clerk.

When Charles died, he was remembered as "the head of engineering, purchasing and budgeting." At his retirement he was "head of production," and he had, in his forty years with the company, "watched the staff grow from

Above: *Women worked the machinery at the process cheese filling line in the Green Bay, Wisconsin, factory in the 1930s.* Right: *This ad for process cheese ran in* The Saturday Evening Post *in 1920.*

An artist's rendering of the Chicago factory warehouse and office, 1911–1921.

less than a dozen to more than 11,000."

Not quite eleven months later, the death of James Lewis Kraft was marked by nearly a full column as "founder and chairman emeritus of the Kraft Food Company," which "under his guidance, introduced pasteurizing processes and packaged cheese."

The name is recalled today not only in Kraft products that are sold throughout the world, but also in the Kraft Road, where the old farm was located, and in a book about jade, on which he was an expert, published in 1947. ◆

MAYTAG

Does the light go out when the fridge door closes? That question has already been settled at many a New Year's Eve party, so try this: Does the water in the washing machine go through the clothes, or do the clothes go through the water?

It could be that the first person ever to ask such a question was Lewis Bergman Maytag, and he put it to himself early in the 1920s, shortly after he became president of the company founded by his father. It is true that he was president for only five years, but in that short time he changed the domestic washing machine forever.

It is not easy to pin down the date of the first American washing machine, and there is even some doubt who invented it, or rather which of two Smiths invented it. One source gives credit to Hamilton E. Smith of Pittsburgh, Pennsylvania, who in 1858 made for his own family's use a tub in which two paddles could be turned through the water by means of a hand crank. It was based on the butter churn, but it never went anywhere because most people found it even harder work than the familiar corrugated washboard.

A likelier candidate is Stephen Morgan Smith, a Moravian clergyman of Canal Dover, Ohio, who had to give up preaching in 1871 at the age of thirty-two because of a throat ailment. Unable to carry on with his vocation and being without financial resources, he decided to try and market a washing machine he had put together some years earlier for his wife's use.

Manufactured in York, Pennsylvania, under the name Success, it was the first washing machine to be commercially marketed in the United States. It made Smith a great deal of money, which he proceeded to give away to poorer friends, until he himself was impoverished a second time.

He gave up the washing machine and started making a hydraulic turbine of his own design, which he marketed under the same name, Success. The foundry grew, he became rich again, and this time he hung on to his money. When he died in 1903, the S. Morgan Smith Company was one of the largest in the world. And all because the founder forsook the washing machine for the turbine.

The Maytag washer came into existence by a route almost as roundabout as S. Morgan Smith's zigzag life.

The founder of the company was Frederick Louis Maytag, born in 1857 on the farm that had been taken up by his parents when they migrated from Germany in 1850. As young Maytag grew up, he managed to squeeze in less than two years of schooling as he helped to work the family farm first in

Frederick Louis Maytag

Why not make the water go through the clothes?

—At Ames

In classroom practice on household management in the *Home Economics Division of Iowa State College of Agriculture and Mechanic Arts*, the

Maytag
Multi-Motor Washer
with
Swinging Reversible Wringer

Standard There's a Maytag Washer of every type —hand, power-driven, electric—all built to the enviable Maytag standard.

FREE The Maytag Laundry Manual is the most complete work yet compiled on the subject of laundering. We will gladly send you a copy *free* — just a post-card brings it.

is demonstrated as an advanced utility for household laundering and home power purposes. It is for homes that lack facilities to operate the *Maytag Electric Washer*. *The Maytag Multi-Motor Washer* operates on gasoline. Safe, simple, economical and wonderfully thoro in its work.

THE MAYTAG COMPANY — Dept. 175 — NEWTON, IOWA

BRANCHES AND WAREHOUSES IN MOST PRINCIPAL CITIES   DEALERS—Our proposition affords wide opportunity for profit. Write!

41

Illinois and then near Marshalltown, Iowa. Finally, in 1880, at the age of twenty-three, he broke loose and got work clerking in Newton, Iowa.

Now flash ahead seventy years. In 1949, a team of photographers and reporters from *Life* magazine invaded Newton and in a long photo story, *Life* published an aerial picture of the town, with arrows pointing to the important sights: the two Maytag factories, the Maytag Dairy, the Maytag Bowl, the Maytag Hotel, Maytag Park, the Home of Fred Maytag II (the founder's grandson), and the old Maytag Homestead. As the article said, "Newton, Iowa, literally grew up around the washing machine."

But seventy years earlier, Fred Maytag was a clerk in a hardware store owned by William C. Bergman. Uneducated he may have been, yet Maytag was able to buy a half interest in the store the following year, when it became Maytag & Bergman. Two years later, he married his partner's daughter.

A few years later still, he sold out and dabbled in the lumber business; but in 1893 he finally came to rest, in a sense, with his father-in-law in a business called the Parsons Band Cutter & Self-Feeding Company. If you think that does not sound much like a washing machine, you are quite right.

George W. Parsons, who also married into the family, had invented a self-feeding attachment for the threshing machine, which he began manufacturing in partnership with Maytag & Bergman. Founded with capital of twenty-four hundred dollars, the company under Maytag's direction quickly became the largest maker of self-feeding attachments in the world, selling to North and South America, Britain, and Australia.

The fact is, Maytag might never have made washers at all if it had not been for an inventive young mechanic named Howard Snyder, who joined them in the mid-1890s. In the next ten years, Snyder invented a corn husker and shredder, a grain grader, and a hay press, all of which were added to the Parsons line. Then, in 1907, he made certain improvements to the old Success washing machine of S. Morgan Smith.

In the United States at that time there were 110 manufacturers of washing

The years 1907–1918 saw many improvements in the way Americans washed their clothes. No more wringing clothes by hand, no more standing over a boiling kettle sloshing dirty linens around with a stick. Opposite page: In a series of early advertisements, the company used the authority of different college home-economics departments to promote the merits of the Maytag Multi-Motor Washer. Bottom left: The Maytag Gyrafoam® was introduced in 1922 and was enormously popular. Demand for the machine boosted total Maytag production over 300 percent between 1923, when this photograph of an acre of washers was taken, and 1926. Bottom right: From the company archives is a photograph of Maytag salesman Joe Long, who is credited with selling eight washers in the Texas Panhandle in one week in April 1929 using this "Jackass Express."

Left: *Appearing in 1949, this advertisement was among the last to focus on Maytag's star product for over forty years: the wringer washer. This was the year the Maytag automatic washer was introduced.* Right: *The Maytag wringer washing machine went to war for the first time in 1917. These men were stationed at the Plattsburgh, New York, Reserve Officer Military Training Camp, where thousands of reserve officers were trained during World War I.*

machines, mostly wooden stave tubs with an agitator operated through the lid. The agitator, studded with pegs, plucked at the clothes and swished them through the water.

When Fred Maytag bought out his partners, Parsons and Bergman, in 1909, this was the washing machine that the Maytag factories had produced for more than fifteen years, though a model powered by electricity, also invented by Howard Snyder, came out in 1911.

All this time, Fred Maytag's son, Lewis Bergman Maytag, born in 1888, was growing up with the company. It was in 1922, the year after he became president, that he first wondered why the clothes were dragged through the water.

Snyder's design was a round tub, not square, and was made of the exciting new material aluminum, but it still had the old post agitator studded with pegs. Lewis Bergman Maytag wondered, Why not make the water go through the clothes? Snyder's answer was to shift the agitating mechanism from the peg-studded shaft to a series of fins at the bottom.

Though it was not a Success, the new Maytag was so phenomenally successful that in 1923 the company discontinued making all their other products to concentrate on washers. Within five years, Maytag had cornered 60 percent of all American washing machine business. ◆

SCHICK

Jacob Schick

Every great invention deserves a legend, so here is the Legend of the Electric Shaver.

One frigid morning in a lonely mining camp in Alaska, just before the First World War, an American lieutenant, recently retired for health reasons from the 14th U.S. Infantry, crawled out of his bunk and sprained his ankle. With the temperature hovering around forty below, he found it impossible to collect snow and melt it into water for his morning shave.

As a military man, that made him uncomfortable. After all, it was one of history's greatest generals, Alexander of Macedonia, who ordered compulsory shaving in barracks so that the enemy could not grab his soldiers by their beards. Wishing to be clean-shaven as usual, the retired lieutenant of infantry, his face covered with unmilitary stubble, realized that he had to find some way to shave without water.

That man was Jacob Schick, and though it took him another twenty years, he persevered until in 1931, at the height of the Depression, he began manufacturing the Schick Dry Shaver and lived wealthily ever after.

The electric shaver was not Jacob Schick's only invention. In the early 1920s he patented his Pencilaid and Pencilnife, sharpening devices attached to pencils. A bit later, he perfected a magazine razor, one of many new types of razor challenging the popular razor invented in 1902 by King Camp Gillette.

You have to go back to Jacob Schick's real life activity as a career soldier, however, to realize that his dry shaver, the first ever electric razor, was one final but very profitable incident in a career that was both adventurous and inventive.

He was born into a life of unusual ventures. His father, Valentine Schick, who emigrated to the United States at the age of four with his Bavarian parents, served with the Union army in the Civil War, then took an active interest in land development in New Mexico as it was opened up to settlement. There he discovered a copper mine, where his son Jacob at age sixteen first began man's work by taking on the construction of a branch railroad from Los Cerillos, New Mexico, to a coal mine his father had opened up to provide fuel for his copper smelter.

By 1897, Jacob Schick was prospecting in Alaska with his father. On reaching maturity the following year, he struck out on his own by enlisting in the 14th U.S. Infantry for service in the Spanish-American War.

The following December he was in the Philippines, newly ceded to the United States as the Spanish empire in the New World was broken up.

He had to find some way to shave without water.

Operates on both A.C. and D.C. Weight 7 ounces

"It isn't a rich man's gadget"

It's an honest, straight-forward Schick Dry Shaver that cuts the toughest beards and shaves the tenderest skins. Never before has there been such a revolutionary idea in shaving. An outdoor workman shaves pleasantly and quickly—and no millionaire can buy more shaving comfort. Gone are the days of preparing the face for a shave. No water, no soap, no waiting for the beard to soften.

YOU CANNOT CUT YOURSELF. Speed, not sharpness, shaves you close and clean. No moving part touches the skin. There can be no cuts, no scratches, no scraping.

SAVES MONEY. There are no blades to get dull, to sharpen or renew—no parts to replace for an indefinite time. The price is $15.

ASK FOR A DEMONSTRATION. Dealers selling the Dry Shaver will give you a demonstration. If none is near you, send $15 ($17.50 in Canada) direct to us. The Dry Shaver is fully guaranteed.

SCHICK DRY SHAVER, INC.
Stamford, Conn.

Pacific Coast:—Schick Dry Shaver Distributors, Reno, Nevada. *Canadian Distributor:*—Schick Dry Shaver, Ltd., Westmount, Quebec.

SCHICK DRY SHAVER

Above: A 1934 advertisement for the Schick Dry Shaver.

Opposite page: Advertisements from 1937 (right) and 1938.

Because he spoke fluent Spanish, he served as interpreter and division color-bearer, refusing a commission in order to command, as a private, a company of scouts, half Americans and half Filipinos.

In 1900 he was sent home suffering from amoebic dysentery, but he was promoted to second lieutenant in the 8th Infantry while still in the hospital. His old regiment, the 14th, made a special request for Schick to be transferred back to them because of inventive changes he had recommended in machine gun practice. This was one of the few cases when an officer promoted from the ranks was permitted to serve in his old command. Schick was also singled out by being made post quartermaster and commissary, an office usually held by those of captain's rank.

As quartermaster, he supervised the building of barracks in Fort Wayne and Fort Brady, Michigan. Then he found himself posted back to the Philippines in 1903, where he was given the task of constructing ocean-going tugs in Hong Kong for army use.

By 1906, he was with the 14th in San Francisco, helping to clean up after the disastrous earthquake. One of his jobs was to supervise the transfer of $50 million in silver from the U.S. Mint, which had been destroyed by fire, to the city post office.

Struck down by another attack of his old illness, amoebic dysentery, he spent a year in the hospital, where he was bumped to first lieutenant. When he recovered, he was transferred on medical advice to the colder climate of Alaska, to keep his recurring illness in check.

Reinvigorated, he supervised the construction of military telegraph lines over a one-thousand-square-mile area in the interior of Alaska. In his spare time, he designed a novel kind of transport boat, called the "General Jacob," for use in the shallow waters of the Tanana and Yukon rivers. Though it could carry fifty tons, it drew only a foot of water and could even carry a company of troops.

Finally, in 1910, though he was only thirty-three, his health forced him to resign. Even then, he stepped out of uniform only to engage in mining prospecting out of an office in Seattle, Washington. It was on one of those trips, in 1911, that he started dreaming about close, waterless shaving. But the army was not done with him yet.

When the United States' neutrality in World War I was threatened by the 1915 sinking of the *Lusitania*, Lieutenant Schick offered his services and, by special act of Congress, was put on active duty with the rank of captain, serving first on the Mexican border and then in London, England, where he was ordered by Pershing to take charge of troop transport. Between August 1917 and June 1918, he moved 680,000 U.S. troops through England to France.

Another spell in the hospital merely led to a change of job, this time to head of the division of intelligence and criminal investigation in the U.S. Army in England, with the rank of lieutenant colonel. He was later offered command of the port of Brest, France, as brigadier but declined. He did,

"I bought a Schick for my husband— *Both of us use it* and think it is about perfect"

What a happy present that you can give to one person—and others may use. Mrs. Otto Ludwig of San Diego, California, says: "I bought a Schick for my husband. Both of us use it for different purposes and think it is really about perfect. My husband's face used to be so tender. We used to buy the best shaving soaps and blades but none seemed to help much.

"He dreaded shaving, always putting it off and skipping days. But since we have been using the Schick, all that is an old story."

Notice that *he dreaded shaving* and he *bought the best blades and soap.*

There are the reasons why the Schick Shaver is the perfect gift.

Shaving becomes a joy. It practically ceases to be an expense the first day of shaving—and for the thousands of shaves the Schick gives.

Think of it. No blades so it cannot cut or injure. No soap, lather, creams or lotions! Just plug in and get a quick, close shave.

A WOMAN'S GIFT, TOO

Women find the Schick way is the gentlest, cleanest way of removing hair from the legs and under the arms. What a welcome gift to any woman who wears sheer stockings, low-cut dresses, bathing suits in summer and for all who appreciate personal daintiness.

SEE AN AUTHORIZED DEALER

He will show you how simply you can learn to use a Schick Shaver and enjoy this invention which is changing the shaving habits of the world.

SCHICK DRY SHAVER, INC., STAMFORD, CONN. Western Distributor: Edises, Inc., San Francisco. In Canada: Henry Birks & Sons, Ltd., and other leading stores.

"Maybe I'll have to come to it"

SCHICK ● SHAVER

He'll NEVER shave with blades

When this boy is old enough he will shave the fast, painless, modern way—with an electric Schick Shaver.

Why Schick? Because he will want the *original*—the inventor's own conception of a shaver, and not some imitation that cannot possibly copy Schick's quick, close-shaving qualities.

Only Schick has this thin, flat shearing head

The Schick shearing head, or cutter, has a patented construction that is vital to its shaving qualities. During twenty years of experimental work before the Schick was marketed, the inventor tested hundreds of types of shearing heads — angled heads, many-sided heads, wide ones, narrow ones —all kinds. The one he finally adopted gives *all* the benefits of dry shaving. It is exclusive with Schick, patented and protected by the U. S. Courts.

It allows the hair to nestle just closely enough into the cutter. It crops the beard at face level—*yet it positively will not cut the skin.*

Purse your lips and run the Schick over them. Even this tenderest skin on your lips will not be irritated in any way. Then how could the Schick cut the *face?* How could it cause any burning or "scraped" feeling?

2,000,000 users prove Schick's claims

Today more than 2,000,000 men use Schick Shavers. Many of them have used the same shavers for five and six years—for 2,000 to 3,000 shaves. Even these men report their Schicks in top-notch condition. Only Schick can point to such a record of service.

Go to a Schick dealer

Any authorized Schick Shaver dealer will show you how quickly and easily you may learn to get quick, close shaves the convenient and happy Schick way, without blades or lather.

$15
AC-DC
Made for 6, 32
or 110 volts

SCHICK DRY SHAVER, INC., STAMFORD, CONN. Western Distributor: Edises, Inc., San Francisco

In Canada: Henry Birks & Sons, Ltd., and other leading stores

Schick Dry Shaver, Inc., has no connection with the Magazine Repeating Razor Co., which manufactures and sells the Schick Injector Razor.

SCHICK ● SHAVER

The Fashion Razor may have been the best invention since lipstick. This 1948 advertisement, directed exclusively to women, appeared in the Ladies' Home Journal.

however, invent a machine to fill gas masks at the rate of twenty a minute, instead of the then accepted rate of thirty-five minutes each.

Lieutenant Colonel Jacob Schick retired from the army for good early in 1919, but even then he plunged into yet another new venture. Acting as agent for the Klinger Manufacturing Co. of England, he bought a complete American hosiery factory and shipped it to England to give employment to the young women thrown out of work when gas mask production ended. He even went to England to supervise the setting up of the factory, but turned down an offer to be managing director.

When did he find time to work on his dry shaver? On July 18, 1921, he patented the Schick Magazine Razor, and while tinkering with improvements, he came up with the first practical electric shaver, which he patented in April 1928.

He tried at first to work out a production arrangement with the Magazine Repeating Razor Company, of which he was a partner. But finally, in April 1930, he organized his own company in Stamford, Connecticut.

It is ironic that a man who spent a lifetime wandering through exotic places of the world should concentrate at last on a machine to take the stubble off the sixty square inches of the human face.

He did have one surprising encore. After fifty-seven years serving the United States, he renounced his citizenship in 1935 and moved to Canada. *The New York Times* obituary in July 1937 reported that "he aroused the indignation of President Franklin D. Roosevelt who charged that 'this had been done to escape our income and inheritance laws.' Friends of the colonel declared that these charges were unfair, explaining that his physicians had recommended the cold climate of Canada."

The cold did him little good, for he lived only another eighteen months. ♦

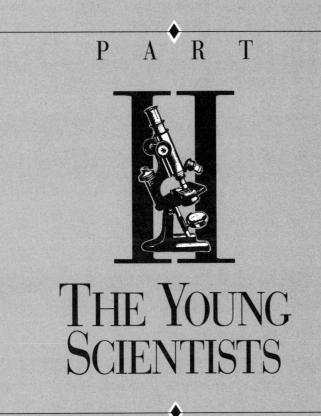

THE YOUNG
SCIENTISTS

BAUSCH & LOMB

John Jacob Bausch (left) *and Henry Lomb*

Lomb lent Bausch $60 to get started. Fifty years later, the company was worth $600,000.

A capital appreciation of 1 million percent sounds pretty good, even when spread over fifty years, but there was no thought of profit in Henry Lomb's mind when he handed over his life's savings of sixty dollars to John Jacob Bausch in 1853.

He was simply helping out a friend whose business was in danger of going on the rocks. But at the same time, he became a partner in Bausch & Lomb, which fifty years later was capitalized at six hundred thousand dollars and was recognized as the world's largest manufacturer of optical lenses.

It is called getting in on the ground floor, but there was more to it than that in this case. Henry Lomb had just turned twenty-one when he met J. J. Bausch, who was then only nineteen, and they could have had only the vaguest notion of what the future had in store. For them, it was more like hanging on to what they already had in those early days in Rochester, New York, where they had come as immigrants from separate parts of Germany.

Bausch, born in 1830 near Württemberg into a family of bakers, learned the optical trade early in life, probably from his brother first, then as an apprentice in Switzerland. When he landed in Rochester, however, he had to find work as a cook's helper and later in a woodworking shop as a lathe turner. That may be where the two men met, for Henry Lomb was a cabinetmaker by trade. Born in 1828 in a town near Wiesbaden, Lomb was orphaned before he was nine and brought up by an uncle who apprenticed him to a cabinetmaker. When he turned twenty-one, he left Germany forever and probably met Bausch as a member of the German community in Rochester.

Bausch had already tried to make some use of his optical skills. He opened a small store, but had to close down for lack of customers. When he took up woodworking again, he crippled his hand in an accident. But he was an expert in optics, not woodturning, so in 1853, he made his second try as a merchant in a tiny store in Reynolds Arcade, stocking it with thermometers, field glasses, and microscopes, all imported. He also fitted a few spectacles in horn-rimmed or wire frames, but eye care was as much a luxury in that community as a telescope, and business was terrible.

The town was full of poor immigrants who had been encouraged and even forced out of crowded New York westward to Buffalo and Rochester. Then there came the cholera epidemic of the late 1840s along with high unemployment.

It was not the best time for the small shopkeeper, and Bausch would have gone under a second time if Henry Lomb had not come forward with his sixty dollars and if he had not also supported the business with his earnings as a cabinetmaker and glazier. It was an odd sideline, but it did have a connection with glass. While Bausch was selling imported optical goods and working with optical lenses, Lomb busied himself repairing plate glass windows; and when business was slow, they loaded up their pack sacks and peddled their wares, including Lomb's carpentry skills, along the country roads.

For about eight years, the two men struggled to stay solvent in a business that was not exactly looked on as a necessity. Although Bausch had been born and trained in Europe, where there was an established tradition in optics, he did not think highly of the quality of the imported lenses, but he was too poor to buy his own lens-grinding machine.

Matters changed in 1861. When the Civil War broke out, Lomb enlisted in the New York Volunteer Infantry and went off for two years to fight in the Army of the Potomac, then at Bull Run, Antietam, and Fredericksburg, sending his pay back home to keep the business going.

Though sales in wartime were slower than ever, Bausch was far from idle. He spent his spare time making his own lens-grinding apparatus to turn out lenses to his own standard. Then there is the legend that one day he found lying on the street a hard black substance which he recognized as the new miracle product, vulcanized rubber, developed in 1839 by Charles Goodyear.

Who else but Bausch would have picked it up out of the gutter with the idea of crafting it into spectacle frames? At that time, frames were crudely made of iron, steel, or even leather, until horn was introduced in the 1840s. The Chinese had been using tortoiseshell and papier mâché for five centuries.

By the time Henry Lomb, now a captain in the infantry, came back from the war in 1863, his partner was already turning out frames of economical vulcanite, selling horn rims only to his wealthier customers. The new, cheaper material became so important to their growing spectacle business that they formed the Vulcanite Optical Instrument Company in 1864, licensed exclusively to use the substance for spectacle frames.

Lomb went off to open a New York branch, and for the next fifteen years, he was their commercial traveler in spectacles and frames.

Meanwhile, back in Rochester, the company was developing new optical lines. By 1867, they were no longer housed in a store but in a small factory, turning out loupes for watchmakers and engravers, pocket magnifiers, and microscopes. In 1878, recently incorporated for the first time as Bausch & Lomb when twenty-year-old Edward Bausch joined his father, the company began standardizing lens curves to permit the use of cemented bifocals. Their long collaboration with George Eastman in his photographic lenses was just on the horizon.

The company's fastest growth began in the early days of this century, but as early as the 1880s, the founder's son, Edward Bausch, while on a trip to Europe, made a profitable deal with the firm of Carl Zeiss, inventor of the prism binocular, and then with Ernst Abbe for the new anastigmatic photo-

Top: *A sketch of J. J. Bausch's first optical shop in the Reynolds Arcade in Rochester, New York. The shop opened in 1853.* Bottom: *This ad for spectacles appeared in a Rochester newspaper in 1853.*

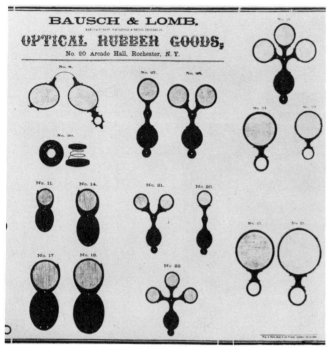

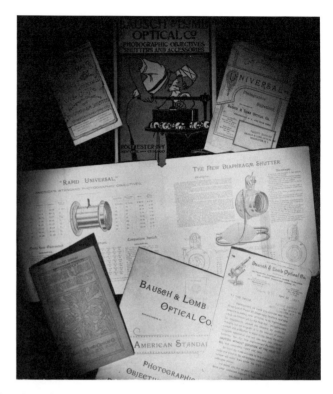

Left: *A page taken from Bausch &
Lomb's first catalog, which appeared in
1864.* Right: *A collection of brochures
advertising Bausch & Lomb's
photographic product line.*

graphic lens also developed by Zeiss. Still later, during World War I, he set up
the first American plant to manufacture precision optical glass.

Henry Lomb's career lasted from 1853 to his death in 1908, but he had an
even more active career in public affairs, especially in health and adult education. He founded the Rochester Mechanics' Institute in 1885, forerunner of
workers' educational associations, and the Rochester Public Health Association in 1897, and also introduced kindergartens and medical inspection into
Rochester schools.

John Jacob Bausch and his sons Edward and William ground away at
their lenses over an incredible stretch of time. The founder himself was active
until his death at the age of ninety-six, while son Edward, born in 1854, was
chairman of the board when he died at eighty-nine. William, dying in 1944 at
the age of eighty-three, was not quite so long-lived, but he was no less
important. In 1912, he began research which, in the words of the company
history, "resulted in America's independence from Europe for its supply of
optical glass."

As a boy, said *The New York Times* obituary, Dr. Edward Bausch (he was
given an honorary doctorate by the University of Rochester in 1931) "heated
sheets of vulcanized rubber on the family cook stove and rushed them out to a
woodshed workshop, where his father fed them into a hand punch press with
which Mr. Lomb stamped out spectacle frames. And he built his first microscope at the age of fourteen."

It is literally true that the son spent his life in the business, for he was born
six months after Henry Lomb loaned his father the famous sixty dollars. ♦

*In this photo taken in the 1930s or
1940s, Edward Bausch is holding the
microscope he built as a boy. Behind
him is a stereomicroscope.*

WESTINGHOUSE

L et's start with the barest of facts.

In 1861, when George Westinghouse was only fifteen years old, he invented a rotary steam engine, which he patented four years later, in October 1865. During his last illness in 1914, nearly fifty years later, he was working on a patent application for an electrically operated wheelchair.

A simple count of the lists of patents given in the appendix of H.G. Prout's *A Life of George Westinghouse* shows that between those two dates, Westinghouse took out patents on new mechanical inventions at the rate of about one every six weeks during his whole working life. They were not just ideas; they were practical inventions, complete with working drawings and specifications, and all arising out of his own work on railroad air brakes and signaling, natural gas, and electricity. During those same years, Westinghouse was personally involved in building a complex corporate network.

But he had got out of the habit of throwing tantrums when he didn't get his own way, as he used to when he was a kid. Francis E. Leupp's *George Westinghouse*, written four years after the inventor's death, records that "old neighbors of the family still remember these paroxysms, which took the form first of screaming and stamping, then of throwing himself flat and banging his head against any hard surface that came most convenient . . . . Near the family cottage was a large flat stone on which he repeatedly thus tried conclusions with his skull."

Leupp quotes Westinghouse later in life: "I have always known what I wanted, and how to get it. As a child I got it by tantrums; in mature years, by hard work."

What exactly did George Westinghouse want? Simply, he wanted to be left alone to get on with his work, and he knew what his work was.

George Westinghouse was the son and the namesake of a successful manufacturer of agricultural machinery of Central Bridge, New York, and the descendant of a family originally from Westphalia, Germany, named Westinghausen, one branch of which moved to England in the fourteenth century.

The American line goes back to fifteen-year-old John Westinghouse, who came to Vermont in 1755 with his widowed mother. Like all pioneers, he cleared land, built a log house, farmed, and raised a family.

Three generations later, George Westinghouse Senior, the fifth of twelve children, moved out to Ohio when he married, but soon moved back east, closer to the larger population centers of New York State. He picked a site near two watercourses and a network of roads for his plant and workshop.

George Westinghouse

He took out patents on new mechanical inventions at the rate of one every six weeks during his working life.

Miss Norma Smallwood had recently been named Miss America of 1926 when she saw a display of Westinghouse products at Atlantic City. She liked the automatic range so well a dealer said he would send her one.

An artist's rendering of the first practical demonstration of the air brake, when it dramatically saved a drayman's life. Opposite page: Every house needed a Westinghouse in the 1940s.

All his ten children were biddable except young George, who simply refused to stay out of the workshop. He played hooky, hid in corners, lied and coaxed, and threw his famous tantrums, just to be able to watch the machinery with the workmen in action.

One neighbor in old age recalled him at age six, "how he would fly into fearful passions," but also recalled "his earnest little face, with its wrinkle between the eyes as if he were already solving problems."

Even in his passions, he solved problems. One day when his father was whipping him, "the switch broke," writes Leupp, "in two or three places . . . . George, who had been crying lustily, desisted long enough to point to a leather whip . . . and say, 'There's a better one, Father.'"

When George was ten, his father moved the plant to Schenectady, New York, where the boy, with the connivance of a friendly mechanic, rigged up a little shop of his own in an empty attic. Gradually, he was allowed near his father's machines.

George was "keen on everything mathematical," and according to Prout "he could easily have been eminent in physics and mathematics . . . . He did things that the textbooks said were against the laws of nature, and in the course of time, the text writers caught up with him."

In the next three years, George became a master mechanic, mostly self-taught, and also turned out his first invention, the steam rotary engine, the principle of which he later ingeniously reversed to make a water meter.

He also wheedled fifty cents a day out of his father for odd jobs such as cutting pipe into standard lengths. Not that George did the actual work. Within half a day, he had rigged up a power tool to feed and cut the pipe automatically, and after he had persuaded a workman to keep an eye on the machine, he went fishing.

No wonder he became an entrepreneur as well as an inventor, and he was both for all his life. They say that for relaxation he used to take machines apart and put them together again.

The foundation for his fame and fortune lay in the Westinghouse air brake for railroad trains. Using compressed air and a revolutionary triple valve, the air brake shunted rail transportation into the future. Before Westinghouse, rail collisions and accidents due to faulty braking were epidemic. The first time the Westinghouse air brake was used, in December 1868, on a rail line near Pittsburgh known as "the Panhandle," it saved the life of a wagon driver who had been flung onto the track right in front of the train. Equipped with the new air brake, the train stopped in time.

In the week after Westinghouse's death, credit for the invention was claimed by a Frenchman named Debruges. According to a story in *The New York Times* of March 29, 1914, Debruges tested it in Paris before Prince Jerome Bonaparte, but when he let his patent lapse in 1870, Westinghouse bought it. Debruges "would sometimes point to the name of Westinghouse on coaches when traveling and sadly say, 'My name should be on there.'" Prout's records

Water Heater · Range · Home Freezer · Laundromat · Dryer · Cabinets

Tank Cleaner

Cleaner

Cozy Glow

Waste Away

Heater

Toaster

Hot Plate

Roaster Oven

AMAZING NEW TWO-TEMP REFRIGERATOR

Waffle Baker

Iron

Fan

Coffee Maker

Mixer

Comforter

IT'S A REAL FREEZER...and A GREAT REFRIGERATOR...Two in ONE!

There's Plenty of Room for 76 Meals... *at one time*...in this superbly planned new Two-Temp. Whopping big, man-sized meals, too ... more than 6 days' food for a family of four. The Freeze Chest alone holds more than 56 pounds of frozen foods and ice cubes ... *freezes* food, too, if you wish. Large quantities of milk,

staples and leftovers easily fit on the shelves. Huge amounts of fruit and vegetables stay fresh and crisp in the two giant Humidrawers. See the new Two-Temp...trimmed with Apricream, the exciting new "go with" color ... and many other wonderful new electric appliances at your Westinghouse retailer's now.

Every house needs Westinghouse
Maker of 30 MILLION Electric Home Appliances

WESTINGHOUSE ELECTRIC CORPORATION · PLANTS IN 25 CITIES · OFFICES EVERYWHERE · APPLIANCE DIVISION, MANSFIELD, OHIO

Tune in Ted Malone ... Every Morning, Monday through Friday ... ABC Network

Left: *An advertisement for a Westinghouse radio-phonograph in the 1940s featured the familiar slogan, "You can be sure . . . if it's Westinghouse." Right: The Columbian Exposition of 1893 in Chicago provided a spectacular showcase for the new electrical system George Westinghouse and his engineers were perfecting. At night the Magic City within a city became a blazing wonderland of light provided by Westinghouse.*

show, however, that the Westinghouse patent was taken out in April 1869.

In July that year, the Westinghouse Air Brake Co. was formed. During the next ten years, the device spread throughout the transportation world, often against resistance from skeptical governments. At home, Westinghouse incorporated one company after another to market his inventions in electricity, which he revolutionized by pioneering in alternating current, known in those days as "Westinghouse current."

In the ten-year period from 1880 to 1890, Westinghouse took out 145 patents, or more than one a month.

In his whole life, he had only one interlude from mechanical invention and business. As a teen-ager he served three years, first in a New York regiment, then as third engineer on a naval vessel, during the Civil War. Even that was not much of an interlude, for on board ship, he rigged up a lathe in the mess and went on with his real work.

George Westinghouse received many honors in his sixty-eight years, but perhaps the most ironic of all came on his death in 1914. Like many former servicemen, he was given a military burial at Arlington National Cemetery, where the inscription, passing over entirely his life as an inventor, reads simply:

"Acting Third Assistant Engineer, 1864–1865."

That's fame indeed. ◆

LIBBEY-OWENS-FORD

By the time Libbey-Owens teamed up with the Edward Ford Plate Glass Company in February 1930 to form Libbey-Owens-Ford, described by the *Toledo Times* as "the largest flat glass manufacturing unit in the world," all three originals had disappeared from the scene within the previous decade.

They were all pioneers in the glass industry, but the name of Ford goes back further than the others. Though it is true that Edward Ford, through his own initiative, founded a new plate glass industry in Illinois, as well as the town of Rossford (his wife's maiden name, Ross, combined with his own surname), which grew up around it, he owed a big debt to the pioneering work of his father, John Baptiste Ford, the first man to fabricate plate glass in America.

It was in 1870 that John Ford supervised the installation of the first two panes of American-made plate glass in John Helb's tailor shop at 318 Pearl Street, New Albany, just outside Louisville, Kentucky, and about 350 miles south of Toledo, where his son Edward was to set up shop more than a quarter of a century later.

By then, John Ford had lived a busy life. Born in a Danbury, Kentucky, log cabin in 1811, he was apprenticed at twelve to a saddlemaker who undertook to teach the boy to read and write. When the saddlemaker reneged on the promise, young John, disregarding the heavy punishment then meted out to young apprentices who ran away, took to the woods and headed for Louisville. He ran like a hunted animal and only got passage to safety across the Ohio River by giving a boatman a pack of cards to hide him in the boat's pigpen.

At fourteen, he settled in Greenville, Kentucky. Later married, he earned his living at various times as grocer, flour miller, seller of tin kitchen cabinets, and harness and saddle merchant. In 1854 he moved to New Albany, where he manufactured a feed-cutting box for farmers, then opened a nail factory, a forge, and a foundry. He later bought steamships to transport his goods up and down the river.

Within five years he had a fleet and became known around the state as Captain Ford, making his pile by repairing boats crippled in the Civil War. He was just about to expand into railroads, which he saw as the coming mode of transportation, when his eldest son Emory, just graduated from college in June 1864, came home with an enthusiasm for glass.

John Baptiste Ford took it up at once, bought land along the river front,

Edward Ford

Edward Drummond Libbey

An artist's rendering of Captain Ford watching his men install the first two panes of polished plate glass ever made in America in the storefront of John Heib's tailor shop at 318 Pearl Street in New Albany, Kentucky.

and built J.B. Ford & Sons (Emory and Edward were the sons) to manufacture bottles and fruit jars, and later window glass.

Then came trouble. Ford's wealth of more than three hundred thousand dollars shrank as business fell off in the post–Civil War depression. He sold off steamboats, cashed in stock in other ventures, wrote off bad loans, and finally saw his glassworks taken over by the contractors who had built it. When it burnt to the ground shortly after, they handed it back to Ford as worthless.

He was then past sixty, but instead of folding, he got loans apparently out of the air and built a new glassworks along two blocks of the river front. All of a sudden he got fired up with the idea of making plate glass right there in America, instead of importing it from France and Britain.

Plate is simply flat glass, which is first imbedded in a plate of plaster for polishing on one side, then on the other. Ford mastered the process so well that his plate began winning awards, but that did not save him from a second financial disaster, this time through foreign dumping of plate. Again he fought back. He helped to design the Louisville Plate Glass Company and became its superintendent. Then he walked out when he found that the business was shaky. Again he borrowed to build a plant of his own.

He had ideas for glass sewer pipe; he fought for protective tariffs; he traded profitably in farmland rich in silica sand; he made a huge commission on a land broker deal in Mexico. And with renewed energy at the age of seventy-one, he established the Pittsburgh Plate Glass Company at Creighton, Pennsylvania, in February 1883, with his son Edward as president and Emory as secretary.

He himself refused to take executive office; he said he was only a builder. He was, however, in charge. A year later, he wrote to his wife, in his own personal spelling, "All who have ben here that have taken Stock are highlley pleased. We are A-Gitting in Good Shape making a splendid Quality of Glass . . . ."

The company did well, and John Ford further amused himself by buying up farmland nearby and establishing a building company, a brickworks, and a pipeline company to bring in gas for the glass furnaces. He was the first to use gas in glassmaking.

In 1887, the year he turned seventy-six, he established "the largest glass factory in the world," and a town to go with it. It was called Ford City in his honor, and he was guest of honor at a huge party with ten thousand guests on his eightieth birthday on November 14, 1891.

Edward Ford's own company was built on that foundation. Suddenly, for complex corporate reasons, he resigned as president of Pittsburgh Glass, moving sideways to head the Michigan Alkali Company, which his father had created a few years earlier to supply soda ash for the glass factory.

For the next ten years, Edward, the son of John Ford, refined his plans to get back into glass under his own name. After all, he already had nearly twenty years' experience. Finally, in August 1898, on 173 acres on the east

bank of the Ohio, he turned sod for what, in a familiar phrase, was called "the largest plate glass factory in the world." With fifteen separate buildings, it was bigger than anything his father had built.

In his first year, he turned out more than a million square feet of plate, as the town of Rossford grew up around him. "Captain" John Baptiste Ford was on hand to witness the first shipment of plate on November 17, 1899 — it was his eighty-eighth birthday — six days after the incorporation of the new Edward Ford Plate Glass Company.

A familiar name turned up as vice president. It was John B. Ford, not the old pioneer, but his grandson and the son of Edward Ford. It was this John B. Ford who led the negotiations in 1930 to merge his father's company with Libbey-Owens.

Edward Drummond Libbey was the man who transported his father's failed glass factory nearly one thousand miles from New England to a fresh start in Toledo, Ohio. Michael Joseph Owens was the inventive genius who changed almost overnight from labor leader to business executive.

Libbey never wanted to be a glassmaker. Even as a young boy, he was deeply religious and actually shocked his parents when at seventeen he announced that he intended to enter the ministry instead of enrolling at Harvard. When a throat infection destroyed his powerful speaking voice two years later, he gave up on the vocation just before he turned twenty.

That was late 1873. He could do nothing else but go back to work in his father's New England Glass Company, where he had already put in months of part-time work as sweeper and packer in the shipping department.

The New England Glass Company, one of the oldest and most reputable glassworks in the country, was formed in 1812 out of the ruin of the earlier Boston Porcelain and Glass Company by a group of men headed by Deming Jarves, whose invention of a source for red lead, an essential fusing ingredient in glassmaking, gave the company a virtual monopoly lasting nearly thirty years. By 1850, they were doing five hundred thousand dollars in annual business, paying continuous dividends, and employing five hundred workers.

It was William Libbey's bad luck that he bought the company just as it began to go downhill. The elder Libbey had been an employee in other Jarves

Michael Joseph Owens

Early 1900s advertisements for Libbey glass. (Top: Harper's Magazine; Bottom: The Review of Reviews.)

companies for fifteen years, doing so well that in 1870 he was appointed manager of New England Glass to try and save it. But times were hard, business fell off, dividends dried up, and five years later he was accused of mismanagement by the directors.

He bought time by undertaking to buy the company, but even as owner, he saw the slide continue. In 1880 he took into partnership his twenty-six-year-old son Edward, who urged him either to sell out or to relocate in the West, where several Ohio cities were offering lavish inducements to different industries. Libbey would not hear of it. His roots were generations deep in New England soil. He died in 1883, leaving his son to carry on, only to have the plant closed down by strike action in 1886.

The plant flickered back to life briefly, when Edward Libbey created Amerina, a new ruby glass that sold well at Tiffany's, but his thoughts kept turning to the West, where there was a supply of good glass sand; where taxes, land, and labor were cheap; where new markets were opening up; and where newfound wells were pouring out a supply of cheap fuel.

It was, indeed, the gas and oil men of Toledo who acted with the town's businessmen to take Libbey on a tour of the city to pick out a site. Nor did it hurt their chances any that on that fact-finding visit, Libbey met the young woman he decided he wanted to marry.

As the secretary of the gas company, William Maher, reported back after a visit to Libbey's New England plant at East Cambridge, Massachusetts, "It is like a large ripe cherry about to drop in the mouth of Toledo."

It was a complicated deal. The expenses at Toledo were underwritten by loans and public subscription, while Libbey issued stock, cashed in his insurance, and borrowed money from friends and family. The day building started was the onset of the three-day Great Blizzard of March 1888.

Libbey left behind in East Cambridge all the equipment, furnaces, and heavy tools acquired over seventy years, but still had to transport fifty carloads of machinery. Not only that, he had to persuade trained glassworkers to uproot themselves and their families to follow the thirty-four-year-old owner of a failing business. The move was finally completed on August 16, 1888, to a banner welcome by the *Toledo Blade* reading, "All Toledo Welcomes You to the Future Glass Center of the World," a parade to the new Ash Street factory, speeches, and a banquet.

It was quite a party, but only Edward Libbey, now president of the Libbey Glass Company, had the hangover. He was in debt, he had start-up troubles, he was homesick for New England, and he was responsible to a painful degree for the well-being of the families he had brought with him. Most of all, he missed the skilled men who had opted not to make the move to Toledo.

In that mood, he could not have imagined the great future that lay in store, which would carry forward into the great consumer society of the twentieth century. He could not possibly imagine the day of the glass-enclosed automobile, the glass-faced skyscraper, and the demand for high-quality optical and insulating glass, safety glass and float glass, and allied products for aircraft and aerospace.

All Edward Libbey had back in 1888 was a corporate headache in an industry that was running pretty well on methods that had been standard for nearly two thousand years. Before the summer was over, he was heartily wishing he had gone quietly bankrupt in East Cambridge.

It was then, in his search for skilled men, that a young fellow in rough coat and woolen working pants walked into his office. "My name is Mike Owens," he said. "I'm looking for a job."

Neither man realized that this was the first move in the future Libbey-Owens-Ford double play. The first thing Michael Joseph Owens did when he was taken on as superintendent of the Libbey Glass Company late in 1888 was to fire every last workman in the place.

That was some beginning for a working partnership. Libbey could not believe his eyes when he came in to work one day and saw Owens with his feet up on a desk reading a paper and the plant empty of workmen and idle. After all, he had come in off the street and had been given a job, and was even promoted to superintendent when he threatened to quit, disgusted with the way the plant was being run.

Owens was only twenty-nine, but already he had been in the glass industry for nineteen years. Born in 1859, he was working beside his father in a West Virginia coal mine by the time he was ten. When he was dragged out, half alive, from a coal slide, his mother put her foot down and refused to let him go back.

Instead, they moved to Wheeling, where he got a job stoking the "glory hole," a small furnace used by glass blowers to keep the glass hot. Owens reminisced in 1922, "I worked five hours in the morning, washed and had my dinner, then went back for another five hours in the afternoon."

Within five years, at fifteen, he was a skilled glass blower, encouraged by a parish priest to read in his spare time. Later, he became involved in debating societies, where he first realized he had gifts of persuasion, which turned him, at twenty-three, into a union organizer in the Union Flint Glass Works across the river from Wheeling. In 1883 he was a union delegate at the American Flint Glass Workers Convention held, ironically, in East Cambridge, Massachusetts, the month before Edward Libbey's father died.

Owens's life had this pattern: sixty hours a week working in glass, with all his spare time devoted to union business. His union career culminated in his great debate in 1887 in Brooklyn against James "Gaffer" Smith, an old line union man.

Owens applied for the job with Libbey right after the company moved to Toledo, when he read their ad in a Wheeling paper. He liked the idea of a new company and making a new start in Toledo. Although he did not realize that the company's future was chancy, he found that out fast enough. Morale was low, and drinking on the job was high. Everybody, from glass blowers to

Workers blowing glass in the Libbey glassworks.

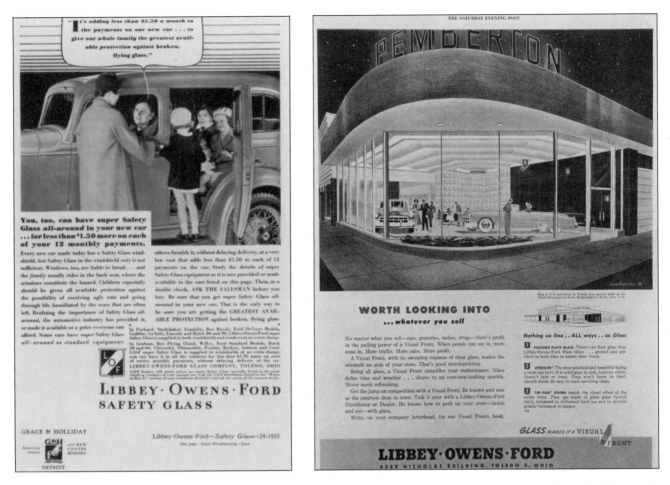

Left: *This ad appeared in* Good Housekeeping *in 1933.* Right: *This ad appeared in* The Saturday Evening Post *in 1949.*

cutters to "carry-in boys" to "blow boys" (they pumped up the furnaces), loafed or talked back or clocked in late, leaving the glass melts to cool. No wonder the company was on the skids, and no wonder Owens fired the lot.

The paper he was reading that morning in an empty plant was running his own help wanted ads. He said thirty years later, "I hired back all the men willing to work the way I was trained to work."

With his new crews of hand-picked men and boys, the place brightened like a freshly stoked fire, and the books moved from the red into the black — a three-thousand-dollar loss to a fifty-thousand-dollar profit — in only eight months. But Owens was only too aware that the industry was using antiquated methods.

His first invention, patented on September 13, 1892, was a mechanical dummy to replace the "mold boy," who opened and closed the glass molds. But he really turned the industry on its ear with his 1895 invention of an automatic blowing machine. Originally designed to blow molten glass into tumblers, it was quickly adapted to the manufacture of lamp chimneys and, as electricity came into common use, light bulbs for industry and the American home. It was this invention more than any other that projected Michael Owens, one-time union leader and later shop foreman, into his first capitalist role. It was none other than his boss, Edward Libbey, who provided the financing for his automatic blowing machine and who later went into partnership with him.

The Toledo Glass Company, which simply held rights to Owens's patents, sold them to its subsidiaries. Libbey granted Owens the controlling interest, which he refused to accept, retaining about 35 percent of the stock, which soared in value. Toledo Glass was quite separate from Libbey Glass, though Edward Libbey was president of both.

Owens's invention of an automatic blowing machine was only the beginning. He was already working on a completely automatic machine to take in molten glass at one end and produce bottles at the other. This was a tougher proposition, and it took more than six years and five hundred thousand dollars, as one try after another was discarded.

The problem was temperature: how to keep the molten glass hot enough as the blow tubes dipped into it. Owens solved this by designing a revolving melt pot in which the draw tube always dipped into freshly heated glass.

The Toledo Bottle Company was formed in 1905 and had become the largest bottle-making company in the world by the time Owens died in 1923.

In 1893 Owens was asked to supervise the construction of a complete glass factory in miniature for the World's Columbian Exposition in Chicago. But they came together in corporate harness as Libbey-Owens not through any invention but through the ideas of another Toledo man, Irving Weightman Colburn, who dreamed up a new way of making window glass.

Colburn, born in 1861, a mechanical genius from Fitchburg, Ohio, who had established an electrical manufacturing plant in Toledo in 1899, became intrigued by the glass industry's search for a new way to make sheets of glass. Both Owens and Libbey knew the old way: blow a huge bottle, cut off bottom and top to make a cylinder, slice it down one side, flatten it out, and polish. Colburn wondered why you had to start with a curve when you wanted flat glass. He worked on one device after another, often to hoots of ridicule and at his own expense. Finally, he came up with a machine involving fire-clay cylinders partly immersed in molten glass. Simply put, the temperature stayed high, and the glass rolled over the cylinders without sticking, in a continuous sheet.

Though the invention was hailed as causing a great furor in the glass industry in September 1906, Colburn ran too small an operation to iron out all the kinks and bring it into production.

It was then he wrote to Owens for help. After intricate negotiations to settle copyright and royalty, Colburn went to work for the Toledo Glass Company, where his machine formed the basis for the new firm of Libbey-Owens, which brought the two friends together in corporate union for the first time on May 18, 1916.

Fifteen years later, their names were linked with Ford, the other glass pioneer. ◆

The first successful device to produce glass bottles is shown here. The heads dipped to take their charges, and the tank revolved so glass was not taken repeatedly from the same place.

Irving Colburn (far right) *and some of those who helped him to perfect his sheet glass machine, standing outside the experimental plant on Castle Boulevard.*

JOHNSON &JOHNSON

Robert Wood Johnson

James Johnson

Once upon a time there was a cattle farmer named Sylvester Johnson in Carbondale, Pennsylvania, whose three sons all went into the professions. Robert became a pharmacist, Edward an attorney, and James a civil engineer.

So which pair of brothers founded the pharmaceutical firm of Johnson & Johnson?

They all did, but not all together and not at the same time; and it is one of history's little ironies that the last of the Johnson brothers to join the firm was the eldest, who happened to be the only pharmacist in the lot. Nor is he one of the two Johnsons in the corporate name.

The main thing, however, is that Johnson & Johnson was a strictly family concern, and even if older brother Robert never got his own name on the incorporation papers, he was the founder in every real sense.

For Robert Wood Johnson, the turning point in his life came at an international medical congress in Philadelphia in 1876 when he was thirty-one. The principal speaker was Joseph Lister, the professor of surgery at Edinburgh University. Lister had nothing to do with the antiseptic Listerine, though it was named after him, but he had everything to do with the use of antiseptics. To put it at its simplest, he revolutionized modern surgery by making it possible for surgeons to slow down.

In the old days, surgeons raced against infection. The faster their knives, the less chance of gangrene or suppuration. In 1865 Lister sprayed an operating room with carbolic acid, disinfecting not only the instruments but the patient's skin as well, and proved that infection during operations could be greatly reduced.

Then there were the dressings, which at that time were crudely bunched wads of lint, jute, and even oakum. They were more like plugs to stop the flow of blood than active parts of the healing process. Listerism, as antisepsis was first called, helped to make such practices obsolete and to let surgeons work more slowly.

All this came as an inspiring message to Robert Johnson, whose contact with medicine had started when he was apprenticed to an apothecary in Poughkeepsie, New York, at the age of sixteen.

The family is traced back to one Edward Johnson, a writer of history, who came to the United States in 1630. When the three Johnson brothers were born six generations later, their father was well-off and part of a settled community, which may be why each brother could choose his own profession.

While Edward and James studied law and engineering, Robert was up to his elbows laboriously mixing medicated plasters, ointments, and tinctures. But the moment his apprenticeship ended, he moved to New York City and established a wholesale drug and brokerage business. In 1874 he became a junior partner in Seabury & Johnson in Brooklyn, which he helped to set up to manufacture pharmaceutical preparations.

Their first important product was a new kind of bandage or sticking plaster with an India rubber base, as distinct from the "court plaster," specially made of silk covered with isinglass (a kind of gelatin) for the delicate faces of ladies at court. In a sense, the new India rubber plaster, intended for mass use, was the ancestor of the Band-Aid developed by Johnson & Johnson and given that marketable name in 1921.

Above: *An artist's rendering of the original factory building, circa 1887.* Bottom left: *The* Robert W. Johnson *was used to transport Johnson & Johnson products from their New Brunswick factory to New York City.*

It was in 1876 that Robert Johnson turned up at Joseph Lister's lecture and had a glimpse of the future in pharmaceuticals. By then Seabury & Johnson, organized in 1874, were doing so well from their Brooklyn factory, they had already moved to larger premises in East Orange, New Jersey.

Robert Johnson acted at once to persuade his brothers to join him at Seabury & Johnson, though whether Seabury was consulted and what he had to say about it has not been recorded.

Engineer James was put to designing machinery for production of modern antiseptic dressings, while lawyer Edward discovered hidden talents for sales and advertising. Within five years, the company of Johnson & Johnson was formed, with capital of one thousand dollars, by James and Edward Johnson in the city of New Brunswick, New Jersey. A photograph of the factory taken in 1902 shows a six-story brick building — formerly a wallpaper factory — with a sturdy cargo tugboat, the *Robert W. Johnson*, tied up at the wharf. By then, Johnson & Johnson was carrying on regular traffic to New York City.

Robert W. Johnson, the pharmacist, was not included in the original

For free reproduction of this painting, write to Johnson & Johnson, Box 1006, Dept. E, New Brunswick, N. J.

"Mommy always says you're safe when you use Johnson & Johnson"

Sealed in individual envelopes, Red Cross Sterile Gauze Pads are soft, absorbent, absolutely sterile. Ideal for First Aid and Baby Care.

New, exclusive formula: Now Red Cross Adhesive Tape gives better sticking qualities and greater freedom from skin irritations.

Red Cross Cotton comes to you sterile. This long-fibered cotton is the whitest, softest, most absorbent surgical cotton available.

Individually wrapped and sterile, BAND-AID Adhesive Bandages are convenient protection for small cuts, blisters, and abrasions.

New Red Cross Cotton Balls are sterile and convenient. Have 1000 and 1 uses, in the nursery, for first aid, for cosmetics.

This product has **no connection** whatever with American National Red Cross.

The most trusted name in surgical dressings... *Johnson & Johnson*

Left: *Workers at the Johnson & Johnson factory at the turn of the century.* Right: *This advertisement for baby products ran in 1914.*

Opposite page: *An advertisement for first-aid products in 1950 shows the use of the red cross. A disclaimer in small type disavows any connection to the American Red Cross.*

corporate structure because of his connection with Seabury & Johnson. In July 1885, however, he sold his half interest, pledging not to engage in any business "of like character" for ten years. In fact, he was released from that covenant long before the term had elapsed.

The game of corporate musical chairs went through two more movements. In 1887 the three brothers recapitalized at one hundred thousand dollars with Robert as president, to "manufacture and sell medical, pharmaceutical, surgical and antiseptic specialties and analogous products."

In fact, they brought Listerism to America. Among their first developments were a sterilized catgut suture and zinc oxide adhesive plaster, both before the turn of the century.

In 1899 Edward, the minority partner, left the company to set up Mead Johnson & Co. (his middle name was Mead) to make dietary and baby foods and vitamins, and later, pharmaceuticals.

Robert and James Johnson worked as a team well into the new century. The older brother continued his interest in antiseptics and surgical dressings, based on theories he set out as early as 1888 in a book called *Modern Methods of Antiseptic Wound Treatment*, while his brother developed the machinery and the production methods to make dressings both compact and simple and sterile-packed.

The company did not begin their great expansion and diversification until after Robert Johnson's death in 1910. James took over, managed the firm through the difficult war years, established the first foreign branch in 1919, and then in 1932, handed over company management to the second Robert Wood Johnson, who within a year had bridged the Atlantic with their first international affiliate in Britain.

When Robert Wood Johnson died in 1968, he left a billion dollars to the Robert Wood Johnson Foundation to be used for the good of humanity — primarily in the areas of health and medicine. It was in his name, but it was also his father's, who had started it all more than a century earlier, up to his elbows mixing ointments and tinctures in a small apothecary's shop in Poughkeepsie, New York. ♦

DOW

Herbert Henry Dow

His search for the key to the bromine market led to the huge industrial chemical complex operating under his name.

All in the interests of science, Herbert Henry Dow took a cautious taste of the liquid the well-driller handed him one day back in 1887 and nearly threw up. He was prepared for the taste of salt, because the liquid was part of a brine deposit in an oil field, but what he did not expect was a nauseating bitterness.

That was his first contact with bromine, a substance first discovered in 1802 in sea water. Bromine, a red liquid giving off an irritating brown vapor, became important in the second half of the century in patent medicines and in photographic chemicals, most of which were expensively imported from Germany. It was a valuable but a disagreeable substance: The name comes from *bromos*, the Greek word for stink.

Dow may have spat out that first taste, but instead of being repelled, he was attracted to the very challenge it offered him as a budding young chemist.

At that time, Herbert Dow was a twenty-one-year-old undergraduate at the Case School of Applied Science in Cleveland, Ohio, working on his thesis on the chemical uses of fuel in boilers. The sample he tasted he later analyzed to find it rich in bromine and lithium. The brine was actually worth more than the crude oil, but only in theory.

In the United States, bromine was a negligible by-product of the salt industry. When brine was evaporated over heat, it yielded masses of ordinary salt, plus tiny amounts of bromine. A new and profitable use was found for the waste lumber and "slash" — small limbs chopped off the main logs — from the many "salt and lumber" companies that were logging the immense forests of that part of the country. It was burned to process the huge brine deposits of Michigan and Ohio, which were still very active when Dow first came on the scene.

When Dow realized that the old cheap source of heat could soon be exhausted, he decided that he must either find a new source of economical heat for the evaporation process (he noted electrolysis as one possibility) or invent a cold method.

It was his search for an economical way to produce bromine that laid the foundation for the huge industrial chemical complex operating under his name today. But it was a long, hard pull, even after he had come up with the new method.

Chemical processes are never easy to describe in lay terms, but it worked something like this. He blew a steady current of air through sheets of burlap wet with bromine-laden brine to which chemicals had been added to help free the bromine. As the brine vaporized, without heat, he collected and reliquefied the bromine.

The process worked, but Dow's first shoestring factory in Canton, Ohio, failed after little less than a year. But he was stubborn. He had been brought up to trust his own ideas.

The family, originally from Norfolk, England, had lived for several generations in New England, where six of his ancestors in succession had been town clerk of Hampton, New Hampshire. Joseph Dow, Herbert's father, was the first in the family to strike out for himself, as master mechanic and inventor.

In the winter of 1865, the father took a temporary trouble-shooting job at a sewing machine factory in Belleville, Ontario, where Herbert was born. He was, however, Canadian for only a few weeks, for his father moved back across the border to Connecticut. In 1878 he took a permanent job in Cleveland, where he invented the first steam turbine ever produced in the United States, the prototype of a model used to power American submarines.

Herbert Dow grew up a chunky young man, with dark thick hair and eyebrows, but with a face so young-looking he grew a beard to make himself look older. He was argumentative, loved to play chess, and kept notebooks for jotting down both his thoughts and his ideas. And he had plenty of both.

At ten, he earned money distributing advertising flyers to pay his own way to the Centennial Exposition of 1876 in Philadelphia. Don Whitehead's *The Dow Story*, published in 1968, pictures Dow as a very ingenious young fellow. In his mid-teens he read that an Australian who had noticed that ostriches were not very good egg-sitters had "devised a crude incubator to relieve the parent birds of their responsibility." Dow figured if an incubator would work for ostriches, it would work for hens, so he devised one of his

The scene of Dow's first successful electrolysis of brine.

Left: *The advertisement for Dow's calcium chloride, used to control dust on roads, appeared in* The American City. Right: *The Dow Powerhouse was part of Dow's Midland plant. It was the biggest electric generator Dow could build, and the electricity it generated was used to power the energy-demanding process of electrolysis. Here the crew pauses for a group portrait in 1903.*

own, incorporating a primitive thermostat it had taken him thirty-nine tries to make work.

When he found out that his incubators were being copied without payment, he stopped making them and instead drafted and sold blueprints and working drawings. That persistence helped after he recorded failure in his notebook: "Quit work at Canton," and dissolved the partnership.

He had already decided to move to Midland, Michigan, a town whose prosperity was threatened when the timber was gone. Underground, however, lay the Michigan brine deposits that Dow was determined to tap. He arrived in August 1890, and within a few months, the townspeople were calling him "crazy Dow," when he leased an idle brine well and set up his new enterprise in an old barn, calling it "The Midland Chemical Company."

He struggled on, assembled new capital, and finally saw his process in actual operation, while continuing his chemical experiments in related fields. He fought on after an explosion, and through financial difficulties, until in 1897 he created the Dow Chemical Company to make chlorine bleach, with other chemicals being added as the facilities grew.

By the time the founder died in 1930, sales had reached $15 million, mostly of bulk chemicals — turned out by continuous automation — to industry.

But the beginning was that primitive heatless method of releasing bromine, which is fundamentally still the best method of all.   ◆

EASTMAN

N o matter how you read it, George Eastman's last words, as reported on the front page of *The New York Times* on March 15, 1932, must be among the saddest on record.

"My work is done, why wait?" was the brief note he left just before killing himself in his Rochester, New York, home.

Shortly before noon, he had been chatting with his personal physician when he suddenly asked him to leave, saying "I have a note to write." Once alone, he sat at his desk, wrote the short note, stubbed out his cigarette, put the cap back on the fountain pen, took off his glasses, and shot himself through the heart.

He was, after all, nearly seventy-eight and chronically ill. He had never married and, since the death of his mother twenty-four years earlier, had lived alone. In her day, his Rochester mansion had been a center for regular musical soirées of high standard, though his own interests were more solitary.

He was an art collector and connoisseur, a skilled amateur cultivator of orchids and roses, a cotton grower, and a cattle breeder on his own North Carolina farm.

The news of his death, reported in the *Times*, "not only shocked the city of Rochester but other centres throughout the world. Not only had the industry he founded penetrated into the remotest parts of the earth, but his philanthropies, estimated at nearly $100 million, had been scattered abroad as well as in his native country."

The *Times* then paid Eastman one of their rare tributes by devoting almost the whole of page 14 — under the banner headline "Science and Industry Alike Owed Much to George Eastman" — to the story of his life and achievements. A series of laudatory articles — "Eastman Charted Path for Industry" and "Science of Nation Aided by Eastman" — revealed his interest in an eighteen-month calendar, his help to young inventors, and how he "got fun by giving money away."

The whole world had been transformed by the impact of his work as inventor and businessman. In the field of photography, he had already made his mark before the turn of the century. It was in 1888 that he put on the market his first Kodak box camera at twenty-five dollars, ready loaded with a 100-exposure roll of film that had to be returned to the factory for stripping, developing, and printing.

By the mid-1890s, he had formed the Eastman Kodak Company, capitalized at $8 million, and set out to internationalize the industry he had created.

George Eastman

---◆---

"You press the button, we do the rest."

---◆---

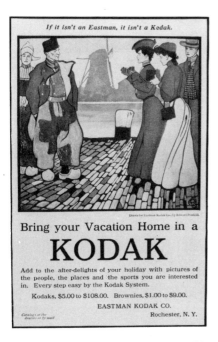

Bring your Vacation Home in a
KODAK
Add to the after-delights of your holiday with pictures of the people, the places and the sports you are interested in. Every step easy by the Kodak System.

Kodaks, $5.00 to $108.00.   Brownies, $1.00 to $9.00.

EASTMAN KODAK CO.

Catalog at the dealers or by mail   Rochester, N. Y.

Top: *This advertisement appeared in* Harper's Magazine *in 1905. Bottom: The Folding Pocket Kodak was sold in 1900 for $17.50 plus $.70 for twelve exposures. The major innovation of this camera was that it could be loaded in daylight.*

It began as a hobby to please his mother, widowed when George was a boy of eight. His father, George Washington Eastman, had been a master of penmanship who also published a standard text on bookkeeping. In 1842 the elder Eastman opened the Rochester Mercantile College, thought to be the first business school ever founded. When he died within two years, the school continued, but his only son, then fourteen, had to go to work, first in a real estate office, then in an insurance company, and then, at twenty, as bookkeeper in the Rochester Savings Bank.

Just before his vacation one summer, he took up photography so that he could bring back to his mother pictures of the sights he saw. In those days, photography meant a field kit including a huge box camera, tripod, glass plates, chemicals, and a lightproof tent. One single print could take more than an hour of concentrated work. After one expedition, George Eastman figured it was hardly worth the trouble, even for his mother. But since he had already realized that the only way he was going to become rich was to start his own business, he decided to invent a new, less troublesome way of taking pictures. It was apparently a deliberate decision by a half-educated young man with no scientific training whatever.

He was already a "capitalist." By saving small sums out of his salary, he accumulated $39 in the first year, rising to $516.95 in the third. Eastman used some of this capital for books, learned journals, chemicals, and supplies, at a total cost of $94.

He spent the next six years between 1874 and 1880 developing a sensitive dry gelatin emulsion and a machine for spreading it over glass plates. With the twenty-five hundred dollars from the sale of that patent, and a further seventy-five hundred dollars from a partner, Henry Strong, he went into business for himself at the age of twenty-six under the name Eastman Dry Plate Company. Everything that came after was built on that foundation.

Four years later, he made glass plates obsolete by inventing strip film — emulsion over collodion over gelatin on a paper base. The company became the Eastman Dry Plate & Film Company and offered a new self-contained box camera, complete with a film containing one hundred exposures.

Eastman thought up both the name Kodak for the camera and the slogan "You press the button, we do the rest."

Disappointingly, there followed a long season of manufacturing headaches because the strip would not stay flat and the prints faded all too soon. The answer, which led to what the *Dictionary of American Biography* calls "Eastman's emergence as an industrialist of the first order," lay in a new photographic process, developed perhaps in parallel by Eastman chemists and a Christian clergyman of Newark, New Jersey.

Hannibal Williston Goodwin, the sixty-five-year-old retired rector of the House of Prayer whose hobby was photography, had stumbled upon a varnish that prevented strip film from curling. He applied on May 2, 1887 for what he described as "a photographic pellicule produced from a solution of

Left: *An advertisement for Kodak color film, circa 1954. Above: In 1953, the Brownie Movie Camera took 8 mm movies in either full color ($49.50) or black and white ($39.75).*

The Brownie Flash Six-20 Camera had an eye-level view finder for indoor and outdoor snapshots. It cost $13.35 in 1953.

nitro-cellulose dissolved in nitrobenzol or other nonhydrous and non-hydroscopic solvents . . ." Over the next months, while the patent was pending, he made a film strip seventeen feet long and dispatched it to Eastman in Rochester to be coated and sensitized. In the course of a long correspondence, Goodwin sent Eastman an account of his process, and on April 17, 1889, Eastman wrote to Goodwin that he had succeeded in coating a film strip one thousand feet long with the sensitized emulsion.

Only seventeen days later, a chemist in Eastman's employ named Henry Reichenbach applied for a patent on a similar film, which was granted on December 10, 1889.

Goodwin pursued his patent application, and when it was finally grant-

George Eastman (left) and Thomas A. Edison in the gardens of the Eastman estate in Rochester, New York. The occasion was Eastman's demonstration of his new color movies for amateurs.

ed, after an inexplicable delay, on September 1, 1898, he went into business as the Goodwin Film & Camera Company. After he died on December 31, 1900, his patents were bought for $403,000 by Anthony and Scovill Company, who marketed the Goodwin product as Ansco film. Goodwin's widow retained a large interest.

In 1898 the incredible growth of the Eastman Company had scarcely even started. That year, the company was recapitalized at $8 million, and the developments poured out: daylight loading film, the pocket Kodak, the five-dollar camera, motion picture film — together with continuing headaches of legal suits against disloyal employees, disputes over patent rights, labor troubles, the Eastman entry into Europe, and antitrust legislation.

Among these events, the legal battle over the ownership of the Goodwin patent dragged on for more than a dozen years.

It was in 1902 that Ansco and Goodwin's widow first challenged the legitimacy of Eastman's claim to ownership in the Goodwin process, but the matter was not finally decided until March 1914 at the Circuit Court of Appeals. "The claims of the rector-inventor" were upheld against the Eastman Company, which then had to give an accounting of all photographic film sold since 1898. "The aged widow of the inventor," said the *Times*, "and his daughters are likely to be considerably enriched."

Ironically, Henry Reichenbach had been fired (for a technical bungle) shortly after he put through the patent application. George Eastman wrote that he did not "cherish any ill feelings" toward him.

Eastman himself was quite clear in his own mind about the patent. "There are a lot of fairy tales going the rounds about the Goodwin patent," he said to the *Rochester Post-Express* after the 1914 decision (quoted in C. W. Ackerman's *George Eastman*). He was convinced that influence had been brought to bear on the court by persons high in the Woodrow Wilson administration. And besides, he claimed that the Eastman Company's application demonstrated how the film could be made, while Goodwin offered "no practicable details as to the method of operating it."

The courts thought otherwise, but the company had little difficulty in paying the award (one source puts it at $5 million) out of their 1914 profits of $14 million.

By the time *The New Yorker* interviewed him in 1928, calling him "camera shy," he was "a spare, gray little man with thin lips and a look of certainty in his eyes . . . living out his remaining years in measured magnificence and shrewdly cautious luxury." He was quoted as saying, "The remaining years are very precious to me, and I am now doing what the movies call a fade-out."

With typical generosity, he distributed through his will his great wealth to several of his beloved charities. ◆

FERRIS

When America was planning the World's Columbian Exposition of 1893, there was a determination to find something to outclass the Eiffel Tower, which its inventor and designer Gustave Eiffel had succeeded in erecting four years earlier on the Champ-de-Mars in Paris.

Eiffel was world famous. When only twenty-six, three years out of college, he had designed the great iron bridge over the Garonne at Bordeaux, then had gone on to build other iron bridges in France before being hired by the United States to construct the giant locks of the Panama Canal and the iron framework for the Statue of Liberty, which actually gave him the idea for the monumental iron tower in Paris which bears his name.

As late as 1891, with the opening of the Chicago exposition only two years away, Director of Works Daniel H. Burnham was telling the country's civil engineers that they were getting rusty. The French had captured the world's imagination by their use of iron, which was the world's excitingly new building material. So get out there and beat the French, he urged. Strike while the iron is hot!

One engineer who paid attention bore the very American name of George Washington Gale Ferris. Born in Galesburg, Illinois, in 1859, he had moved with his parents as a small boy to Carson City, Nevada, where he graduated from college in 1881. He spent a few months working on the railroad, planning the layout of rail lines in the eastern states. He also designed a trestle bridge and built three tunnels before developing professional skills in concrete work under pressure in pneumatic caissons.

At the time Burnham was calling out to the country's civil engineers, Ferris was running his own company under his own name, specializing in the testing and inspection of structural steel, which was just then being introduced into bridge work.

What could he do to beat Eiffel? Build a deeper tunnel, a taller tower, a longer bridge, a more elaborate concrete caisson? None of the above appealed to him. Meanwhile, the exposition was under construction.

Here the story slips very slightly into romantic legend. According to Ferris, the idea came to him in a single flash of inspiration. He would reinvent the wheel. If the French insisted on going up in the air, the Americans, he decided, would go round and round and round.

"We used to have a Saturday afternoon club," he recalled in the September 1893 issue of the *Review of Reviews*, "chiefly engineers at the World's Fair. It was at one of these dinners, down at a Chicago chop house, that I hit on the

George Washington Gale Ferris

Ferris reinvented the wheel.

Left: *These two photographs of the Ferris wheel at the World's Columbian Exposition of 1893 were taken by amateur photographers. Right: A poster from the Columbian Exposition.*

idea. I remember remarking that I would build a monster wheel. I got some paper and began sketching it out. I fixed the size, determined the construction, the number of cars I would run, the number of people it would hold, the plan to stop six times in the first revolution for loading, then making a complete turn. In short, before the dinner was over, I had sketched out almost the entire detail, and my plan has never varied from that day. I even made a note of how much we would charge. And the Wheel stands in the Plaisance [the fancy name for their fairground] at this moment as it stood before me then."

Ferris was not in the least interested in giving people pleasure. He did not set out to provide a delightful means of scaring the daylights out of timid riders or giving views of a lighted fairground at night. He was simply solving a technical engineering problem in response to a challenge, and he ran into stubborn opposition on every side.

His idea was to build a perfect pinion wheel — a wheel with projecting teeth — 250 feet in diameter, sustained by tension and not solid spokes, to rise 268 feet above the ground, turning on an axle 45 feet long, weighing 42 tons, which was roughly the weight of an ordinary locomotive.

His fellow engineers around the chop house table all agreed that it would never work. The moment it revolved, they agreed, the strain of the motion would make it lose its circularity. It would become an ellipse and then collapse. There was no way, they said, of moving such an enormous mass.

The officials of the exposition objected to the idea on the ground that it was too "revolutionary," an odd criticism to make of a wheel. Besides, the country was just recovering from the depression of 1892. Where would they get the money? Who would pay good money for a ride to nowhere?

These officials dug in their heels so firmly that Ferris was put on hold for months, and though they did finally reluctantly agree, the monster was not finished until the World's Columbian Exposition had opened.

Ferris worked fast once he did get the go-ahead. As an article of the day put it, "On December 28, 1892, Ferris had 2,200 tons of pig-iron in his hands; but by June 21, 1893, this 'pig' had been converted into a revolving mechanism as perfect as the pinion wheel of an Elgin watch."

Probably nobody else could have done it in time. After all, Ferris was the chief inspector of all the steel and iron for the country's bridges, and he was able to enlist the help of nine of the largest steel mills. Still, it was a marvel of planning, for the separate parts of this first Ferris wheel were constructed from blueprints in separate mills in Detroit, then shipped to Chicago, where "every spoke and bar, truss and girder, went together as though each had been previously fitted."

The foundations had been sunk in January through twenty-five feet of quicksand and water down to a firm footing, and live steam was used to prevent the cement from freezing.

But would it move? The wheel had to be a perfect circle held under tension by steel cables. The sum of four hundred thousand dollars hung on its first test run, but "a finger was lifted, a throttle opened, and the great wheel began to turn, obeying the lightest touch of the driver with a precision and accuracy that is not the least of the wonders of this mechanical world."

And did it fall over? The Ferris wheel even withstood the hurricane that swept through the fairground in July 1893.

Actually, George Washington Gale Ferris knew all along that it would revolve and not keel over. "It is as perfect a pinion wheel as the little wheel that flicks back and forth in a watch," he said.

He was asked, "Would it have been possible to build a wheel five hundred feet high?"

"Possible, but not feasible," he replied, "since it would have proved nothing that the present wheel does not prove."

"What other projects do you have in mind?" he was asked.

"Perhaps I had better not say," he replied slowly, "some of them might be too frightening."

Ferris did not live to frighten anyone else, for he died less than four years after the first Ferris wheel began to turn. ◆

Two photographs taken of the Ferris wheel at the Columbian Exposition by amateur photographers.

P A R T

MACHINISTS AND TINKERERS

McCormick

The International Harvester Company, which recently changed its name to Navistar, is suffering from premature aging, and it is their own doing. This busy conglomerate of several merged farm implement companies came into being on August 12, 1902. But by some corporate sleight-of-hand, they celebrated their 150th anniversary in 1981, simply by pushing their birthdate back to 1831, the year Cyrus Hall McCormick first tried out his new mechanical reaper on a neighbor's farm.

In a sense, International Harvester was entitled, for the first president of the 1902 incorporation also happened to bear the name Cyrus Hall McCormick. He was the eldest of the seven children of that inventive mechanic of 1831. Besides, the McCormicks had a strong sense of family, which became stronger over the years.

The dynasty started late because Cyrus the first did not marry until he was nearly fifty, when he fell head over heels in love with a twenty-three-year-old singer, who proved to be an indomitable lifelong support.

The best story about their marriage dates from 1871, the year of the Chicago fire. She happened to be in New York when news came from her husband in Chicago that the McCormick Reaper works had been completely destroyed. She joined him at once, and together they viewed the smoking ruins. McCormick was rich enough to retire then and there, but his wife would have none of it. "Rebuild," she said, "I do not wish our sons to grow up in idleness."

Her oldest son, Cyrus, was then only twelve. A mere thirteen years later, at the age of twenty-five, he became president of the company when his father died in 1884. In 1902 he supervised the merger of the McCormick interests with the harvester company founded by Charles Deering to create the celebrated McCormick-Deering family of farm machines.

Now back to the real beginning, for although the reaper was Cyrus Hall McCormick's development, he might never have brought it to market without the challenge of his father's many failures. If ever a young man followed in his father's footsteps, it was twenty-two-year-old Cyrus McCormick in the year 1830, building on the work of his fifty-one-year-old father.

Robert McCormick had spent his entire life on a twelve-hundred-acre spread in Virginia, which he had inherited from his own father (son of Scotch-Irish Presbyterian immigrants to the United States), who had moved there in 1779 after service in the Revolutionary War.

Robert was an exceptional man. He had little schooling but read every-

Cyrus Hall McCormick

◆

McCormick's reaper revolutionized agriculture.

◆
---

thing he could lay his hands on, especially in the fields of music, philosophy, and astronomy. He was also a gifted mechanic. After he took over the farm, he installed a machine shop and a sawmill and ran a blacksmithy and even a small distillery, all on the same property.

It is a historical oddity that in 1809, the year his first son was born and named Cyrus after the great Persian king, Robert McCormick decided to invent a mechanical reaper. Nothing of the kind existed anywhere in the world, and it is likely that he began his tinkering even before Patrick Bell, in far-off Scotland, managed to cobble together a machine that made one successful run at a field of grain in 1826.

It took Robert McCormick from 1809 to 1816 to put together his idea of what a reaper ought to be. He clamped a gang of sickles to a bar of wood and fixed other flanges here and there to bend the grain over, all geared to a leather belt-drive that turned them as the contraption moved over the ground. It didn't work.

For fifteen more years he fiddled and machined and adjusted, while in his spare time he farmed the land; invented a jump brake, a hydraulic engine, and a device for a gristmill; and improved the blacksmith's bellows.

Finally in May 1831, he thought he had all his problems licked. In another demonstration in one of his fields, the machine cut the grain all right, but only when conditions were perfect, and even then it left the stalks so tangled that the wheat could not be bound into sheaves. At that moment, Robert McCormick gave up on the reaper.

According to family legend, his son Cyrus had taken note of all these failed attempts and decided to try something entirely different. The extraordinary result was that he, coming to the problem from another angle, was demonstrating his unique mechanical reaper a few weeks later during the harvest of 1831. And it worked like a charm.

The essential difference between McCormick's reaper and all other fail-

Left: *A demonstration of the first reaper in 1831.* Right: *An advertising poster for the reaper, 1884.*

THE McCORMICK AT WORK IN ASIATIC RUSSIA.

From a Photograph taken on the Estate of IVAN PLESHANOW, 120 miles east of Samara, Russia, who operates Five McCormick Harvesters and Binders, ALL DRAWN BY CAMELS.

The work of the McCormick Machines around the World and throughout the year NEVER CEASES.

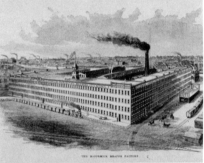

Top left: *An 1886 advertising poster.*
Top right: *The grain binder, 1901.*
Bottom right: *An artist's rendering of the McCormick Plant, 1899.*

ures was his discovery of the reciprocating knife. His father affixed rigid sickles; son Cyrus installed blades that moved reciprocally with the forward movement of the machine. Added to that were the knife guards to support the grain, the reel that swept the grain up for cutting, the platform for gathering the cut grain, and the trick of cutting to one side of the line of travel, with a bar to divide standing grain from the row being cut.

That machine revolutionized agriculture. Young McCormick tried it out locally, then demonstrated it throughout the state. But not until 1843 did he begin selling rights for its manufacture, and then perhaps only because of rival claims from a competing inventor, Obin Hussey, with whom he had a brief legal tussle.

The fact was that McCormick made a better reaper, but Hussey made a better mower, and gradually over the years these two functions, with others, were incorporated into more complex farming machinery.

By 1850, there were nearly thirty firms competing for business, and by 1860 more than a hundred, but McCormick stayed in the lead by adding a mower, self-raking devices, and later a binding apparatus.

He exhibited his reaper at the Great Exhibition of 1851 in London, where it won the Council Medal. *The London Times* declared that the machine, "if it fulfilled its promise, was worth the whole cost of the exhibition."

Cyrus Hall McCormick always went his own way, and though he used to talk merger with Charles Deering, who moved farmers from wire binding to binder twine, he died before any conglomerate or merger ever came into being.

It remained for his son, Cyrus the second, born a dozen years before the disastrous Chicago fire, to tie everything up neatly in corporate binder twine, naming the package the International Harvester Company. ◆

DEERE

John Deere

♦

John Deere's victory over the clogging loam soil of the prairies made his reputation.

♦

The inventor of the plow is on the same list as the inventor of the wheel and the discoverer of fire.

Plows go back into the remotest days of mankind, when an angled tree branch was first used to scratch a furrow in the earth. Both the Greeks and the Romans, not to mention the Chinese and the Egyptians, used plows tipped with metal, and some unknowns among them had even worked out, by trial and error, the rough shape of the moldboard and how to give it that special curve that turns the soil over.

When it comes to the invention of the modern plow, most people point to John Deere, who made his first successful experiment in 1837 at the historic spot of Grand Detour, an unincorporated village in Ogle County in the prairie state of Illinois, which boasts one of the flattest terrains in the United States and some of the blackest, stickiest loam.

It was John Deere's victory over that clogging loam that put his name at the top of the list of experimenters with the plow and made Moline, Illinois, where he set up his factory, almost a place of pilgrimage for plowmen the world over.

The plow is an unrecognized precision tool. It looks simple, but it has been shaped over the years in the most meticulous way to fit it for its special task. It is a machine with named parts: The coulter is a knife for cutting the soil vertically; the share is the tooth that separates the sod from the subsoil; the moldboard turns the earth over; and the stilts, or handles, are attached to the beam, which in turn is linked to the horse's harness.

Maybe in the dawn of history it was a tree branch, and maybe the form has been refined and shaped over the centuries, but that simple tool remained almost unchanged until modern technology took over about two hundred years ago.

Those were still primitive days. Tillers of the soil were using plows that had to be kept down under the ground by the weight of men standing on them, while horses or other men or women pulled at them. So it was an exciting event when in 1785, an Englishman named Ransome took out a patent for the first cast-iron plowshare. Not the whole plow, just the share.

Then came visionaries who dreamed of a plow driven by steam, harnessed for the first time only ten years earlier, when Watt and Boulton constructed the first steam engine in 1769. Steam was the energy source of the future, but the wooden plow, even with a cast-iron share, could never stand up under it. The world, clearly, was waiting for John Deere.

He was born in 1804 in Rutland, Vermont, the third son of an English-born merchant tailor. The Deere family Bible records that his father was Welsh, but Deere himself claimed in the 1880 census that both his parents were English.

New material included in the 1984 history of the John Deere company by Wayne G. Broehl, Jr., suggests that Deere's mother was the daughter of a Revolutionary War soldier. She was widowed when John was a child of four. In Broehl's book, the last anyone heard of her husband was a letter in 1808 written while he was waiting to board a ship to England. It is presumed he was lost at sea, leaving his wife to carry on his tailoring business.

John Deere was apprenticed at seventeen to a local blacksmith and made a reputation in Vermont by hammering out by hand all the ironwork for a new sawmill in nearby Colchester. His apprenticeship ended in 1824. Three years later he married and in the next twelve years fathered four children (he had ten altogether). He also supported his mother until her death in 1826. Then he struck out for new fields in Grand Detour, where they needed a good black-smith to hammer out metal parts for leather harnesses and to fit their wooden plows with steel shares.

Top left: *John Deere's 1838 plow, which is kept in the Smithsonian Institution.* Below left: *An artist's rendering of the John Deere factory, circa 1847.* Below right: *"Plowing on the Prairies Beyond the Mississippi," a sketch by the artist Theodore R. Davis, published in* Harper's Weekly, *May 9, 1868.*

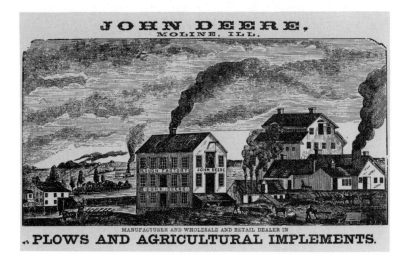

His First Lesson

The farmer of today proudly teaches his son what his own father taught him— to use a John Deere Plow.

Within weeks, he learned that the plows that were adequate back east were almost useless in the heavy soil of Illinois. In those wide open spaces, the furrows could be a mile or more long, and the plowman had to stop more often than he liked to scrape away the earth clogging the moldboard.

John Deere's contribution to world agriculture may be simply that he was the first man to use steel in a commercially successful plow. It was not a common metal in 1837, though it had been in use for nearly a century. It took John Deere to realize that a plow is a cutting tool no less than the clothier's shears or the lumberman's saw, which were made from blister steel, the purest then known.

One legend, enshrined in the *National Cyclopedia of American Biography*, says that the first plow Deere made was cut from a cracked circular saw. Using a rounded log as a template, he beat the saw into the curved moldboard shape, then cut it and attached the steel share and coulter, finishing it off with beam and handles of white oak.

According to the legend, he made three plows out of that one saw and tried them out that fall in a field across the Rock River from Grand Detour. They cut clean, scoured themselves free of heavy earth, and needed little horsepower. He sold all three then and there.

There was no great rush into mass production. He and his associate, Leonard Andrus, made two more in 1838, ten in 1839, and forty in 1840, all handmade.

Three years later, he had taken Andrus into partnership, built another workshop and a small foundry, and was turning out four hundred plows. Then, for the first time, he ordered a slab of cast plow steel from the steelworks of Jones & Quiggs and started seriously thinking about going into the plow-making business.

John Deere moved to Moline in the late 1840s, some ten years after he first shaped that old chunk of saw steel, and in May 1848, the new firm of Deere & Tate began making plows. Moline was served by good river transportation and offered the ideal water power essential for the new factory, which went into production that year with an output of seven hundred plows.

After ten years, he formed a company with three partners, calling it John Deere & Co., which by then — according to some sources — was turning out ten thousand plows a year. Deere's name soon became internationally known. In 1878 he entered the plowing matches at the Paris Exhibition, winning every class with his gang plow against the French *bisoc*.

To quote from the September 14, 1878, *Scientific American*, "With the former, the plowman rides, and with the latter, he walks behind. The American plow was far ahead, though the French workers slashed away at their horses with their whips, while Mr. Deere had only his umbrella to poke up the four horses on his plow.... Though somewhat heavier than the French plow, the American was more speedy, and considerably more efficient."

Even in France, John Deere was outstanding in his field. ◆

The Gazelle gang plow was popular in the 1890s.

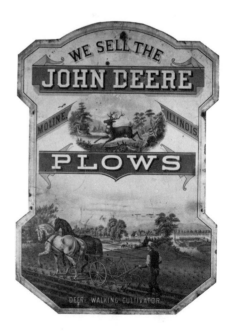

Opposite page: *An advertisement from the Civil War period.*

BIGELOW

Erastus Brigham Bigelow

A title on the door rates a Bigelow on the floor.

Take it from the ads: a title on the door rates a Bigelow on the floor. But what's a Bigelow and how did it get there?

Go back more than a century and a half to the small town of West Boylston, Massachusetts. Two brothers, young teenagers, are playing violin in a local orchestra. Horatio Bigelow, at fourteen, is already a pretty good mechanic and works as overseer in his father's small cotton factory. His younger brother Erastus, a scholarly type, is still trying to make up his mind whether he wants to be a musician or a doctor.

So which brother will invent a machine to revolutionize the carpet industry not only in the United States but the world over?

Erastus Brigham Bigelow would have gone on to become a country doctor and an amateur fiddler if his father, Ephraim Bigelow, a summertime farmer and part-time cotton weaver, had had the money. Instead, he was put to work in the factory because the family could not afford more schooling for him.

Erastus Bigelow disliked the work, but he kept having brain waves. He was a natural born inventor. Before he was sixteen, he had invented a new way of making piping cord, as well as a hand loom for weaving suspender webbing. These inventions paid him a trifle, and with the few dollars he picked up playing violin at dances, he started building up his own fund for more schooling. He learned Latin for his medical training and could have made it to college, but once again money ran out. He had to go back to work, this time as a dry goods clerk in Boston.

He had another brain wave. He wrote a book called *The Self-Taught Stenographer* — a shorthand manual — and published it himself before he turned eighteen. He sold it door to door, took on other small commission lines, taught penmanship in New York, and set up a small factory making twine and cotton thread — not all at the same time, but all to help him get back into medicine.

He learned one thing about himself: He could concentrate on a problem and usually solve it. But he never did become a doctor, perhaps because he could not shake off those early years growing up in a weaver's house.

He became interested in quilts at a time when imports from Marseilles, France, were all the rage, and he invented a power loom for weaving knotted counterpanes. When his backers ran short of money to pay him the agreed one-quarter of all profits, he adapted the machine into a loom for turning out coach lace used to trim upholstery on stagecoaches.

There is little demand for coach lace these days, but in the 1840s it was a thriving industry. With his brother Horatio, the mechanical brain, young Erastus formed the Clinton Company in 1841 and marketed their lace through a Boston manufacturer. This was Erastus Bigelow's first breakthrough into money, and he was just twenty-seven. Before long they were turning out miles of coach lace and tens of thousands of quilts a year.

Then came the carpet brain wave.

This industry had been in trouble for some time. British carpets were all the rage, outselling American carpets two to one. Ingrain carpeting with no pile was the common floor covering in the States, but more and more people were turning to pile carpets, such as Axminsters and Wiltons. The industry was labor-intensive, using skilled weavers, mostly foreign trained, and it relied on imported yarns.

Alexander Wright, a Scottish immigrant mechanic associated with the Lowell Carpet Company of Boston, knew that power was the answer to the industry's ills. He put it to Erastus Bigelow: Invent a power loom for carpets.

There were five problems: how to allow for the interweaving of several plies; how to create smooth fabric take-up, a firm and even selvage, and perfectly matching patterns; how to construct mechanical shuttle boxes. And it all had to be done by machine and not by hand.

Bigelow was incredible. He had working drawings in hand within a matter of weeks and, with money pouring in from the Lowells, a working power loom within two years and full operation two years after that. The power loom was capable of turning out thirty yards a day, as against eight yards by the hand method. The result was an operating profit of about one thousand dollars a year per loom. It was the first successful mechanization of the carpet industry.

Horatio was the marketing man, while Erastus, the mechanical genius, could adapt machines to fit any marketing need. Between the two of them, they made Bigelow the first marketing driven company.

A few years later, Erastus Bigelow applied his invention to the weaving of

Top left: *An old engraving of the Bigelow Carpet Company plant at Clinton, Massachusetts.* Top right: *The Brussels loom was in common use before Bigelow's invention of a power loom.* Bottom right: *Before power looms, the jacquard was used in looms such as this early nineteenth-century European model.*

Above: *The perforated jacquard cards, which control the pattern, are checked against the design.* Right: *A 1934 advertisement for Bigelow Weavers.*

Brussels carpet, a mixture of wool worsted interwoven with linen, using jacquard cards — primitive punch cards — for the first time in a power loom to control the pattern. They worked so well that at the 1851 Great Exhibition in London, his Brussels carpet was voted superior to any hand-woven carpet on display.

Just before his death in 1879, Bigelow presented to the Boston Historical Society a portfolio titled "The Inventions of Erastus Brigham Bigelow patented in England between 1837 and 1868." It ran to six volumes of specifications and sketches for patents in his name for every kind of weaving from silk brocatel to wire cloth.

Oddly enough, in all six volumes, there is not a word about either medicine or music. ◆

YALE

Memorials come in all sizes. The Woolworth Building in New York City is a monument to the creator of the five-and-ten-cent store, but the memorial to Linus Yale is a small, flat piece of metal, mass-produced by the thousands every day.

The Yale cylinder lock was the brainchild of a man whose mechanical genius overpowered his minor talent for portrait painting, and the world's valuables are safer because of it.

The Yale family of Salisbury, New York, were distant relations of the Elihu Yale who gave his name and a lot of money to Yale University. When Linus Yale was born in 1821, his father, after whom he was named, was a struggling young mechanic. By the time Linus was in his teens, the father had become a manufacturer in Newport, New York, of locks for bankers' vaults and safes, none guaranteed against the expert safe cracker.

The first improvements to the old spring lock by the Chubbs in England had not yet reached across the Atlantic. For years neither Linus Yale nor his father, both master mechanics, bothered to give the problem a second thought. Linus himself left the toolbench to study art and struggled along as a painter for nearly ten years.

Linus Yale

Maybe it was one of his father's banker clients, whiling away the tedium of a portrait sitting, who lectured him on the problems of safekeeping old masters. Maybe it was the sheer weight and bulk of the keys normally in use, often weighing more than a pound each, that made him think life could be made a lot easier. Or maybe he just got tired of daubing oil paint on canvas.

Whatever the reason, after months of experimental machining, young Linus came up with an invention in the year 1857 that made him famous instantly: the Yale Infallible Bank Lock, sometimes known as the Magic Lock.

The novelty lay in the key, constructed in two parts. As soon as the key was turned, the web part inside the lock separated from the shank and opened the safe, while a sheet of thin steel dropped down to seal off the keyhole. A safe cracker could not reach the wards or the bolt itself through the keyhole. Not only that, the two parts of the key could be assembled in various ways, as the banker chose, and the weight of the key was cut down to mere ounces.

That invention led to the Treasury Lock, specially designed for the government; and to keyless dial locks, an early form of combination lock; and to clock locks, now called time locks; and to the amazing double lock, which could be opened by either of two keys or by both together.

The world's valuables are safer because of Yale's invention.

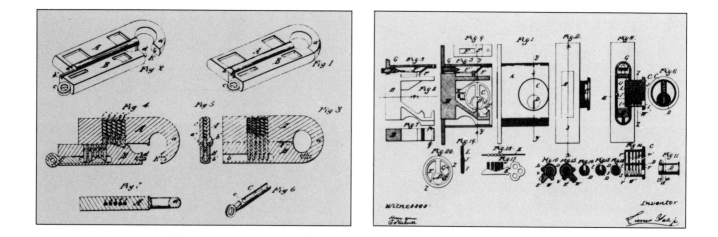

Left: A reproduction of the original patent drawings for a pin-tumbler padlock devised by Linus Yale, Sr., who was also a famous inventor and a manufacturer of bank vaults. Right: A reproduction of Linus Yale, Jr.'s pin-tumbler cylinder locks.

A Triple Movement Yale Time Lock used for bank vaults.

It was only after inventing all these complicated locks designed for banks and treasuries that Linus Yale turned his attention to the world at large and devised the flat key in the cylinder lock, with its infinite variations in the web.

It was advertised as pickproof, and so it was for all practical purposes. But a wandering daguerreotype artist named James Sargeant, also an inventor, took it on himself to meet the Yale challenge. After days and nights of experimentation and measurement, he succeeded in picking a lock specially selected by Linus Yale.

Sargeant went on to become a professional lock-picker and invented a lock with a magnetic safety device; but Yale's answer to Sargeant was to cut a channel in the shank of the key, adding one more simple complication to the flat key mechanism. Yale patented the revised version in June 1865.

In the meantime, after his father died, five years after the invention of the Magic Lock, Linus moved with his wife and young son John from Newport to Philadelphia and then to Shelburne Falls, Massachusetts, where Henry Robinson Towne entered his life.

Towne was the son of a wealthy foundry owner who had given $1 million for scientific research to the University of Pennsylvania, from which young Towne had graduated. During the Civil War, Towne — still underage — was busy designing and installing engines for government naval craft. Later he became superintendent of an ironworks, toured engineering establishments at the Sorbonne in Paris, and topped that off with several months of designing machinery for a shipbuilding firm. And he was not yet twenty-four.

Linus Yale and Henry Towne were drawn together as kindred spirits in spite of their age difference. Within months, they became partners in the Yale Lock Manufacturing Company, formed in October 1868, and looked forward to a profitable future with the combined talents of inventor Yale and designing engineer Towne.

They were not only in the lock business. Yale also had patents on minor ideas, such as a clamp for a joiner's square, a screw tap, a mechanic's vise, and an alarm clock. But the partnership lasted less than two months. On Christ-

Left: *A diorama of the original Yale plant in Newport, New York, circa 1847.* Below: *A Yale Dial Lock for burglarproof safes.* Bottom: *A Yale Dial Lock for fireproof safes.*

mas Eve in 1868, Linus Yale died suddenly in New York City at the age of forty-seven.

The whole enterprise could have failed then and there. Linus Yale's son John did not have his father's inventive or mechanical genius, and the new company had taken on a heavy debt by a move into a new factory in Stamford, Connecticut.

Henry Robinson Towne did not hesitate for a moment. He took it as his mission in life to establish the name Yale in the world and to build a company on the Yale reputation.

He had just turned twenty-four when he became president of the reorganized company Yale & Towne, with thirty employees. When he finally resigned that position, forty-seven years later in 1915, the plant covered twenty-five acres, employed five thousand, and had capital stock that had grown from $80,000 to more than $5 million.

It was Towne's decision to stamp the name Yale on every key blank the company's machines stamped out as a memorial to Linus Yale.   ♦

OTIS

Elisha Graves Otis

◆
---

*He helped to change
the world's thinking
from horizontal to
vertical.*

◆

The thoroughly advanced outlook of Elisha Graves Otis may have laid the foundation for today's sleek high-speed elevators, but his own workaday life had all the glamour of a freight elevator ride in a run-down factory. Yet he helped to change the world's thinking from horizontal to vertical.

The name Otis means elevator to millions of people who travel to work up and down, clocking perhaps more miles altogether than trains, buses, and planes.

Yet this obscure mechanic did not really invent the elevator at all. The Romans and the Tibetans knew all about hoists and counterweights, and steam-operated hoists were already in use when Elisha Otis was a boy in Halifax, Vermont. As early as 1833, Holt's Hotel in New York had a steam-powered hoisting apparatus to carry baggage, and an early power-driven elevator named the Teagle was in operation in an English factory in 1835. Not only that, the one specific safety device he did invent for the steam-operated elevators in use on construction sites in his day has been obsolete for nearly a hundred years.

The truth is, if it had been left up to Elisha Otis himself, we might all be riding up and down today in elevators named Tufts or Ellithorpe or Waterman, who were also early American tinkerers with vertical travel. Otis was certainly inventive enough, but he was also lucky in his sons Charles and Norton, who were not only just as good mechanics as their father, but good businessmen as well.

Elisha Graves Otis was born on August 3, 1811, in Halifax, Vermont, the sixth and last child of Stephen Otis, a fairly prosperous farmer, a justice of the peace for forty years, and a member of the state legislature from 1808 to 1812. They are related through the Otis lineage, which goes back to John Otis, an emigrant from England in 1665, with the revolutionary patriot James Otis and the great American statesman Harrison Gray Otis.

As we would say today, Elisha was a school dropout, but that was the situation for many young men in the period of common schools. After various menial jobs, he found work at age nineteen with a construction company, but left because the work was too hard for his health. After a turn driving a horse and wagon between Troy, New York, and Brattleboro, Vermont, and another turn working a gristmill, he tried his hand at machine repair, but before long went back to haulage.

The company affirms that these varied jobs "gave him the experience he needed to become a master mechanic, and prepared him for his invention of the safety elevator, which originally used a wagon spring as one component."

Elisha Otis was nearly thirty-five before he settled down to a steady job as a master mechanic in an Albany, New York, bedstead factory. But he left even that to strike out on his own in a small machine shop, only to leap-frog again, when it did not work out, to another bedstead factory in Bergen, New Jersey.

By this time, Charles Rollin Otis was a lively lad of fifteen, with two years of machine shop behind him already, following in his father's footsteps. In later life, Charles claimed that he was made engineer at fifteen in the Bergen bedstead works, while his father was still working as a master mechanic. But the company cautions that the remark might have had its roots in the quarrels that often sprang up between Charles and his father and brother Norton. Nevertheless, when Elisha was sent to help in the building of a new factory in Yonkers, Charles went along as part of the Otis package, working side by side with his father on the construction of an elevator.

The year was 1852, and that elevator was unique in the world because of the new Otis safety device. In those days, elevators were raised and lowered by ropes, which often frayed and broke, killing many workmen every year. It was Elisha Otis's idea to attach two metal pawls, like those that regulate a watch escapement, to the moving platform. The pawls stayed retracted as long as the cable holding the platform remained taut, but if the cable broke, the pawls sprang out and brought it to a stop.

Simple and primitive it may have been, but it was so new and effective that Otis exhibited it in 1854 at the New York World's Fair in a dramatic demonstration.

To quote from *Scientific American*, "A great impression was made on the spectators when the inventor, after running his car to the top of the shaft, cut the supporting ropes and yet descended safely to the main floor."

Otis, inventor of the automatic stop, became known as "Otis the safety elevator man," but it was son Charles, impressed by the interest shown by many New York businessmen, who encouraged his father to capitalize on his invention and go into the elevator business, which, on the face of it, had nowhere else to go but up.

The elevator was not Otis's only invention. He had already patented improvements on railroad car trucks and brakes, and later invented a bake oven and a steam plow. But it was the steam elevator with its safety feature, patented on January 15, 1861, that formed the basis for the business his two sons then built up.

The first safety elevator specially designed for passengers was installed in the New York store of E.V. Haughwort & Company in 1857. Serving five floors at forty feet a minute, it was, needless to say, an Otis. Then came the first Otis electric elevator in the Demarest Building in New York City in 1889. There had been earlier electric elevators, but those by Otis were the first to be considered

Otis's Crystal Palace Demonstration in 1854.

The first push-button elevators, introduced in 1894, won immediate acceptance for residences.

Left: *An early advertisement for Otis passenger and freight elevators. Right: Three uniformed elevator operators in a photograph taken circa 1915.*

commercially successful.

In the World's Columbian Exposition of 1893, Otis had a huge exhibit that demonstrated a dozen elevators in actual use, one reaching the height of 185 feet. But Elisha Otis, who died in 1861 at the age of forty-nine, never saw it, nor the Otis elevators in the Eiffel Tower, nor in a Glasgow marine tunnel, nor in a railway incline in the Catskills, nor anywhere else, as his name spread throughout the world.

The company, known as Otis Brothers & Company from the 1860s to 1898, has long been out of Otis hands, and is now a subsidiary of United Technologies. But it was Elisha Graves's younger son Norton, and later his brother Charles, five years older, who carried their father's invention to heights he could never have imagined. Charles was in the business from the beginning, while Norton, who had mastered the mechanics of the elevator while still in his teens, joined with his brother after their father's death. Together, the two brothers registered more than two dozen patents, as they helped the elevator to evolve from the hand-operated type to the modern automatic elevator.

Charles retired in 1890 at the age of fifty-five and spent the rest of his life in travel. But not always in elevators.

Norton stayed with the company into the new century and died in 1905. ◆

CRANE

lance through a recent annual report of Crane Co., with its net sales of
more than $1.6 billion in steel, cement, control equipment, and build-
ing and aerospace products, and it seems absurd to look back even for
a moment to the way it started out.

In the year 1854, a business panic raged through the American continent,
with interest rates above 20 percent and thousands of men out of work and
out on the streets, facing poverty without any of today's social underpinning.

One of those thousands was twenty-two-year-old Richard Teller Crane,
who had been continuously employed full-time, believe it or not, since he was
nine years old. He had been doing a man's work already for thirteen years.

Crane was the son of a mechanic and builder of Dunbar, Massachusetts,
descended from an earlier generation that had held influential office in the
state government of Connecticut. The elder Crane, however, had gone his
own way and had been ruined financially by the earlier business panic of
1837.

Facing desperation, he was finally forced in 1841 to put his son Richard,
then only nine, out to work in a cotton mill. That job led to others over the
next ten years until at fifteen, Richard Crane became an apprentice worker in
the brass and bell foundry of John Benson of Brooklyn, New York.

That job he took to because, like his father, he was a born mechanic.
Benson manufactured equipment for grinding white lead used in paints and
putty. Young Crane added an invention of his own to turn out better castings
for the grinding rollers.

From that job, he moved to a firm that made printing presses for the
growing newspaper industry, in which Horace Greeley's *New York Tribune*,
founded in 1841, was a new sensation; then to a locomotive works; then to yet
another press machine shop — just in time to be thrown out of work at the
height of the depression.

For four months he pounded the streets, until he followed Greeley's
advice to all young men and went west to Chicago in the spring of 1855, where
one of his uncles owned a lumberyard.

It could be that Crane turned up in the right place at the right time. It is
true that by arriving on May Day, 1855, he just missed the Lager Beer Riots of
April, sparked by the city council's sudden hike in tavern fees from fifty
dollars to three hundred dollars, but he was just in time to hear "Deacon"
William Bross proclaim that Chicago was "the greatest primary market in the
world."

Richard Teller Crane

---

*When it struck him
that the energy
source of the world
he lived in was
steam, he tapped
into it.*

Bross had just bought the *Chicago Tribune,* and he must have known what he was talking about.

Incorporated in 1837 with a population under five thousand, Chicago had exploded to nearly sixty thousand. When a group of Canadian politicians visited there in 1855, they were astounded by the twenty-five miles of planked streets, the fifty-seven miles of sidewalks, the four miles of busy wharves, and the ten bridges over the river.

In that same year, George Pullman came to jack up the city, Cyrus McCormick and John Deere were selling rival agricultural equipment, Dwight L. Moody was chasing drunks out of saloons, and twenty-two-year-old Marshall Field had just been hired as a counter-jumper in the genteel emporium founded by Potter Palmer.

In that optimistic climate, Crane made his own fresh start by prevailing on his uncle to let him build a brass foundry in the lumberyard. The story goes that on the Fourth of July, 1855, while the rest of the nation was celebrating Independence Day, Richard Teller Crane was hard at work with his crude machinery, casting brass couplings and copper tips for lightning rods, much in demand at that time.

As owner and sole employee of the R.T. Crane Brass and Bell Foundry, he did it all. He made the cores, fashioned the molds using sand dug out of his own foundations, melted and poured the metal, assembled the finished product, and went out to sell it.

A year later, he had so many orders that he brought in his brother Charles from Paterson, New Jersey, to lend a hand in a new company called R.T. Crane & Brother.

He was now part of Chicago, the boom town, mainly through his connection with the railroads, which were then handling ninety-six trains a day, funneling immigrants by the thousands (thirty-four hundred in one incredible day on the Michigan Central alone) and grain by the millions of bushels.

These are an artist's renderings of the exterior and interior of the original R. T. Crane foundry.

Left: *An advertisement from the 1920s urged owners and architects to make their complete selections of heating and plumbing systems from the Crane line.* Below: *From that same advertisement, an illustration of a special cast-steel return bend was meant to be indicative of Crane's ability to meet unusual requirements in the industrial markets.*

One of Crane's first big orders came from a builder of mill equipment and freight cars for journal or junction boxes, which hold material to lubricate the axles of rolling stock. His search for a copper supplier to fill that order led him as far as Detroit, but in the process he became aware of the wider markets in railway centers outside Chicago. When it struck him that the energy source of the world he lived in was steam, he tapped into it himself by making and jobbing wrought-iron pipes and fittings for the steam heat business.

As early as 1857, two years after he tipped his first lightning rod, Crane was installing steam heat in the Cook County Court House. The contract, at six thousand dollars, was the biggest ever let up to that time. The system included a new type of globe and check valve specially designed for its job. He also hitchhiked on another revolutionary invention of the day: the safety elevator as first demonstrated in 1853 by Elisha Otis. Crane invented an improvement that geared the controls directly to the cable drum and then designed a new kind of brake for steam elevators, a variable speed control, and sliding double doors.

For one period, Crane controlled more than 95 percent of all the elevator manufacturing business in the United States, but the company abandoned this line as they moved more and more into pipe fittings and connections, turning out one innovation after another. Most of these inventions are obscure, like the double-sliding chuck for three-way tapping machines, the low-water alarm for steam boilers, a two-spindle return bend tapping machine, and a pipe-coil screw machine.

Crane was just one of the many things happening in Chicago in those exciting years, but his one-man lightning rod company grew and changed the world as it did so. ◆

ARMSTRONG

Thomas Morton Armstrong

On September 1, 1917, one of the landmark ads of the new consumer society of the twentieth century appeared in the *Saturday Evening Post.*

It shows part of the living room of a modest house, furnished with a couch, a birdcage hanging in the picture window, and flowers on the window ledge. Through the curtained archway, there is a glimpse of the entrance hall with its curving staircase.

A woman, dressed in the floor-length fashion of 1917, stands by the foot of the stairs, gazing through the arch into the living room, where another woman stares through the window. Her right knee is on the couch, and her left foot, which lightly touches the floor, seems to be pointing directly at the company logo inset into the picture.

It reads "Armstrong Linoleum."

The logo is repeated in 72-point type across the foot of the ad, and the space between is crammed with detailed factual copy: how linoleum is made (of powdered cork and oxidized linseed oil pressed on burlap); how to test it for quality (try to tear it: imitations tear easily); and what to look for (is it economical? sanitary? easy to clean? durable?). The copy even adds a touch of snob appeal to "American women who love beauty" by telling them that "in many of the finest homes in Europe, you will find linoleum in every room."

That was the first national ad placed by the Armstrong Cork Company of Lancaster, Pennsylvania. Even in 1917, it was thought to be a soft sell, even "noncommercial."

Instead of asking for the order, the ad suggested that readers send for the booklet "The House That Jack Re-Built" — a house presumably rebuilt and decorated with "rich polished linoleum floors, in mellow tones that would harmonize perfectly with rugs and walls and furniture."

That was the beginning of a deliberate attempt by a research-conscious company to service their customers. And it would have bewildered the company's founder, Thomas Morton Armstrong.

He was not indifferent to the customer, but the company he headed never made linoleum nor anything else for the American home. Armstrong started out as a maker of cork stoppers, one of the simplest and most universally useful products known. So there is quite some contrast between the Armstrong company of today, based on synthetic materials, and Tom Armstrong's modest cottage industry, which he started back in 1860 with capital of three hundred dollars, when he laboriously fashioned cylindrical corks from slabs of bark stripped from the cork oak.

Armstrong's Linoleum
For Every Room Ⓐ in the House

The living-room floor is a warm brown linoleum, with a hint of tan in the carpet design. In the hallway, Parquetry Inlaid Linoleum gives the effect of hardwood. Note how the decorator has carried the linoleum design into hangings and upholstery.

Linoleum is made of powdered cork and oxidized linseed oil, pressed on burlap. Be careful you get it. For there are inferior floor coverings nowadays that look like linoleum on the surface, but which are merely imitations. Remember these two easy ways to tell genuine linoleum. First, look at the back and make sure it's burlap. Second, try to tear it. Imitations tear easily. Better still, ask for Armstrong's Linoleum *by name.*

Three Armstrong patterns, suitable for the interior shown above.

IN many of the finest homes in Europe, you will find linoleum in every room. Not gaudy "oil-cloth" patterns, but rich, polished linoleum *floors,* in mellow tones that harmonize perfectly with rugs and walls and furniture.

Such linoleums are made right here in America by Armstrong Cork Company. And women who love beauty are laying them throughout their homes, creating floors that are at once tasteful, sanitary, economical.

Armstrong's Plain Linoleums in soft green, brown, red and gray—without any figure or pattern—make superb backgrounds for rugs. The darker shades give those low color tones necessary to make the floor the real base of the color scheme, and to harmonize with the darker woods in trim and furniture.

*Send for booklet, "The House that Jack Re-Built"
and the names of merchants near you who handle
Armstrong's Linoleum.*

Then for your guest-room, your bedroom, or nursery, there are the Armstrong carpet and matting designs—light, tastefully simple things in greens, blues, tans, and rose. Or the wonderful parquetry inlaid patterns—accurate reproductions of hardwood—for dining-room, living-room, hall, and den.

Look into this matter of linoleum floors. Have you seen the new Armstrong designs? Do you know how economical linoleum is? How absolutely sanitary? How easy to clean? How durable?

Stop thinking of linoleum as gaudy, old-fashioned. Go to some Armstrong merchant in your town and see for yourself what beautiful decorative effects you can have in floors that blend with your color scheme; floors that really *belong* to the room.

ARMSTRONG CORK COMPANY
Linoleum Department   Lancaster, Pa.

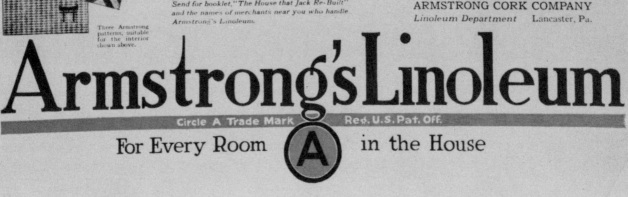

Armstrong's Linoleum
Circle A Trade Mark   Ⓐ   Reg. U.S. Pat. Off.

For Every Room Ⓐ in the House

Armstrong Quaker Rugs were very inexpensive, printed, felt-based floor covers.

An artist designs a floral pattern to be block-printed onto a Quaker Rug.

Previous page: *This 1917 advertisement, which first appeared in* The Saturday Evening Post, *was the first national consumer advertisement ever run by the company.*

The records do not show why young Armstrong got into cork. His father, William Armstrong, brought the family to the United States from Ireland (Londonderry, not Cork) in 1834, and Thomas M. was born two years later in New York City. When the boy was about six, they moved to Allegheny, Pennsylvania, which in 1906 was amalgamated with Pittsburgh on the other side of the Allegheny River.

Sometime in his late teens, Armstrong got a job in the shipping department of a Pittsburgh glass factory. At twenty-four, he teamed up with John D. Glass, one of his fellow workers, in a scheme to cut corks as Glass & Company. At first, Armstrong moonlighted from his regular job, while Glass worked full-time, but when Glass died in 1864 after only four years, his interest was bought out by Armstrong's brother Robert and a friend named William L. Standish.

The new company, known as Armstrong, Brother & Co., installed cork-cutting machinery at a capital cost of one thousand dollars. The industry at that time was supposed to have an unlimited future. As the Armstrong business grew, they stopped buying their raw cork from American importers. In 1878 they opened their own plant in Seville, Spain, to collect and prepare corkwood and cork waste.

That same year, after their Allegheny factory was destroyed by fire, the brothers and Standish built a new plant on the river at Twenty-Fourth Street and at the same time welcomed their newest employee, the founder's seventeen-year-old son Charles, who learned the business while it was undergoing its first expansion phase.

They were already an international company, with interests in cork plantations across the Atlantic and a new foothold in Canada, where they opened a branch in 1893. By then, Thomas M. Armstrong was pushing sixty, and his son, then over thirty, was a vice president with an eye to the future. Diversification came slowly, as the company moved into corkboard insulation, then into insulating pipe covers, cork flooring tile, and cork gasket material.

The simple, ordinary cork, which had remained unchanged without a serious competitor for more than a century, was threatened by the crown cork (which we know as the bottle cap), invented in 1892 by William Painter of Baltimore in response to the needs of the growing soft drink industry. Then there was the glass stopper, attached to the bottleneck by a hinged wire, which was invented in 1904 by Charles Edward McManus, also of Baltimore, who went even further by inventing a composition cork material called Nepro and a machine to slice it into circular discs as part of the crown cork assembly.

The Armstrongs recognized the crown cork as the logical successor to the cork stopper. The crown cork also offered a way to recycle cork scraps left on the cutting room floor from their other operations.

During all these years, the new product called linoleum was being manufactured in the United States by firms licensed by the British inventor Frederick Walton, who patented the process in 1860, the very year Tom Armstrong

A Music Shop *must* have Quiet Floors

IF there is any place where "silence is golden," it is in the floor of a shop where radios and phonographs are sold. Only when the floor of such a shop quiets noisy, shuffling footsteps to the faintest whispers can customers listen in comfort to the music and instruments on sale.

This golden silence underfoot has been secured in the smart California phonograph shop you see here without sacrificing any of the other important features so necessary in a business floor.

The floor selected by Mr. Grove, proprietor of this shop, is Armstrong's Marble Inlaid Linoleum. One glance at the picture tells you this floor is a handsome, dignified floor—a decorative part of the whole well-planned interior. One step on this floor would tell you that it is soft, springy to walk on—*and remarkably quiet.* And if you had been in this shop the day the floor was laid, you would also know why this is a floor that will last for years. For it was firmly cemented in place over builders' deadening felt. Laid this modern way, linoleum makes a smooth, practically one-piece floor, unbroken by dirt-collecting cracks and seams. It waxes to a rich, soft sheen. Dust and office litter brush up from its surface quickly, easily. It never needs refinishing.

Wherever the public walks

Today, to smart retail shops, to office buildings, to schools, churches, public institutions —wherever the public walks— floors of Armstrong's Linoleum bring new beauty, new comfort, new economies in floor maintenance.

There are merchants in your city who make a specialty of installing distinctive business floors of Armstrong's Linoleum. These merchants will gladly show you many modern designs. They will also give you estimates for laying any pattern you select.

They can do the work quickly, with scarcely any interruption to business—at night if necessary. And the surprisingly small cost will be more than returned to you in better floor appearance and reduced cleaning expense.

Write for "Business Floors"

A post card or letter mailed to us today brings you a 48-page book, "Business Floors." This book contains colorplates of Armstrong's Linoleum and gives specific directions for the laying and care of modern linoleum floors. Send for it. No charge. Address Armstrong Cork Company, *Linoleum Division,* 853 Liberty Street, Lancaster, Pa.

Armstrong's Linoleum *for every floor in the house*

was cutting his first corks.

It was the latest thing in floor covering, easily taking over the market from the more primitive oilcloth, which is simply jute canvas covered with layer after layer of paint. The Walton process created something new out of linseed oil mixed with ground-up cork chips.

But it was not until 1908 that Charles Dickey Armstrong, at forty-seven the newly elected president of the company after his father's death in that year, began to move away from industrial cork products into linoleum. He even built a factory especially for the new consumer-oriented product on thirty acres in Lancaster, Pennsylvania, where they had just acquired the property of a rival corkmaker.

By the time the younger Armstrong resigned the presidency in 1929 to become chairman of the board, the plant covered seventy-five acres, had a daily capacity of one hundred thousand yards of linoleum, and had branches in seventeen other countries.

But already, technology and the new chemistry were changing Charles Armstrong's world, just as it had changed his father's. Tom Armstrong's modest cottage industry has become Armstrong World Industries, primarily a chemical converter, with world-wide annual sales of more than one and a half billion dollars.

Though they still make floor coverings, Armstrong has not made a cork stopper for decades. ♦

Left: *A three-story rotary press in Lancaster, Pennsylvania, turns out Armstrong's Straight Line Inlaid Linoleum.* Right: *An advertisement for the same linoleum appeared in* The Saturday Evening Post *in 1935.*

REMINGTON AND UNDERWOOD

Philo Remington

Philo Remington
was typecast as the
man destined to give
birth to the first
commercial
typewriter.

Glance over this short list of names — Dennis, Schiesari, Albertson, Villey, Fisher, Elliott, Otto, Remington, Underwood — the odds are that the eye will linger over the last two as the names of well-known typewriters.

The list could have gone on, for the history of the typewriter is mostly a history of failures and nonstarters by well over a hundred busy inventors, most of whom actually made typewriters branded with their names. The line stretches back to Henry Will, who took out a patent as long ago as 1714, and to Italy's Pellegrino Turri, some of whose typed letters dating from 1808 still exist.

A. S. Dennis produced the first machine to write in syllables, using one hundred keys; Mario Schiesari made one that wrote both longhand and shorthand; Ernest Albertson's was a folding machine, but his company folded first; Pierre Villey, who was blind, invented a shorthand writer for the blind; Robert J. Fisher's machine typed from beneath, so it could print on bound books; and so did George Crawford Elliott's book typewriter, which came out in five models under the name Elliott-Hatch and later as Elliott-Fisher, and was still later linked to Underwood; the Reverend H.J. Otto rigged his pneumatic typewriter to a compressor in his basement.

It is ironic that it was Remington and Underwood who became household names in the industry, since neither one invented either a typewriter or even a part of one.

Philo Remington happened to own a factory famous for precision work with machine parts, while John Thomas Underwood simply bought the patents for a typewriter developed by a German inventor named Franz Xavier Wagner.

Indeed, Wagner is not only known as the inventor of the Underwood typewriter, he also had a great deal to do with improvements to the typewriter manufactured by Remington.

You cannot fault the ancestry of the modern typewriter. It began as a gleam in a writer's eye, became a newspaperman's obsession, grew as the godchild of an editor, and was at last brought into the world by a gunmaker.

If Philo Remington was the man destined to give birth to the first commercial typewriter, he was typecast for the part. Born in 1816, the same year his father made his first gun, he lived his entire life surrounded by machines that made guns and machines that made machines. Tools were his toys on the family farm in Herkimer County, New York, and they were his livelihood when he was taken into the family business.

When he was still a teenager, he was in full charge of the gun factory. When his father died in 1861, he inherited a company rich with government contracts. When the Civil War ended in 1865, however, Remington the second had to reorganize drastically to compensate for the loss of orders for military equipment. With two brothers, he incorporated E. Remington & Sons, retooled to make agricultural machinery, and set up a factory to turn out the then newfangled sewing machine. More significantly, to meet a new fashion in firearms, he developed a breech-loading rifle and a popular line in handguns, from a .50-caliber pistol to the so-called "vest pocket companion."

So far, he was merely following in his father's footsteps. But in 1873, he was approached by fifty-three-year-old James Densmore, an oil-rich retired editor and publisher who had paid one thousand dollars for a quarter interest in a machine that could imprint letters on paper. The mockup that Remington was shown had been constructed by a newspaperman named Christopher Lathan Sholes, whose inventive talents had been awakened by reading an article in an 1864 English arts journal in which John Pratt, an American writer living in England, described his new invention. It was the first working typing machine.

John Thomas Underwood

Sholes worked so fast that he had put together his version of a writing machine, inspired by Pratt's article, by the time Pratt exhibited his own for the first time in 1867. Pratt called his invention a "pterotype" from a Greek word meaning fern, to describe the fan-shaped arrangement of the type bars; but the moment James Densmore saw the Sholes model, he gave it the name typewriter, which stuck.

In 1867 Densmore actually set up a company to manufacture the Sholes typewriter, but the workmanship was so poor that three-quarters of all the machines sold came back for repairs. In trying to get out of that money-losing dilemma, Densmore secretly set up another company to produce a slightly different version called a calligraph, which meant that there were two competing makes, both being produced by the same people.

At this point, Densmore applied to Remington, whose reputation for quality machine work was international through arms sales to governments outside the United States. Indeed, Remington's brother Samuel had been living in Europe for years as the company's representative, becoming among other things the chief purchasing agent for France at the time of the Franco-Prussian War for all arms and munitions bought in the United States.

In 1870 the Remington rifle was recommended for adoption by the U.S. Army, but when the contract went to the Allin gun, other contracts began to fall off. That was the beginning of the end of the company as Philo Remington and his father had known it. The typewriter must have seemed like a breath of fresh air to their dying business.

After a month of tests, Remington contracted to manufacture the Sholes-Densmore typewriter, one condition being a change of name to Remington, on the plausible ground that his reputation would virtually assure its success.

For the first time, the typist could see the typed material as it emerged on the paper.

The Man Who Knows

the good and the
bad points of all

Typewriters

Buys the

Remington

Top: *A Remington Typewriter
advertisement from* The Review of
Reviews, *1905. Bottom:* A rather
boastful advertisement that appeared
in The Review of Reviews *in 1906.*

Opposite page: *An early
advertisement for Underwood Portable
Typewriters that appeared in* The
Saturday Evening Post.

Even at that, Remington moved cautiously. For four years, he applied his skilled machinists and his armory's resources to technical problems, while at the same time dealing with his financial problems. Only then, in 1876, was the first Remington put on display at the Centennial Exhibition in Philadelphia.

Philo Remington was then a man of sixty. He had been at work with machinery all his life. Unlike his father, who had three gifted sons, Philo had only daughters and no son to bring into the business. And he wanted to retire.

In 1886 he sold his entire interest in typewriters to three of his salesmen, then two years later auctioned off the main plants, separating the guns from the typewriters.

Philo Remington died in 1888. Since then no Remington has been associated with any Remington product.

Give Underwood credit. He was closer to the typewriter than Remington, for he did at least manufacture typewriter supplies and came into the business through the supply side.

John Thomas Underwood, born in London, England, in 1857, was brought to America at the age of sixteen by his father, a student of the English scientist Michael Faraday. In New Durham, New Jersey, the two opened a small plant for the manufacture of inks and special papers in 1874. They picked a good year, for the typewriter as a practical tool was just coming into business use. The Sholes & Glidden uppercase machine, ancestor of the Remington, was first made that year, though the first commercially successful machine had come out a few years earlier, made by a Dutch pastor, Johan Malling Hansen, who was way ahead of IBM with his "writing ball." It did not, however, make it across the Atlantic.

The Underwoods at once moved into supplies for the new machine by adding to their line such essentials as carbon paper, ribbons, ink pads, and rollers. They worked closely with several typewriter makers until the father died in 1882, leaving the business to his two sons, John Thomas and Frederick, who reorganized the company as John Underwood & Co. and moved it to Brooklyn, where the action was.

It was there that the Underwoods did business with Franz X. Wagner, one of the geniuses who recorded patent after patent for typewriter components or improvements.

It would be an oversimplification to say that Underwood bought Wagner's patents. A German immigrant to the United States, Wagner first worked in the early 1880s with Sholes & Glidden but was lured away in that decade of corporate raids by George Washington Yost, whose machine, the Yost, was popular both in the United States and Europe.

Finally, working with his son, Wagner created a machine all his own, which he patented in April 1893. It was this machine the Underwoods bought, and though it was first marketed as a Wagner, the name was changed in 1896 to Underwood.

It was, in many ways, the first modern standard typewriter. More than

"Pretty Soft!"

NONE of the wearisome drudgery of hand writing for him! Instead, just an easy tap-tap-tapping on the Underwood Portable, and words flash upon the paper—clean, clear, *typed!*

In a jiffy, his order and reports are completed; his letters to his family and business associates are written—all legible, fluent, full. *Pretty soft!*

THE UNDERWOOD PORTABLE is light, compact and easily carried. It requires no folding or adjusting. Its frame is strong and firm; its action smooth and swift. In every detail of appearance and design, it is an UNDERWOOD.

The Portable is obtainable at Underwood Offices in all principal cities, or direct by mail.

PRICE, $50 IN THE U.S.A.   WEIGHT, 6¾ LBS.; IN TRAVELLING CASE, 9¾ LBS.

UNDERWOOD TYPEWRITER CO., INC., UNDERWOOD BUILDING, NEW YORK

UNDERWOOD PORTABLE

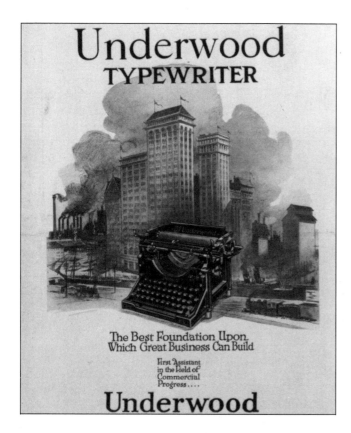

Left: *A 1917 advertisement for Underwood Typewriters.* Right: *This 1931 advertisement for the Underwood Portable appeared in* The Saturday Evening Post.

any other feature, the Wagner front-stroke principle of typing broke new ground. For the first time, the typist could see the typed material as it emerged on the paper. Before Wagner, the printing mechanism had to be lifted before the typing could be seen.

Incidentally, 1878 marked the invention of the shift key, which permits a typist to select either uppercase or lowercase letters. The inventor was Byron A. Brooks, a mechanic working for Remington.

Underwood's machine was so successful he could not keep pace with the demand. He had to farm out production to a company that was already turning out the Lambert, a rival yet obsolescent machine created by Frank Lambert, in which the paper rolled up on the platen and had to be laboriously unrolled after the work was finished.

It was Frank Lambert who made the first one thousand Underwoods (or Wagners). Then in 1901, Underwood put roots down in Hartford, Connecticut, in a factory that in time became the largest in the world.

Before World War I, they were turning out about 500 machines a day, but when John Underwood died at eighty in 1937, only twenty years later, the figure was more like 150 machines an hour.

By then, Underwood had merged with another pioneer typewriter name, Elliott-Hatch and Fisher, which was itself the amalgamation of inventions by three different people active in the business. But that name — Underwood Elliott Fisher — has vanished into corporate limbo. ♦

PITNEY-BOWES

On May 6, 1840, Rowland Smith in England invented the adhesive postage stamp; and on November 16, 1920, Arthur Pitney and Walter Bowes of the United States uninvented it.

In a way, it was stamp history coming full circle. Before Rowland Smith, letters were often franked by an ink scribble to indicate that money had been paid or was to be paid at the other end. A postage meter is a similar ink imprint on an envelope (the marks are called indicia) made, however, by machine and not by a goose-quill pen.

It was the newly incorporated Pitney-Bowes Postage Meter Company of Stamford, Connecticut, that sent out the first batch of metered mail in November 1920. But who came first, Pitney or Bowes?

Curiously enough, they both did, but from different directions and for different reasons. Strictly speaking, metered mail was Arthur Pitney's idea in the first place, and he had been working on it for at least twenty years before Bowes came along.

Born in Quincy, Illinois, in 1871 (and that is about all that is known of his early life), Arthur Pitney moved to Chicago at the age of nineteen looking for a job. He had grown up handicapped by a severe limp from an attack of polio in infancy, so there were few manual jobs he could handle. He found a selling job in a wallpaper shop, but in his spare time amused himself with various mechanical ideas, one of which — a novel rack for displaying wallpaper samples — he actually put into use in the store.

It could be that he got his idea for a postage meter from his contact with wallpaper, which, like a stamp, also has to be stuck to a surface. While visiting the World's Columbian Exposition of 1893 in Chicago, he was impressed by a traveling post office built into a railway car, with its battery of clerks and canceling machines, and spent many hours after that visit trying to make a machine that would stick stamps onto letters from a continuous roll.

When that failed, he first thought of doing away with stamps altogether. After all, if a machine can cancel stamps on individual letters, why can't a machine print them? Fifteen years later, Walter Bowes was struck with exactly the same idea.

Arthur Pitney had no idea that others had already invented stamp machines in Germany, Norway, New Zealand, and even in the States, but only one had ever made it off the drawing board, and that one did not work in practice.

The machine that Pitney, with the help of a mechanically inclined patent

Arthur H. Pitney

Walter Bowes

From the company's archives,
illustrations featuring a postage meter.

attorney named Eugene Rummler, patented in October 1902 actually did work and was praised by Harry Seger, who ran the mail wagon for the Chicago post office. When he sent the blueprints to Washington, he wrote, "The machine prints upon letters an indelible stamp in lieu of the postage stamp as now used. These imprints are numbered automatically and show the licensing number of the machine. It may be set for any number of impressions up to 10,000," after which it had to be reset by the post office.

It seemed foolproof, but it was not bureaucratproof, as Pitney was to learn over the next two decades. He set up the Pitney Postal Machine Company, with offices in the Tribune Building on South Dearborn Street, and made an appointment to test-run it before the post office brass in Washington.

That was in 1904. The officials were impressed, even enthusiastic, but said they could not adopt the machine without approval from Congress.

Over the next five years, Pitney revised and improved the machine and tested it with many different companies, always with practical success. In 1910 he gave up his clerking job, sold stock in a new company, which he named the American Postage Meter Company, using the word meter for the first time, and ran yet another test in Washington. Again nothing happened.

Four years later, with the cooperation of the Addressograph Company of Chicago, Pitney orchestrated a huge test among companies including Montgomery Ward, Armour & Company, and the American School of Commerce, running 853,924 pieces of mail through his machine. Though it worked like a charm, it was only a test; it could not be official without government approval. The government wrote to Pitney on October 8, 1914: "There is no need for such a machine as an adjunct to the Postal Service."

They were principally concerned that they might not be able to keep control over the printed indicia, as they could over printed stamps.

Now enter Walter Bowes, who has been described by the Pitney-Bowes historian William Cahn as "the man who couldn't stand still." He was the youngest of the twelve children of a well-to-do merchant of Yorkshire, England, and was brought to Boston by his parents in 1893 at the age of eleven. He was an athlete and a go-getter, and a born salesman. As a new man with the Addressograph Company at twenty-four, he broke all selling records, then resigned in spite of a handsome promotion to go sailing on his new twenty-three-foot sloop.

He first crossed Pitney's path as a competitor in the stamp meter field. In 1912, as owner of a company that made a stamp-canceling machine, he had sold a contract to the U.S. government just when Pitney was getting yet one more rebuff for his stamp meter machine. It was then that it occurred to Bowes, as it had occurred to Pitney years earlier, to invent a machine that would print a stamp right on the envelope.

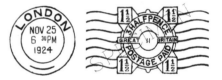

He got the same governmental cold shoulder. When he demonstrated how his canceling machine could be converted into a stamp-printing machine, the government said there was no way they were going to let people print their own stamps.

Then followed seven years of deadlock, but when Pitney met Bowes for the first time, there was an instant chemical reaction. As the historian says, "Bowes was the promoter, Pitney was the dedicated inventor. Pitney was given to depression, Bowes was aggressive and assured. Pitney was restricted by lameness, Bowes was athletic and impetuous."

From a full-page color advertisement that appeared in a 1924 issue of Postal Supervisor: *the Pitney-Bowes Postage Meter and postmarks and indicia from the United States, Great Britain, and Canada.*

It may not have been love at first sight, and indeed their personalities clashed most of the time, but it certainly was a perfect marriage between the Bowes Universal Stamping Machine Company of Stamford and Pitney's American Postage Meter Company of Chicago.

While Pitney set to work fitting his machine with the latest modifications, Bowes himself set about lobbying in Washington for another demonstration, and got it.

On their way there, Pitney and Bowes had another quarrel so heated that Pitney picked up his meter, stepped into a taxi, and disappeared. When he was finally tracked down early the following morning, after a search through every hotel in the city, Pitney and Bowes kissed and made up, and the demonstration went off like a charm.

This time, the post office caved in, which is why Tuesday, November 16, 1920, bears the stamp — or rather the indicia — of history. ◆

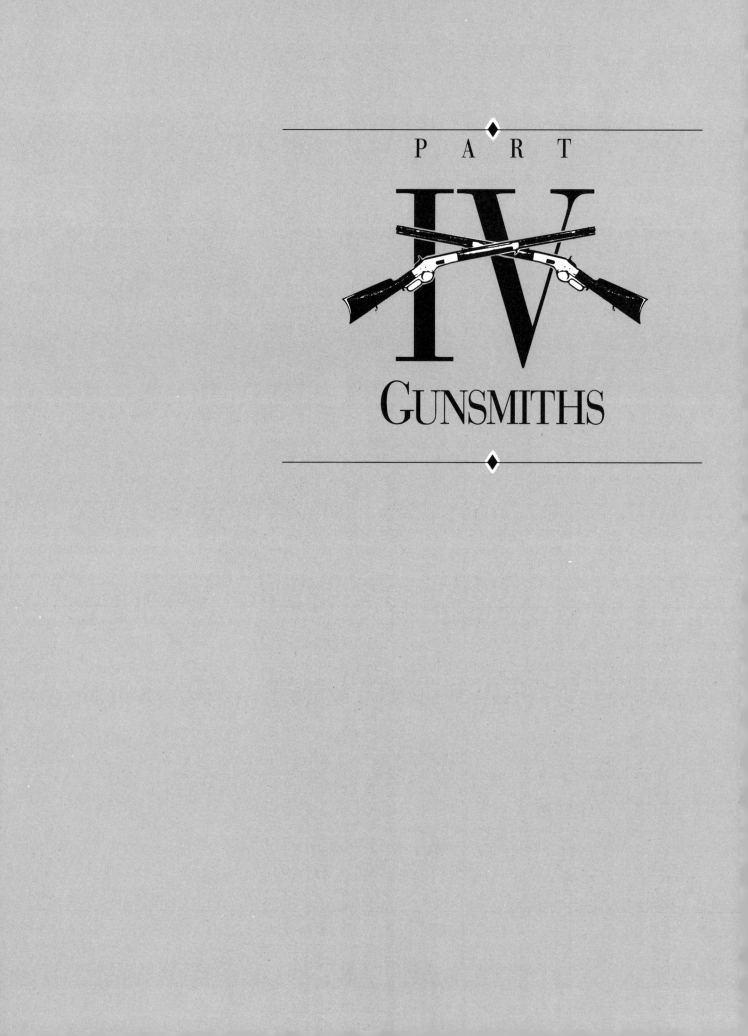

P A R T

IV

GUNSMITHS

REMINGTON

If you want your son's name to become a household name, don't give him the money to buy a gun.

At least, that is what happened when twenty-three-year-old Eliphalet Remington got a firm no from his father. Now look around: The Remington name has turned up on typewriters, chainsaws, handguns, and rifles, as well as cutlery, farm machinery, bicycles, and bridges. You'll also see the Remington name on computers, electric shavers, card indexers, and air conditioners, but only the products of Remington Arms can be directly traced back to that parent's refusal in 1816. On that date Remington Arms was formed, and it's one of the oldest companies in the United States still manufacturing the same product in the same location.

Young Eliphalet had to take his father's refusal for real, since he had no choice. But instead of mooning around the house with a grudge, he went out into the back shed and made a gun.

Luckily, the Remington place had lots of scrap metal lying around because both father and son were part-time blacksmiths and part-time farmers near Utica, New York, where they had been living since 1800. Eliphalet had been a married man for a couple of years, but he still lived at home.

Eliphalet Remington

He made the gun himself — lock, stock, and barrel — but because he did not have the tools necessary to rifle the barrel (that is, to cut spiral grooves in it), he took it to a gunmaker in Utica, who was so impressed by the workmanship that he asked Eliphalet to make another.

Young Remington went home, machined parts for several other guns, and carted them back to Utica for rifling. From that simple beginning sprang a family business lasting more than eighty years and spanning two generations.

The point about Remington is that he was not interested in the smoothbore gun. He wanted one of the newfangled rifles that were just then making their way across America. They were first brought across the Atlantic by the Swiss in the mid-1700s and came into limited use during the American Revolutionary War.

The latest improvement when Remington was a youngster was the invention of the percussion cap in 1807, supplanting the old flintlock ignition. Famous gunmakers such as Colt, Enfield, Mauser, and Smith & Wesson were still more than twenty-five years in the future. Even rifles were still using balls instead of bullets. So Eliphalet Remington was in on the ground floor of the rifle as a modern firearm.

The Remington barrels were so well made and so much in demand that

> *Eliphalet Remington was in on the beginning of the rifle as a modern weapon.*

Top: *The birthplace of Remington Arms.* Bottom: *The room where the double gun was assembled.*

Opposite page: *During World War II, Remington produced only guns for the military. This advertisement ran in* Collier's *in 1943.*

buyers used to come to the farm and hang around waiting for their orders to be filled. One visitor, perhaps a frustrated poet, wrote that "the banks of Steel's Creek blazed with the cheery fires of many forges, powered by a water wheel, and the surrounding hills rang with the joyous music of the anvil."

Not for long, though. Business became so brisk that in 1828 Remington moved the armory closer to the new main transportation highway, the Erie Canal, opened three years earlier. He was free to make the move when his father, also named Eliphalet, died earlier that year.

By then, E. Remington & Son, equipped with water wheels and trip hammers, were not only welding and forging gun barrels, but rifling, stocking, and fitting locks as well. They were so busy, the place was like a little town, and it was known as Remington's Corners. But in 1843, at Eliphalet Remington's urging, the name was changed to Ilion. It is now a good-sized town.

For a while, the factory carried on a small sideline in other metal implements, but firearms were the moneymakers. Remington is credited with many of the improvements that made American firearms effective and durable. They were the first to use steel in sporting gun barrels, and they seem to have put into place a form of assembly-line production, half a century before Ford. At first, they imported locks from England, where they were all made by hand, but in the Remington armory, machines were developed to turn out parts to fixed specifications. The savings in material and labor gave Remington a marketing advantage.

The company absorbed a Springfield, Ohio, gunmaking plant, which had a lucrative government contract for several thousand carbines, then lobbied for and got another federal contract for five thousand rifles, and then another.

In a sense, success was the death of Eliphalet Remington. In 1856 he had branched out into his father's old business by building three new factories to turn out agricultural implements. When the Civil War broke out, the company was given huge federal contracts for rifles, carbines, and pistols, which meant further expansion at such intense pressure that Remington died four months later at the age of sixty-eight.

His three sons, as they grew up, had all gone into the business. Eliphalet, Jr., the youngest, was office manager; Samuel was chief contract negotiator; and Philo, the eldest, who had inherited his father's and his grandfather's mechanical aptitude, went on to manufacture the first practical typewriter. ◆

"Maybe next year, Queenie!"

"**Mallards!** Gosh, don't they remind me of some swell times!

"Gets *you* kind of excited too, Queenie, doesn't it? I understand. My dog was a lot like you, and I know how he loved hunting.

"There'd be cold, gray autumn mornings when the wind almost blew our ears off. Just the right weather for ducks. I'd paddle us out to our favorite hunting place in the marsh. Pretty soon our wooden decoys would be bobbin' away, natural as life, and a big flight of mallards would start down to get chummy. Then—*whammo!*

"No matter how far away the ducks dropped,

that dog of mine used to retrieve 'em every time. I'll bet you did too. And boy, what wouldn't we both give to do some duck hunting this season!

"But there's a war on now, Queenie. We're in the Coast Guard, and we've got a job to do. Maybe *next* year . . . ."

Remington's job right now is to supply a lot of military arms and ammunition fast—to help speed, among other things, the return of hunters and hunting dogs to their favorite

marshes. Here is what we are doing . . . .

1. *Every working day, Remington produces thirty million rounds of military small arms ammunition.*

2. *And, every working day, Remington produces more than enough military rifles to equip an entire infantry regiment at full fighting strength.*

After the war is won, we will again be serving our sportsmen friends with Remington shotguns and rifles, Nitro Express shells, Kleanbore Hi-Speed .22's, and Core-Lokt big game bullets. *Remington Arms Co., Inc., Bridgeport, Conn.*

"Nitro Express," "Kleanbore," "Hi-Speed," "Sportsman," Reg. U.S. Pat. Off. "Core-Lokt" is a trade mark of Remington Arms Co., Inc.

★ HELP YOURSELF LATER BY HELPING YOUR COUNTRY NOW. BUY WAR BONDS! ★

Remington Sportsman 3-shot autoloading shotgun and Nitro Express shot shells

Remington

DUPONT

56

COLT

Samuel Colt

♦
*He was only fifteen
when he solved the
mechanical problem
that had challenged
gunmakers since the
seventeenth century.*
♦

The only conventional thing Colonel Samuel Colt ever did was to live and die in the same town he was born in, Hartford, Connecticut; but he was no stay-at-home. Like most nineteenth-century Americans, he had the itch to travel, but it was typical of Colt's lifestyle that he packed all his exotic travel into his teenage years.

He was born in 1814, the third of four sons of a Hartford manufacturer. His mother was the daughter of Hartford's first insurance company president. At the age of ten, when his father's wealth was swept away by economic reverses after the war of 1812, young Colt was put to work part-time in the factory. But though he liked mechanical work, he ran away to sea, just like in the storybooks, after only three years and signed on as a common seaman before the mast for a voyage to Calcutta.

It was during his idle hours on that voyage that Colt, instead of whittling or turning out the traditional seaman's scrimshaw, constructed a working model of a revolutionary new revolving pistol out of a slab of white pine, using a chisel and a common jackknife.

He was only sixteen, but somehow he had managed to solve the mechanical problem that had challenged gunmakers since the beginning of the seventeenth century: how to make a handgun shoot several bullets in rapid succession.

Until Samuel Colt came along, one gunsmith after another had tried multiple barrels, usually turned by hand, each one charged with powder and shot. In the year Colt was born, the Parisian gunsmith Le Norman had constructed one with five barrels, then one with seven; and there was even one monster with twenty-four barrels, which was later adapted into the famous "pepperpot" pistol.

They were all "revolvers," but Colt's idea, simple enough once he had thought of it, was to convert the multiple barrel into a revolving cylinder or breech of six or seven chambers, each one loaded and ready to be revolved in line with the single barrel. His first model, whittled in white pine, is still preserved in the Samuel Colt Museum.

At the end of his East India voyage, Colt went back to work in his father's mill and studied chemistry on the side. Then at the age of eighteen, he decided to take off again. Traveling under the name of Coult, he stumped the country up and down lecturing on nitrous oxide, or laughing gas, then widely used by dentists to make their patients overlook pain. Playing to packed hysterical houses in the Union and through British North America, he said he had

♦ 140

administered laughing gas to more men, women, and children than all the dentists in the world combined.

He did it simply for money, in order to put into production the Colt Repeating Pistol. Granted a patent in 1836, the year he turned twenty-two, he had backing of three hundred thousand dollars from various capitalists within a year, and opened his Patent Arms Manufacturing Company in Paterson, New Jersey.

He did not build in Hartford because he could not at that time afford to build the kind of plant he wanted, on the site he already had his eye on. It was a tract of land called the South Meadows on the west side of the Connecticut River near where it is joined by the Little River, and which regularly disappeared under water when the rivers flooded. Colt planned to emulate the Dutch and reclaim the land from the swampy waters.

The exact date is not given in William B. Edwards's *The Story of Colt's Revolver* (1953), but Colt was prosperous enough in the early 1850s to begin buying small parcels from willing sellers. But when word of his plan leaked out, prices began to rise alarmingly. One parcel was owned by the president of a Hartford bank, who asked ten times the land's value. Colt went out and bought up all the bank's stock to force the president either to sell the land or lose his job.

Colt began to clear the land in the fall of 1853, and surrounded the two hundred acres with a stone dyke two miles long, 150 feet wide at the base, and 18 feet high, inside which he built a city, or at least a company town, called Colt's New Armory. Including his own private residence and grounds, the work cost nearly $2 million in 1853 dollars. But by then, Colt was worth nearly half a million dollars, so he could well afford it.

The Paterson plant had made a few thousand pistols, which helped to win the Florida war against the Seminoles and helped the Texas Rangers win independence for their state. After a slight recession due to a shortage of local wars, shooting started again in Mexico in 1846, bringing in so many profitable orders that Colt was able to go ahead with his city in a swamp.

The various stone buildings housed fifteen hundred separate machines, each one fabricated in Colt's own shops, which manufactured all the components of a growing industry, from cartridges, balls, bullet molds, and powder

Top: *Colt carved this original wooden model of the revolver while at sea.* Bottom: *Martha Jane Cannary, a.k.a. Calamity Jane packed a Colt.* Bottom left: *A 1904 advertisement for Colt from* McClure's *Magazine.*

Left: *Colt guns were ingeniously packaged to look like reference books. These book casings were first made at Paterson. The closed volume contains a Model 1859 Pocket Pistol given to a member of the Colt factory's Sons of Temperance chapter. The open volume, entitled* Holy Bible, *holds a Sidehammer. Colt liked to make puns with the titles, and once presented a Hartford bishop with a "copy of my latest work on 'Moral Reform'." Right: A Colt advertisement from "the percussion period" features copies of engravings from the cylinders of various firearms.*

flasks to lubricating oil. The plant ran twenty-four hours a day.

Colt even harvested the river banks, which he had planted with thousands of Dutch osiers to knot together the swampy soil. These osiers, as they grew, were cut under Colt's orders and used for the manufacture of a line of woven willow articles.

His inventive mind took other turns. As a boy, he had predicted the submarine torpedo. He later devised a way to blow a ship out of the water by remote electric batteries, but no government wanted to take it up. In 1843 he was the first to lay submarine electric cable, connecting New York City with Coney Island.

One of his most unconventional acts was to deny that his repeater pistol was an original invention. He certainly worked it out alone at sixteen; but just before he built his new armory, he was rummaging through the ancient arms in the Tower of London while on a visit to England and came across an early, imperfect attempt by an unknown gunsmith. He gave a lecture on it, with full credit to the nameless inventor, before the Institution of Civil Engineers in 1851.

Samuel Colt died suddenly of a stroke early in January 1862, when only forty-eight. Of his four children, three had died in infancy and the fourth was under ten, so his widow stepped in to run the Colt armory until the son reached maturity.

In that way, too, the Colt story is unconventional. ◆

SMITH & WESSON

Pick up almost any American murder mystery and chances are the fatal bullet was fired from a Smith & Wesson automatic or revolver.

But are they keeping it from us that the perpetrator was led away in a pair of Smith & Wesson handcuffs? And why are we not told that the victim was found in the bathroom slumped over a Smith & Wesson flush toilet, his face freshly shaved with a blade sharpened by a Smith & Wesson Blade Saver, with his wife bound and gagged on the kitchen floor beside her Smith & Wesson Dish Washing Machine?

Perhaps these fascinating details are played down because they are connected to the few times that the Smith & Wesson partnership had to make the attempt — sometimes desperate, sometimes even comic — to stave off bankruptcy.

Shortly after World War I, Harold Wesson, grandson of one of the founders, invented a device to resharpen razor blades "so individuals could get more shaves for their money," then he tried marketing washing machines for clothes and dishes. But both these lines petered out within a few years. The line of Peerless Handcuffs, however, proved to be a staple commodity.

During the Great Depression, when Harold Wesson tried to keep the company going through diversification, his "avenue of pursuit," to quote from Roy G. Jinks's *History of Smith & Wesson*, "was the plumbing business and the development of a series of toilet flush valves, and there is no doubt that this new product brought some laughs from Smith & Wesson's competition."

The company struggled through to 1939, when a dynamic new plant superintendent named Carl Hellstrom, later president of the company, was given a free hand to turn the company around.

A fat contract for service revolvers for British troops did not hurt any, yet despite that, according to a *Saturday Evening Post* profile of Hellstrom published in August 1949, the company's total physical assets in 1941 had shrunk to $250,000 "including all its machinery, real estate and 21 dank buildings." As Hellstrom said in his *100 Years of Gunmaking*, they spent "ten years in the red." Under Hellstrom, the red soon turned black.

Blade savers and handcuffs were not the company's only nonlethal products. Way back in the late 1870s, Harold Wesson's father, Walter Wesson, took one quick foray into the domestic market by incorporating the Wesson Sewing Machine Company, but three weeks later the company dissolved without making a single machine and Walter Wesson went back to revolvers.

To be strictly accurate, even revolvers were a diversification, because the

Horace Smith

Daniel Baird Wesson

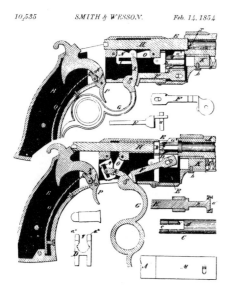

Patent drawing of the Horace Smith and D. B. Wesson magazine pistol. The arrow in the drawing points to the Flobert cartridge.

first firearm Horace Smith and Daniel Baird Wesson developed was a single-shot pistol together with its cartridge.

It would be too simple to say that it was Smith who created the gun and Wesson who created the bullet, but that is not far from the truth, provided you bear in mind that in the mid-1800s there were so many inventors at work on firearms that no one weapon could reasonably bear one man's name.

Roy Jinks, the company's historian, has done a great deal to lead a way through the maze of gunmaking history in his two books, both filled with technical data and one containing graphic portraits of the founders: Wesson, plump, bearded, and confident; Smith, somewhat drawn and anxious, clearly of an older generation.

Of Horace Smith, he says that "we can see he was not a man who drew a great deal of attention, for there is very little written about his life." Since his father, Silas Smith, worked at the government armory in Springfield, Massachusetts, the boy grew up surrounded by guns. At sixteen, he became helper to a bayonet forger, and during the next eighteen years was credited with several mechanical inventions as he became a skilled armorer.

Then he moved from one civilian gunmaker to another, working with firearms of all makes, from percussion pepperpot pistols, which aroused his interest in repeaters, to whaling guns, for which he invented an explosive bullet.

By the time he met Wesson in about 1850, he was already a mature forty-two and had patented his first gun, a modified version of a magazine loader invented by Orville Percival and Asa Smith, no relation.

Daniel Baird Wesson, on the other hand, was only twenty-five, but he had been interested in firearms for years, probably ever since his older brother Edwin began earning a living as a gunsmith in 1835. Jinks, quoting from another brother's letter written when Daniel was seventeen, writes that "Daniel likes to hunt, but he had rather be at work in the shop on gunlocks, springs, or something of that kind."

Daniel worked with Edwin gaining experience in gunmaking with the early Wesson target rifles and making useful contact with Samuel Colt and others in the firearms business. The two brothers became partners with a gunsmith named Arthur Smith (no relation to Horace), and when Daniel was finally released from his apprenticeship in November 1848, the future seemed quite predictable.

When Edwin Wesson died suddenly two months later, Daniel tried to cope with the financial burden he inherited by forming the Wesson Rifle Company, but matters grew so desperate the company was finally auctioned off. Though Daniel Wesson busied himself in gun manufacture, often as an employee, it was not until he formed a partnership with Horace Smith that his fortunes took a turn for the better.

The two men had probably met earlier through their mutual connection with Allen & Thurber, gunmakers of Norwich, Connecticut, but they began

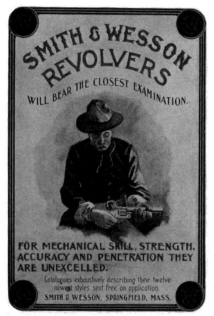

Left: *The Smith & Wesson patent model of the large-frame magazine pistol.* Right: *An early Smith & Wesson advertisement.*

working together when Wesson described to Smith an ingenious modification he had made to the patented but unreliable Walter Hunt bullet.

To make a complicated story unreasonably short (Jinks tells it in great detail) Wesson and Smith put their heads together and produced their first weapon: a magazine pistol modified mostly by Smith (from the improvements Lewis Jennings had made to the 1849 original by Walter Hunt), and adapted to fire a cartridge invented in France by Flobert but improved by Wesson. That is one small example of the way inventors' names got tangled up in the early history of American firearm development. But there is more.

Smith and Wesson, now partners, began production of their magazine pistol in 1853 at Smith's plant in Norwich, Connecticut, but one of Smith's own patents had been assigned to a New York inventor named Cortland Palmer, who also happened to own patents granted to both Jennings and Hunt. Wesson himself had patented an improvement on a Palmer cartridge.

To tidy up this situation, and to provide useful capital, the three formed a limited partnership under the name Smith & Wesson, with Palmer giving his rights to the patents he owned.

On that foundation, the company moved ahead. One popular item was the .31-caliber pistol, which *Scientific American* in 1854 dubbed the Volcanic, because a fast gunslinger could fire it at the rate of one bullet every two seconds. It did not sell well, however, and after two years, money was so tight that the company had to be sold.

Horace Smith went back to Springfield to operate a livery stable with his brother, while Wesson stayed on as superintendent of what was renamed the Volcanic Repeating Arms Company.

That is by no means the end of the story. Indeed, it is the merest curtain raiser, since neither Smith nor Wesson ever stopped dreaming about the repeater they would one day bring into the world.

Some years earlier, Smith had been hired by Cortland Palmer to work on a repeater invented by Walter Hunt, which was already being produced in a licensing arrangement by a competitor. Meanwhile, Wesson had hoped to fabricate a revolver one day based on one invented by his brother Edwin, which in fact was thought to be an infringement on patents held by Samuel Colt.

Two Smith & Wesson advertisements.

Somehow, the two men came together again in October 1856, and it is this Smith & Wesson partnership that has lasted through the years. Horace Smith stayed on until 1873, but lived on in active retirement until he died at the age of eighty-four. From 1873, Smith & Wesson was dominated by Daniel Baird Wesson until his death in 1906, and then by his sons and grandson until the mid-1930s.

The landmark firearm of those years was the .357 Magnum, their "most deluxe revolver," which brought an overwhelming response from their customers. The first Magnum, issued on April 8, 1935, was presented to J. Edgar Hoover.

Ironically, the cartridge for the Magnum was developed by the company that produced the Winchester, which is just as famous a name as Magnum, but with a much more unusual story behind it. ◆

WINCHESTER

I f it drives you up the wall to keep track of the characters in a historical novel, wait until you try sorting out the parentage of the Winchester rifle and all its various models.

The best thing to do is to hang on to this one clear fact: The Winchester was not invented by Oliver Fisher Winchester. Simply put, Winchester was a well-to-do shirt manufacturer who had the good luck to be owner of a nice chunk of stock in a company that was turning out firearms in March 1857, just when it needed a financial bail-out.

Originally called the New Haven Arms Company of New Haven, Connecticut, it was reorganized as the Winchester Repeating Arms Company in 1866.

Winchester had already crammed many experiences into his first forty-seven years. Born in Boston in 1810, he had to go out to work for wages on a neighbor's farm at the age of seven after his father died. He was a carpenter's apprentice at fourteen and a master builder at twenty. Among his accomplishments was a church he built in Baltimore, which still stands.

Then at twenty-three he married and went into business in Baltimore selling men's furnishings, moving after three years to Boston.

In 1847 he made his radical improvement in the design of men's shirts. He disliked the usual cut that resulted in an uncomfortable twist to the neckband. "The object of my invention," he wrote in his patent application, "is to remedy this evil." He altered the cut so that the shirt was supported by the shoulders, without tugging at the neck. Perhaps the disagreeable expressions on the faces in old daguerreotypes was caused by strangling shirt collars.

The moment the patent was awarded in February 1848, Winchester sold his financial interests, moved to New Haven, formed a partnership with a New York distributor, and proceeded to grow wealthy by contracting work out to seamstresses in their homes, who by the early 1850s could work on Singer's new sewing machine. Soon he was paying piecework wages to nearly six thousand workers, and by 1860, he was turning out 40,000 dozen shirts a year.

By then, of course, Oliver Winchester had been for three years the beneficial owner of the New Haven Arms Company, which had risen from the ashes of the Volcanic Repeating Arms Company, formerly Smith & Wesson, who regrouped two years later.

Winchester got control of the company through a tragic fluke, when Volcanic's president Nelson B. Gaston, who had interests in mining, paint

Oliver Fisher Winchester

Winchester's invention was not a gun, but an improvement to shirt collar design.

Above: *Buffalo Bill with Sitting Bull, holding a Winchester Model 1873.*
Bottom left: *Buffalo Bill surveying the Wild West acts, 1911. He is holding a Winchester Model 1873.*
Bottom right: *An advertisement, circa 1904, from* The Review of Reviews.

products, shipping, and guns, dropped dead less than a year after the company was formed. Winchester, a major shareholder who had taken an interest in it, was elected president.

There was trouble ahead. The price paid by Volcanic to Smith and Wesson for their interest was so high that Volcanic had difficulty meeting it on top of their production costs.

Here, wealthy Oliver Winchester stepped forward with guarantees to save Volcanic, accepting in exchange a pledge or mortgage on the principal assets, which included machinery, tools, and patents on inventions by Hunt, Jennings, Smith, and Wesson.

Winchester never invented anything but a shirt collar, but here he was in control of a company that owned the united inventions of several American pioneer gunmakers. Even before the papers were signed giving him control of Volcanic, however, he had already organized its successor corporation, the New Haven Arms Company.

He was the first of a new breed of entrepreneur in the firearms industry. Colonel Samuel Colt was an inventor of firearms who turned to manufacturing, and Smith and Wesson carried on as experts in their own technical field. But, as Geoffrey Boothroyd asserts in *The Rifle and Rifle Shooting*, "It is indeed odd that the man whose name became practically synonymous with the term 'repeating rifle' personally knew very little about firearms." Boothroyd goes on, "Winchester himself was a businessman, not an engineer, but under his direction the company grew in stature and prosperity." Apparently he built up his company using financial and selling skills, depending on others to advise him on technical matters.

Among these expert advisors, John Moses Browning must surely take first place. Boothroyd calls him "the most famous of all the firearms designers," and he was probably the greatest inventor of American small arms and automatics. The Browning Machine Gun of 1917 and the Browning Automatic of 1918 were supplied to the U.S. Army in great numbers after they were

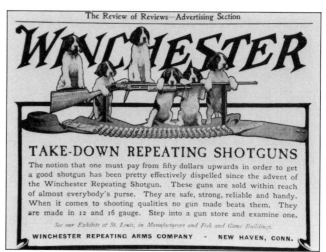

personally demonstrated by the inventor against his main competitor, Samuel Colt.

Early in his career, however, Browning never used to name his inventions after himself. There were many firearms around bearing names such as Colt, Remington, Henry, and Winchester, but they were all invented by Browning.

Browning was born in Ogden, Utah, in 1855, the same year the Volcanic Repeating Arms Company was formed. Son of a Mormon gunsmith, he first started making guns on a homemade lathe as a boy of thirteen. He was less than two years old in 1857 when Oliver Fisher Winchester first became a manufacturer of firearms. And he was still only a young teenager hanging around his father's gunsmithy when Winchester and Benjamin Tyler Henry organized the Winchester Repeating Arms Company in 1866 at Bridgeport, Connecticut, and began turning out firearms with the Winchester name stamped on them.

Browning first made contact with Winchester in 1880. While still a teenager, he and his brother Matt turned out six hundred copies of a breechloading rifle he had invented, which he patented on October 7, 1879. This patent he sold, with his stock of unsold rifles, for eight thousand dollars to the Winchester Firearms Company, where it was named the Winchester Single Shot .22.

Their association lasted for about twenty years, and he designed several models for Winchester, though none, as Herbert G. Houze, curator of the Winchester Arms Museums points out, were made without extensive reworking of the Browning prototypes. And Winchester himself is credited with half a dozen patents in his own name.

It is ironic that Oliver Winchester died in 1880, the very year that John Browning sold Winchester's company his first invention. Though Winchester guided the company through its first stages as it became the Winchester Firearms Company, he did not live to realize that his own name would become legendary among gun fanciers. ♦

An advertisement appealing to hunters, from Munsey's Magazine, *August 1899.*

AUTO MECHANICS AND EXPRESSMEN

GOODYEAR TO SEIBERLING

Automobile tires and the name Goodyear are so closely linked that it may come as a shock to hear that Charles Goodyear himself could never have imagined that the world would one day ride on the new kind of rubber that he spent most of his unhappy life developing. And he never made a tire in his life.

He knew that he was working on research of great importance; but when he himself first used his new and practical substance, he made strange things — a cravat, a money purse, and a suit of clothes. At the Great Exhibition of 1851 in London, he displayed furniture, floor coverings, books, bric à brac, even jewelry — all made of rubber. But no tires.

In fact, the first tires manufactured under the Goodyear name did not come on the market until twenty-eight years after he died. In 1898, Frank August Seiberling bought an old strawboard factory in East Akron, Ohio, with borrowed money and turned it into the giant of the rubber industry, naming it after the inventor of the vulcanizing process.

Beyond the name, the Seiberling company had no connection with the Goodyear Company founded early in the nineteenth century by Charles Goodyear's father.

Amasa Goodyear was the enterprising New Englander who manufactured the first pearl buttons ever made in the United States. Later, with profits from a government contract to make metal buttons for soldiers in the 1812 war against the British, he branched out into general hardware, including the moneymaking spring steel hay fork, which he devised as an improvement over the heavy wrought-iron fork then in use. Beginning in 1821, father and son worked together as partners in the family firm of A. Goodyear and Son.

It would seem that Charles Goodyear had an assured future. Born in 1800, he was one of six children, all of whom worked in the profitable family business. But when the company, with branches in New Haven and Philadelphia, tried to expand too fast through the southern states, it went bankrupt, and Charles at twenty-nine had to assume heavy liabilities. Since debt was punishable by imprisonment in those days, Charles, his health enfeebled, spent many dismal months off and on inside debtors prisons.

Ironically, it was in prison that he made his first researches into rubber. He had been traveling through New York State on business when he saw that an inflated rubber life-preserver in a store window was equipped with a faulty valve. After tinkering with it, he made an improvement; but when he offered it to the manufacturer, he was told he would spend his time better by invent-

Charles Goodyear

Inside debtors prison he made his first researches into rubber.

This advertisement appeared in the July 4, 1917 issue of The Youth's Companion.

ing a way to cure India rubber so that it would not melt, stick, or decompose in summer.

The new rubber industry, which took off like a rocket in 1830, crashed a few years later because products made with the volatile new substance were no good. One company had two hundred thousand dollars worth of shoes returned because they had decomposed in the heat of summer. The shoes smelled so bad they could not be burned but had to be buried.

When Goodyear came back to Philadelphia, he was arrested for debt one more time and flung into prison. There he began his experiments, which involved simply kneading raw rubber with one substance after another to try and arrive at the stable heat-resistant compound an entire industry had failed to develop.

When he was released from prison that time, he had a mission in life. Though he invented many other things — a new button, a faucet, an air pump, a boat made of metal tubing — rubber and its improvement became his obsession, and it finally drove him into misery and isolation.

His family suffered as much as he did. His wife Clarissa stuck to him through the humiliation, the loss of friends, the begging, and the hunger. Once Goodyear sold his children's spare clothing to buy food. Another time, when they had nothing to eat in the house, he went grubbing in old potato fields for crop leavings.

In 1837, through the charity of friends, the family was given a room to live in, with another room for Charles and his experiments, which used materials given him by a sympathetic druggist.

He had been searching for six years, in and out of jail. He had tried scores of substances and had even made shoes that melted and caps that stank. No wonder his wife begged him to give up. Even his neighbors thought he was crazy.

The actual discovery of the vulcanizing process has become the subject of what Ralph Wolf calls "so many ridiculous and utterly false stories," some of which he included in his 1939 story of Charles Goodyear, *India Rubber Man.*

In one version, Goodyear was kneading a batch of rubber in the kitchen when he heard his wife's step outside. He had thought she was out shopping, but she came back unexpectedly. Not wanting to hurt her feelings, he threw the mess into a corner, but it landed on the red hot stove where to his surprise it did not melt. He had no idea what he had done to the stuff, but this time it stood up to all his tests. He took that lump and froze it, heated it, pounded it, and tried to cut it. It stayed flexible and did not disintegrate.

There were lots of stoves around, mostly red hot. The Newburyport, Massachusetts *News,* which copied the item from a Woburn newspaper, said that Goodyear made the accidental discovery on the red hot stove in Colonel Wade's store in the village. A pamphleteer of the time says it was on the red hot stove in A.E. Thompson's emporium that Goodyear dropped a ball of rubber and sulphur. An unnamed rubber expert lectured that Goodyear had leaned against a stove wearing a rubber apron; and as recently as 1937, the Akron, Ohio *Times-Press* reported that Goodyear hid a ball of rubber in a stove to avoid a quarrel "with his termagant wife."

Wolf also cites the Waterbury, Connecticut *Republican*, which "attributed asbestos hands to the inventor," when he "threw a handful of melted sulphur" into a cup of melted rubber and watched the combination solidify.

Wolf then gives Goodyear's own story. The discovery was made during a series of experiments with pieces of rubber and red hot stoves at his "manufactory at Woburn," as witnessed by his brother Nelson, and again before an open fire at home before the eyes of his daughter Ellen.

Wolf quotes her saying, "I casually observed the little piece of gum which he was holding near the fire . . . . He nailed the gum outside the kitchen door in the intense cold. . . . In the morning he brought it in, holding it up exultingly."

Legends remain, but so does the fact that on February 24, 1839, Charles Goodyear took out a patent for a process he called vulcanization, on which an entire new industry was founded.

They called him crazy, but Frank August Seiberling had his own brand of economic madness. He never knew when he was licked.

He proved it when he went into the rubber business for the first time in 1898, at the height of a depression. And he repeated that trick in the depression of 1921.

He was sixty-two years old, and he had just been forced out of the presidency of the Goodyear Tire and Rubber Company. After the Goodyear plant passed into the hands of a syndicate of bankers, the deposed president, whom *The New York Times* referred to as Ziberling, spent the summer planning a comeback.

In association with his brother Charles, he went public in November, a month after his sixty-second birthday, with the Seiberling Rubber Company, capitalized at $55 million.

Ahead of him lay more than thirty busy years in one of the industries that developed as the automobile proliferated, and behind him lay two generations of enterprise with an inventive and industrious family.

His grandfather, descendant of an immigrant from Stuttgart, Germany, in 1741, was a farmer and sawmill operator in Summit County, Ohio, before Akron existed. His son, John Frederick Seiberling, Frank's father, became an inventor of agricultural implements, among them the wheat binder later manufactured by McCormick-Deering.

In 1862 John Frederick Seiberling and his brother James Henry were in business in Akron as the Empire Mower & Reaper Company, but three years later, they dissolved the partnership and went their separate ways. James left Akron to become involved in the manufacture of insulated wire, while John Frederick stayed on in Akron, making mowers and reapers under the name J. F. Seiberling & Company. He was also responsible for starting local industry sidelines in flour, grain, banking, real estate, and strawboard (a thick card-

Frank A. Seiberling

◆

He was known as the "little Napoleon" of the rubber industry.

◆

Above: *A 1931 advertisement for Goodyear tires.* Bottom right: *This advertisement for Seiberling All-Treads appeared in the August 8, 1925 issue of* The Literary Digest.

board made from straw).

In this environment, his son Frank grew up, went to high school, married, started a family, joined the firm, and became secretary treasurer. Then suddenly in 1898, after the business panic of 1893 and "unable to compete successfully," says the *National Cyclopedia of American Biography*, "with the harvesting machine trust," the business failed. Frank Seiberling found himself at thirty-nine out of a job and without resources.

That spring, he ran across a business acquaintance whose strawboard factory on seven acres with frontage on the Cuyahoga River had been closed for four years. He was prepared to sell the buildings and power plant, worth $150,000, for $50,000. After some dickering, Seiberling closed the deal at $13,500 with $3,500 down.

Even then, Seiberling had no idea what he was going to do with the plant. It was only after talking things over with brother Charles (later his associate in the 1921 venture) that their attention focused on rubber, then coming into use as the best material for tires on both carriages and bicycles. Automobiles were still experimental, for Frank Duryea's first car had come out only five years earlier.

The Seiberlings made a good choice, for within ten years there were sixty-five thousand automobiles on the road with names such as Stanley, Hertel, Winston, Hayes-Apperson, Oldsmobile, Autocar, Ford, and Whitney. *The Goodyear Story* records that the new company aimed first at the market in bicycle tires, most of which were solid rubber, and pneumatic carriage tires. But their first product sales — $28.40 on December 1, 1898 — were for unidentified "second line products [which] included horseshoe pads, rubber bands, sundries for druggists and poker chips."

Against competition from Goodrich and Diamond Rubber, Seiberling, under the Goodyear name, forged ahead despite suits brought against him for patent infringement, all of them disallowed. In 1900 he also fixed on the winged foot of Mercury as his company symbol and had a gilded statue of the fleet-footed god installed on the newel post in his Akron home.

By 1908, Seiberling's Goodyear company was doing a $2 million business, which doubled in 1909 after a lavish advertising campaign. The company claimed that in 1910, 36 percent of all cars manufactured would be equipped with Goodyears, with the remaining 64 percent divided among twenty-two other makers.

Growth was steady until after World War I. In 1920 Goodyear's 33,000 workers produced forty thousand tires a day, plus conveyor belts, bumpers, shoe heels, and rubber hose, for a $51 million profit.

Then, only a year later, sales were cut in half; and in the face of a $5 million loss, Frank Seiberling was out of a job, with millions in personal obligations. Without friends on Wall Street, Seiberling had no way of raising cash. And he was not alone. One day he ran into Harvey Firestone in the financial district. When he learned they were both hunting for backers, he said, "All right, Harvey, you work one side of the street, and I'll work the other."

The blow fell on April 21, 1921, when *The New York Times* ran a story announcing "control now in new hands," referring to a syndicate of bankers who had arranged a complicated structure of refinancing.

Seiberling was offered a five-year contract at fifty thousand dollars a year to stay on as chairman but turned it down, saying "they only wanted to use me as a figurehead."

Three months later, he launched the Seiberling Rubber Company with factories in Ohio and Pennsylvania. It was the smallest of the three hundred

Top left: *The old strawboard plant in 1898. The factory later housed the Goodyear Tire & Rubber Co.* Top right: *A 1912 photo shows a worker applying treads on a Goodyear tire.* Above: *This statue of Mercury was Seiberling's inspiration for the Goodyear trademark.*

Left: *A 1907 advertisement for Goodyear tires that appeared in* The Saturday Evening Post. *Right: The 55,555,555th Goodyear cord tire, which rolled off the Akron, Ohio, assembly line on October 4, 1923.*

rubber companies operating in 1921, but within ten years, it was grossing $42 million a year from sales in forty-two countries around the world.

Seiberling stayed on as working head until the day he turned ninety, when ill health at last forced him to stop work. When he died in August 1955 at the age of ninety-five, *The New York Times* obituary laid the foundation for a Seiberling legend by giving him credit for inventions that properly belongs, according to the Goodyear Tire & Rubber Company's history, to associates of his such as master mechanic William C. State (the automatic tire-building machine), Paul W. Litchfield (the cord tire), and "Nip" Scott (the "universal rim").

As early as 1909, only six years after the first flight of the Wright brothers, Seiberling's plant began making airplane tires, and the following year manufactured the special new rubberized fabric for the ill-fated dirigible *Akron*. It took to the air early the morning of July 2, 1912, and exploded after only twenty-three minutes of flight.

The company says that Seiberling's genius was "primarily entrepreneurial," a somewhat cool memorial to this innovative businessman. He was not just a workaholic tycoon. He was known in his lifetime, according to *The New York Times*, as "the little Napoleon" of the rubber industry, as much for his short stature as for his driving ambition.

In fact, you might call him tireless. In an ironic footnote, the names of Goodyear and Seiberling were merged when in 1964 the Goodyear Tire & Rubber Company acquired the Seiberling Rubber Company of Canada. ◆

STUDEBAKER

Remember the Studebaker? Winston Churchill camped out in one as a young reporter covering the Boer War. On twenty-four hours' notice, five hundred were assembled and shipped to Cuba in 1898. They were used as street sprinklers in Honolulu; they went on safari in Africa; and they rolled across thousands of dusty roads in America, to the sound of this "singing commercial":

The Studebaker Brothers

> Oh farmers all! Poor farmers all!
> To save your cash on you I call!
> For Studebaker offers you
> The very best that he can do.

Actually it was not the Studebaker automobile that was the subject of those advertising verses, but the Studebaker horse-drawn wagon, which came in two dozen different models, from a four-in-hand coach to a three-seat mountain wagon. And of course farm wagons:

> Then to it quick your horses hitch
> 'Twill last until you all get rich.

No wonder the company could claim to be "The Largest Vehicle Factory in the World! Annual Capacity 75,000 Vehicles!"

This incredible company, which dominated the horse-drawn wagon market for half a century, then for another half century turned out quality automobiles, was created by a family team of five Studebaker brothers: Henry, Clement, John Mohler, Peter, and Jacob.

These brothers were in wagons and carriages, not automobiles. The only one of the brothers to see a Studebaker automobile was John Mohler Studebaker, when in 1902 the company began turning out battery-operated electric cars. The decision to make those automobiles was made not by a Studebaker but by Fred Fish, who had been taken into the firm when he married John Mohler's daughter.

The Studebaker story goes all the way back to 1852, though in reality it ought to start before that, with the father of the five brothers, since it was he who actually made the first Studebaker wagon.

The family (originally Studebecker) came to the United States in 1736 from Germany. Speaking no English, they gravitated to Germantown, now part of Philadelphia, where they became blacksmiths and worshiped as Dunkards. Dedicated to the simple life, Dunkards baptized by "dunking."

From that background came John Studebaker, born in 1799. He married Rebecca Mohler, a German-American girl, and began raising his own family

> *"We have not been indifferent to the introduction of the horseless carriage, but buyers should be careful."*

Left: *Riding in this early Studebaker is Thomas A. Edison (left). At the "steering lever" is George Meister, Edison Company Paymaster. Right: The last vehicle of Studebaker's first century — the company's 7,130,874th — was produced at South Bend, Indiana, on February 15, 1952, just one day short of the 100th anniversary of the opening of a blacksmith and wagon-building shop by two Studebaker brothers. Harold S. Vance, Studebaker board chairman and president (right) drove the car off the final inspection line with Walter C. Zientowski (second from right), the oldest Studebaker factory employee (50½ years) as his passenger.*

in Gettysburg, Pennsylvania. Long before the Civil War, the Studebakers had trekked west into Ohio, traveling in a Conestoga wagon, every bit of which, from wheel spoke to canvas top to harness, had been made by John Studebaker. The actual wagon may still be seen in the Studebaker National Museum in South Bend, Indiana.

The father did not start the carriage business. When he was financially ruined in 1837 — at forty-eight, with six children — he spent many unhappy years trying to make a go of it first on a farm and then as a blacksmith in Ashland County, Ohio.

His two oldest sons, Henry and Clement, who learned the blacksmith trade at their father's forge, struck out in different directions but came together again in 1851 in South Bend. They were soon joined by the rest of the family traveling in that same Conestoga wagon.

The following year, on February 16, 1852, the Studebaker vehicle company was born when the two brothers — aged twenty-five and twenty — went into business with capital of sixty-eight dollars as H. & C. Studebaker, Blacksmiths and Wagonmakers.

The vehicle they made for their neighbor, George Earl, was the first that ever lumbered over the road with the name Studebaker lettered on it. That year, they made a total of two Studebaker wagons but added to their income by molding candles, repairing guns, and fabricating hinges and other metal objects.

In that year, John Mohler, just turned seventeen, joined the gold rush to California. He struck a deal with a passing wagon train, offering them a new wagon made by him and his brothers in return for transport to California and three meals a day. His mother sewed sixty-five dollars into his pants, handed him a Bible, and off he went to seek his fortune.

When he landed at Sutter's Field after five months of travel, he was down to his last fifty cents. He got a job with a wheelbarrow maker, claiming he could make wagons, but when he turned out his first barrow, the boss said, "And what the hell do you call that?" He got better with practice and became known as "Wheelbarrow Johnny."

In six years, he salted away eight thousand dollars — by working at a job, not by gold digging. When he went home, he traveled by boat to New York City, and from there by train to South Bend. He found his brothers' business had grown enormously, but Henry's health was so bad, he retired to a farm, selling his interest in 1857 to John Mohler, who became a partner in the new Studebaker Brothers Manufacturing Company, incorporated in 1868.

John Mohler was the idea man. He believed in advertising and pioneered in local dealerships. One of his ads began, "If you buy a horse, you don't take chances on a spavined, wind-broke, moon-eyed, knock-kneed animal . . . but if you want a farm wagon, freight wagon, spring wagon, phaeton, open buggy, top carriage, landau, see that it bears the name Studebaker, a certain guaranty of excellence and superiority."

While on his honeymoon at Goshen, Indiana, where brother Peter ran a general store, John persuaded him to display a Studebaker wagon among the hams, flour, and cracker barrel. It was the first vehicle display room, and it brought in more business.

By 1870, the firm had fourteen workmen and was worth more than ten thousand dollars. In that year, Jacob, the youngest of the five brothers, joined the firm. At 26, he was a shrewd trader, whether buying or selling, and was put in charge of the manufacturing plant in Chicago, helping to promote the sale of carriages by breeding purebred Percherons.

But he, the last to join the firm, was the first to die, in 1887. Then Henry was gone, and Peter died within two years. Clement lived on until 1901, the year before the first Studebaker horseless carriage, when he died just after stepping off the boat returning from a selling trip to Europe.

Only John Mohler, then sixty-eight, was left to forge ahead into the automobile world of the twentieth century, but he looked forward with caution. "We have not been indifferent to the introduction of the horseless carriage," he wrote, "but buyers should be careful. It is expensive and will wear out."

He worked on for another sixteen years until he died in April 1917. Always the businessman, he made one sentimental journey in 1912 back to the scenes of the California gold rush half a century earlier. This time, he toured the site in a Studebaker limousine.

The South Bend plant stopped production in 1963; the plant in Hamilton, Ontario, closed in 1966. ◆

Two advertisements for Studebaker from the pre-automobile days.

PULLMAN

George Mortimer Pullman

The only railway car fit to carry Lincoln's funeral procession was the new Pioneer.

They laughed when George Mortimer Pullman in 1863 unveiled his plans for a new kind of sleeping car with fancy brass lamps, tasseled window curtains, and carpets on the floor. They called them "fairy pictures."

And they sneered when they saw his working drawings, calling for a lower berth made up by sliding together the cushions from the daytime seats, and an upper berth hinged from the roof, complete with self-storing mattress.

Surely Pullman must have realized that his specifications called for railway cars too high to pass under most bridges in the United States, and so wide they would shear off the edge of most railway platforms. The man was a lunatic.

Yet only two years later, the car that was used to transport the body of President Abraham Lincoln from Chicago to Springfield, Illinois, was the Pullman Pioneer, the first of his luxurious Palace Cars.

And the railwaymen, without turning a hair, willingly shaved an inch off the station platform to make room for the car that was too wide but which revolutionized railway travel in the United States and the rest of the world.

Pullman was quite used to changing the face of the world in the name of efficiency, comfort, and safety. After all, wasn't it Pullman who jacked up most of the city of Chicago to avoid flood damage? Incredible? Not at all. He was only following in his father's footsteps.

George Mortimer Pullman, born on March 3, 1831, in Brocton, Chautauqua County, New York, was the third of the ten children of James Lewis Pullman, a general mechanic (to quote his son's obituary in *The New York Times*) "who made a modest income and a local reputation as a mover of barns and other frame buildings."

The family could only afford to let their children have a primary education, which could be the reason that George was put to work at the age of fourteen in the village store in Westfield for forty dollars a year and board.

His parents meanwhile moved to Albion in Orleans County. The obituary records that when George turned seventeen, he "went to Albion to join his oldest brother in the business of cabinet making. He also learned to use the crude implements, which his father had collected, for raising and moving buildings."

George Pullman might have become a cabinetmaker if it had not been that his father dropped dead in 1852 while they were working together at a house raising. George, just turned twenty-one, finished the job with his

father's own tools, then just naturally carried on the business, supporting his widowed mother and her younger children by working in various localities in western New York State.

About that time, the Erie Canal was being enlarged in sections, and George Pullman, through Ben Field, an Albion neighbor who happened to be a state senator, got contracts to remove various buildings along the new route.

By the time he was twenty-eight, he had a decent bankroll, enough to make the move to Chicago, where there was public agitation to raise the level of all the streets to make room for a modern sewage disposal system underground.

It helps to have friends. Another Albion neighbor happened to own the Matteson House, one of Chicago's largest brick hotels. Pullman raised the hotel with so little disruption to local traffic that he suddenly had more business than he could handle. Even more important was his raising of the Tremont Hotel, using four thousand jack screws and one thousand workmen. During the next three years, he moved or raised most of the large buildings in Chicago and multiplied his original bankroll many times over.

He was already building sleeping cars in partnership with Senator Field, whose political interest was railway legislation. As a sideline, Pullman converted ordinary passenger cars into sleepers by adding flat bunks, which rented at fifty cents a night, but this he suddenly gave up to spend the spring of 1862 to the spring of 1863 operating a trading post in Central City, Colorado.

In all this time, the dream of a luxury railway car never left him. Even in camp he kept sketching his "fairy pictures," until, drawing on his capital, with encouragement from Senator Field, he decided to build one.

It took a whole year in a shed of the Chicago & Alton Railway Company (Senator Field happened to be a director), with the help of a single master car builder hired at a wage of four hundred dollars a month. Pullman boasted that it was going to be the most comfortable and the costliest railway car ever built.

His dream was a car that could be occupied on long trips, as useful by day

Above: *The Pullman Pioneer, the first of Pullman's luxury Palace Cars.*

The interior of the Pullman Pioneer.

Top: *Two views of the 1899 Alton Limited passenger train. Bottom: An 1891 advertisement for the Chicago and Alton Railroad, which featured the "Pullman Vestibuled Trains" shown above.*

as by night. Oddly enough, though he soon solved the upper berth problem (how to make it so it would fold back neatly into the ceiling), he could not decide where to store the mattresses, until he was struck with the lunatic idea to raise the roof by nearly three feet. He knew as well as anybody how high American railway bridges were, but a detail like that was not going to stop him.

To give the car the look of luxury, he hired the interior decorator who had just created a sensation by his designs for the New York home of Samuel J. Tilden, who was to be an unsuccessful presidential candidate against Rutherford B. Hayes in 1876. The decorator's bill came to eighteen thousand dollars, but Pullman paid it cheerfully. The publicity generated by such extravagance made it apparent that the only railway car fit to carry Lincoln's funeral procession was the new Pioneer.

Three years later saw the incorporation of the Pullman Palace Car Company, producing custom-made cars only. His products soon included drawing rooms, dining cars, and full private cars with complete housekeeping facilities.

And what did George Pullman do for an encore? He bought over four thousand acres of land a few miles south of Chicago and there built a company town for his new plant.

Begun in May 1880, it was created by an army of four thousand workmen, who threw up schools, a market, a church, a hotel, and a railway station, as well as houses into which the first families moved only fifteen months after sod was broken. But there were no saloons. The city of Pullman, Illinois, was incorporated into the City of Chicago in 1889. "Mr. Pullman," to quote *The New York Times* obituary, "regarded the founding and development of this settlement as the crowning achievement of his career."

What else? Pullman also built the New York Elevated Railway, probably in his spare time. ◆

BUICK

"When better bathtubs are made, Buick will make them." If that does not sound quite like the way you heard it, read on, for when it came to making bathtubs, David Dunbar Buick couldn't put a foot wrong, but he never quite got the hang of it as a maker of automobiles.

Buick's great invention was the process for fusing porcelain onto cast iron, which was to make the modern bathroom a thing of shining beauty. The Buick automobile was invented and developed by other, cannier men. You might almost say that the Buick car only made it into the future once David Buick himself left the scene.

But don't underrate him. He started life at the bottom and made his own place in the world by his gift for invention and hard work. But he should have stayed in bathtubs.

Born in Arbroath, Scotland, in 1854, David Buick was brought to the United States by his parents to settle in Detroit at the age of two. When his father died only three years later, the family was plunged into such poverty that David had to go out to work as a full-time farm hand when he reached the age of eleven.

That meant he had almost no schooling, but he did pick up enough practical mechanics on the farm to be apprenticed at age fifteen to the Alexander Manufacturing Company of Detroit, which turned out brass and iron castings and fire hydrants. (Henry Ford was an apprentice in that same plant several years later.) By the time David Buick finished his apprenticeship, he sailed through the final test — to draw blueprints for a job, make the patterns, mold the piece, finish and install it.

In his spare time, he was also doing private research, which led to his independent discovery of the porcelain bonding process, which up to then had been the closely guarded secret of a German cartel. There is no exact date for Buick's invention but by 1882, when he was only twenty-eight, he and an apprentice friend named William Sherwood were in business as Buick & Sherwood turning out enameled bathtubs, which rapidly developed into a business offering a wide range of plumbing fixtures.

Within ten years, Buick was a prosperous Detroit businessman and was on his way to making millions, when all of a sudden he found bathtubs boring and toilets tedious. He fell in love with the internal combustion engine, which everybody in Detroit was talking about.

About this time, David Buick posed for one of his rare existing portraits.

David Buick

"He sipped from the cup of greatness and spilled what it held."

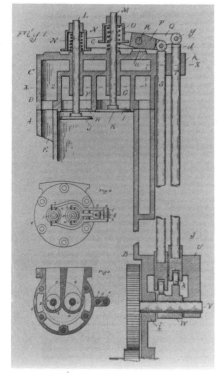

Patent drawing of the valve-in-head engine.

He is shown wearing a high, stiff collar and tie. His hair is short and stiffly combed, and a thick moustache gives him a dour, critical look. He seems uncomfortable, and maybe his friends noticed that, for one of them later wrote, "Fame beckoned to David Buick. He sipped from the cup of greatness and spilled what it held."

It was in December 1899 that he took his first clumsy sip by selling his interest in Buick and Sherwood to the Standard Sanitary Manufacturing Company (Standard is still a famous name in plumbing) for one hundred thousand dollars and formed a company with the catchy name of Buick Auto-Vim and Power to make marine and stationary engines.

Buick hired the best brain he could find, which happened to be inside the head of a talented Michigan native named Walter Marr, who had been building gas engines for more than ten years and who was at that time trying to develop a motor tricycle. Buick, in effect, gambled his hundred thousand dollars on Marr's ability to turn out a superior car with an L-head gas marine motor attached to a carriage.

Marr was an original. He might accept another man's wages, but he worked for himself and for nobody else. And Buick was opinionated to the point of obstinacy. Though he acted the responsible businessman as a bathtub maker, almost overnight he became vague about money and let his assets dribble away. Finally he had to ask Marr for financial help. He was turned down.

Then Buick teamed up — their contract is dated May 23, 1903 — with Eugene Richard, born in France but Philadelphia-trained. Hired as designer, inventor, and head of the drafting department, Richard developed the valve-in-head engine. This engine had a valve directly over the piston, resulting in greater power from the more compact combustion chamber and a faster burn. It was patented in Richard's name, installed in a chassis sketched by Buick, and sold as the Buick Model F.

At the first trials for this car, Walter Marr joined Richard and Buick, advising them on technical matters concerning fuel and production, with the result that he rejoined the Buick organization and worked for more than twenty-five years side by side with Eugene Richard.

He did not, however, work with Buick, who was still "spilling the cup of greatness." When Buick reorganized Auto-Vim and Power as the Buick Motor Company in May 1903, he was so badly in debt to two brothers, Frank and Benjamin Briscoe, parts manufacturers, that he ended up with only three hundred dollars of the company's hundred thousand dollars of stock. Buick had the option of purchasing the rest of the Buick stock simply by paying off the twenty-five hundred dollars he owed the Briscoes. They gave him until September. (These were the same Briscoes who teamed up with Jonathan Maxwell in 1903 to make Jack Benny's favorite car.)

Buick failed to find the money, and so the wheeling and dealing began that, within the next twelve months, was to make William Crapo Durant the

Left: *An advertisement for a 1926 Buick.* Right: *Buick's chief engineer, Walter L. Marr (left) and Tom Buick in the first Flint Buick as it ended its successful Flint-Detroit round trip in July 1904.*

owner of the Buick car.

Just before the Briscoe deadline, the Flint Wagon Works bought Buick and moved it to Flint, Michigan, which was then known as "the vehicle capital of the U.S.," and merged the Flint car with the Buick. By spring 1904, Buick of Flint was building engines but no cars, until finally in July they turned one out and test-ran it over a 115-mile course, going so fast that at times the driver, Buick's son Tom, could not read the "6 mph limit" signs. But they were losing money just as fast, for their production of five cars a month could not meet their costs.

In September 1904, enter Durant, who for two solid months test-drove a Buick car over every kind of road he could find. Then he bought the company.

Within months, David Dunbar Buick was out and had moved to Los Angeles as president of the Buick Oil Company. When that went sour, too, he gradually drifted into an association with an industrial school and was — as they say — never heard from again.

But the Buick car became the cornerstone of General Motors, created in 1908 by Durant, who was also personally involved with the Chevrolet, the Oakland, the Dort, the Durant, the Little, the Mason, the Star, the Locomobile, and the Flint. ◆

OLDS

Ransom E. Olds

"The father of the popular priced car."

"It never kicks or bites, never tires out on a long run. It does not require care in the stable, and only eats while on the road, which is only at the rate of 1 cent per mile."

That sounds like quite a horse, but it is in fact a facetious description of the first American car ever sold for export in the words used by its inventor, Ransom E. Olds, in an interview he gave in 1892 to a reporter from *Scientific American*. And it was a distinct improvement over his first unsuccessful try at a horseless carriage.

In 1887 he had put together an automotive freak, a crude boat-shaped box on three wheels, which he tested secretly between midnight and dawn to avoid spectators. It ran one block, then had to be pushed back into the shed.

Five years later, he stripped this machine of its usable parts to turn out a vehicle that really did run. And it was unique.

As pictured in the May 21, 1892, issue of *Scientific American*, it resembled a surrey with a fringe on top, with two seats at the front straddling a pair of high wheels steered by a rudder. The rear wheels were smaller to accommodate a platform concealed by a curtain "so that there would be nothing," said the article, "to scare the horses."

Behind that curtain stood the power source (a water boiler and a gasoline tank) for the two steam engines, each linked to one of the front wheels by direct drive, making both gearing and transmission unnecessary. "The rig runs as quietly as an ordinary carriage."

The secret lay in the revolutionary gasoline steam engine, invented by Ransom Olds while he was working full-time with his father in their machine repair shop and engine works in Lansing, Michigan.

At the time of Ransom Olds's birth in 1864, his father, Pliny Fiske Olds — son of a church minister — was earning his living as a blacksmith in Geneva, Ohio, later rising to become superintendent of a Cleveland ironworks. After many moves for the father's health, the family settled in Lansing in 1880, where the father, with his older son Wallace, established P. F. Olds & Son.

Ransom Olds, at sixteen, rose before dawn to light the furnace fires and helped out after school and on weekends, all for fifty cents a day. Then he was sent to business college to learn accounting and at nineteen began a full day's work as machinist and bookkeeper. Two years later, in 1885, he bought out his brother's interest for eleven hundred dollars and became a partner, skilled in general repair and manufacture of small steam engines running on either coal or wood.

Right away he made changes. First he designed an engine powered by steam generated by an ordinary gasoline burner, which could be turned on and off as the work required. It was a simple enough device. Gasoline was gravity-fed from a raised tank to an outlet under the water boiler, ready to burst into flame at the touch of a match.

The first Olds gasoline steam carriage. It was completed in 1886.

In the next five years, P. F. Olds & Son made and sold more than two thousand engines, and the company was continuously expanding in buildings and employees. By 1889, Ransom Olds at twenty-five was being described as "one of Lansing's most deserving young men."

His reputation spread beyond the Lansing city limits as soon as the article in the *Scientific American* began to circulate. In the spring of 1893, a patent medicine firm in London, England, offered to buy the gasoline steam carriage. When Olds asked the impossible price of four hundred dollars, they replied that the money was already in the bank and would he please ship the carriage to their branch in Bombay, India.

Olds had not really wanted to sell, so he drove the car around for a couple of months, then reluctantly shipped it out of the country. It was the first American car ever sold for export.

But that was only the first step in Ransom Olds's lifelong experimentation with the horseless carriage. Abandoning steam, in 1897 he patented the first true Oldsmobile. Completed in 1895, it was a high-wheel car with a four-stroke gas engine, with three forward speeds regulated by a device similar to a bicycle derailleur.

The second Oldsmobile (there is a sample in the Smithsonian Institution) was so successful that Olds at last incorporated a company in August 1897 as the Olds Motor Vehicle Company. But to find a good supply of qualified machinists, he had to move from Lansing to Detroit.

Oldsmobiles inspired music in 1905, and people are still singing this song.

In 1899 the Olds Motor Works built the first factory specially designed for automobile production, together with the first assembly line. The plan was to turn out a car for popular use, priced at about $1,250, but Olds incorporated so many advanced automatic devices that he lost money fast.

Turning on a dime, so to speak, Olds changed course and designed the famous "curved dash" Oldsmobile. It was an open-type carriage design, but the driver's feet could be tucked in under the upward roll of the dashboard.

Powered by a one-cylinder gas engine, it proved that a cheap car could be sold in quantity. In the first year, Olds marketed four hundred at $650 each; by 1904, sales were running at five thousand a year and rising.

That car made Detroit the car capital of the world, and Olds became "the father of the popular priced car."

So what did Ransom Eli Olds do at this peak of success? He sold out his interest in a company now capitalized at more than $2 million in order to retire. After all, at age forty, he practically had one foot in the grave.

His friends looked at it differently. Without his knowledge, a small group put together five hundred thousand dollars and organized a new automobile

Left: *In the fine print of this 1946 ad,
the origin of the automatic
transmission is explained: It was
developed for wartime use on tanks.*
Right: *A 1903 advertisement for the
Olds Motor Works, which appeared in
Harper's Magazine.*

company to make a car to be called the Reo, a name based on Olds's initials.

They knew his name would sell any car, but when it came to naming the company the R. E. Olds Motor Company, the other company cried foul. Although Olds insisted they were only entitled to the name Oldsmobile, they argued that Olds was stealing his own name from them.

Finally, the new company was renamed the Reo Motor Car Company, and Olds ran it himself for the next twenty years, until sales in 1924 had reached nearly $50 million.

Then he retired a second time, leaving behind not only the Oldsmobile and the Reo, but other companies that made everything from screw gear to the Olds power lawn mower and included a hotel chain, the Reolds farm, the town of Oldsmar at Tampa Bay, Kold Hold refrigeration, Ransom Fidelity insurance, and a collection of charitable works that should have been too much for any one man's life.

When Ransom Eli Olds died in 1950, he had just turned eighty-six. ◆

PACKARD

James Ward Packard

William D. Packard

Ask the man who owns one? It's not easy, because there aren't that many Packards around anymore. The Packard production line stopped forever on July 13, 1958; yet less than ten years earlier, in May 1949, Packard had been lustily celebrating its fiftieth anniversary, claiming to be the only carmaker that had lasted half a century.

In fact, Packard was the sole survivor of the forty or so carmakers active in 1899 when the two brothers, James Ward Packard and William Doud Packard, built their first horseless carriage in a corner of their electric appliance shop in Warren, Ohio, some fifty miles southeast of Cleveland.

The Packard brothers were sons of a successful businessman of Warren, Ohio, who started out in the hardware business, from which he branched out into extensive sawmill operations in three neighboring states. When his sons were teenagers, he was also involved in the Ashtabula, Youngstown, and Pittsburgh Railway.

About the same time, the two boys set up their own small job-printing press in the house and with their profits, took in the 1876 Centennial Exposition in Philadelphia. But then their paths diverged.

James Packard, born in 1863, grew up tinkering with machinery and electricity and enrolled in mechanical engineering at Lehigh University in Bethlehem, Pennsylvania. At seventeen, he was the youngest in his class and graduated before he was twenty-one. Within a year, he was foreman in the Sawyer-Mann Electric Company of New York City, makers of an incandescent lamp. Packard used their research facilities to invent and patent a new kind of lamp and socket and a new vacuum pump for exhausting air from lamp bulbs. When the company was bought by Westinghouse in 1889, the Packard inventions were thrown in as part of the package. James could have stayed on, but he decided to go into partnership with his brother William, who had taken a different route in life.

Two years older than James, William Packard began as bookkeeper in the family hardware store, went from there into wireless telegraphy, then worked with his father first in their Lakewood, New York, hotel and later in the Packard lumber mills. Finally, after a stint at Sawyer-Mann, where James was foreman, the two left together to form the Packard Electric Company in 1889 to manufacture transformers, fuse boxes, and electrical instruments and cables, many of them modified by Packard improvements. In 1890, they changed the company name to the New York and Ohio Electric Company and ran it successfully for more than ten years.

William Packard was also an inventor, with patents on a transformer, an improvement in the incandescent lamp, and an electrical cutout.

James Packard's interest in the horseless carriage was awakened in the early 1890s when he bought a French De Dion Bouton motor tricycle, stripped it, and reassembled it, then went on to analyze every other automotive vehicle he could get at.

The automotive age was then in its infancy. It was less than ten years since Carl Benz had driven the world's first horseless carriage. The first American car Packard saw was probably the Winton Phaeton, first built in 1897 by the prominent Cleveland bicycle maker Alexander Winton, then thirty-seven. In July 1898, Winton made history with his first ever test run of an American car, from Cleveland to New York City by an indirect route of eight hundred miles in nine days, with seventy-nine hours of actual driving time.

The Winton was the first car produced for sale in quantity in the United States, and Packard may have been one of Winton's first customers. There is no record of what Packard said about the car, but Winton is reported to have

Left: An etching by Earl Horter of the 1913 Six-38 Packard Phaeton, set in Rome. Right: A January 1904 advertisement from Harper's *Magazine.*

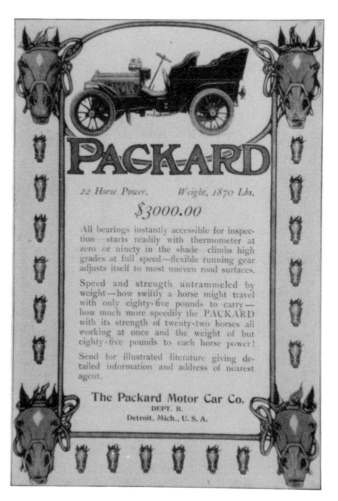

said, "If you think you're so smart, Mr. Packard, why don't you make a car yourself?"

So he did, practically overnight. By November 1899, the Packard brothers were testing a vehicle on a buggy-type body, with bicycle wheels fitted with three-inch pneumatic tires, and powered by a one-cylinder gas-powered horizontal engine.

The Packards formed the Ohio Automobile Company, and when their first models, priced at twelve hundred dollars, began selling well, they changed the name to the Packard Automobile Company, which was still based in their Warren, Ohio, premises.

By then, however, they were not working alone. The name change was part of a capital restructure led by Detroit financier Henry Bourne Joy. He bought into the company, became its manager, then assembled five hundred thousand dollars to finance the move to Detroit, a city that had the car in its future.

From that moment, the Packard should probably have been called the Joy wagon, because it was Joy's research into what the modern car owner wanted and his iron grip on production methods that made the American motorist want to be "the man who owns one." The Packard brothers took little part in the future of their car.

The year of the move to Detroit, William Packard sold his interest in the company and retired at age forty-four to Warren, which he proceeded to make the beneficiary of a stream of gifts — both money and property — including the fifty-five-acre Packard Park. He died in Warren in 1923.

Though his brother James did not move to Detroit with the company, he stayed on as president until 1908 and then as chairman of the board until 1915, when he too retired and began giving away millions for the building of various institutions, in both Warren and Cleveland.

He was also a collector. At his death in 1926, he owned hundreds of clocks and watches and had collected one copy of every typewriter manufactured in the United States.

♦

Above: *The car at the left is the first Packard. It was completed by J. W. Packard in Warren, Ohio, in 1899. At the right is the Packard "38," a six-cylinder salon touring car built in 1914.*

The "Old Pacific," the first car to cross the continent under its own power (1903), at its present home in the Henry Ford Museum, Greenfield Village, Michigan.

FORD

Henry Ford

♦

Ford's tool was the assembly line.

♦

H istory," said Henry Ford, "is bunk." But of all people, he made more history in his eighty-four years and changed the world in more ways than many a political dictator. His tool was the assembly line, first installed in April 1913.

What came after that date is Ford history: the Model A, the Fordor, the Tudor, the Meteor, the Mercury, the Edsel, the Thunderbird, and today's energy-conscious compacts.

What came before was the alphabet soup of Ford's all-black cars. The original Model A, or Fordmobile, built in June 1903 by the newly incorporated Ford Motor Company, led to the Model B touring car and the Model C sedan in 1905, and to the famous 1908 Model T.

But it took a long time to reach that point. In the Ford story, the missing link between the automobile and the surrey with the fringe on top has been traced to a small house on Bagley Street, Detroit, in December 1893.

It was there that Henry Ford clamped to the kitchen drain board his first gasoline engine. The cylinder was a reamed-out gas pipe; the spark plug was a fiber pad threaded with wire; and since the car battery had not yet been invented, he got his current by connecting the spark plug to an overhead light socket, while his wife stood by ready to feed gasoline to the engine.

She had just given birth to Edsel Ford, and here she was acting as midwife to the birth of the Age of Ford.

Almost exactly fifty years later, in 1943, that son died, and Henry, several years into retirement as president of the company, had to come back to work again for a few final unhappy years, as boss over 160,000 employees and assets of nearly a billion dollars, all vertically integrated to include railroads, factories, ships, steel mills, iron and coal mines, entire forests, and rubber and soybean plantations, not to mention the early American villages and early Ford homes he had preserved or constructed faithful to historical detail.

Would even Henry Ford have said that such history is bunk? Indeed, he later disowned the remark, and anyway, his sense of family and tradition showed that he thought it nonsense.

Like many young Americans of the last century, Henry Ford grew up on a farm. His father William had emigrated at age twenty-one from Ireland with his parents and grandparents to escape the potato famine, settling in Michigan on land rich with loam sixteen inches deep. When Henry was born in 1863, the country was split into the northern Union and the southern Confederacy, and his father was farming forty of the family acres near Dearborn.

Top left: *The Model T assembly line, circa 1913.* Bottom left: *Barney Oldfield racing Ford's 999, circa 1902.*

Those acres have never since been out of the family. Henry Ford, as his passion for history developed, bought more and more acreage, not only for his sprawling factories but for the colonial villages he was reconstructing.

The last thing he wanted to be, however, was a farmer, though in his boyhood he did his share of the chores and more than his share of tinkering with the farm machinery. Even as a boy, he dreamed of the day when machines would replace the hard work of many hands. When he was twelve, two momentous things happened. On one of the rural roads, he saw a steam wagon for the first time, the motive power supplied not by horses but by a boiler stoked with coal, like a locomotive used to drive a threshing machine. Four years later, he had built one for himself, not so much for use as to stretch his machinist skills. Also at twelve, he was given his first watch. Now at last, here was a machine he could tinker with and study night and day if he liked, winter and summer, at any idle moment. By the time he left school, he was an expert watchmaker, with the ambition to manufacture a popular watch so cheaply it could be sold retail for a dollar.

At seventeen, to his father's disappointment, he walked the nine miles to

A 1926 advertisement that appeared in The Delineator.

A 1924 advertisement.

Detroit to his first job as repairman in a machine shop, moonlighting as watchmaker for friends and workmates. One friend loaned him a copy of the English magazine *World of Science*, in which he read for the first time a technical description of the newly invented Otto internal combustion machine. By a lucky chance, there was an Otto engine, fed by vaporized gasoline, already in the neighborhood. When it broke down one day, young Ford, not yet twenty, was the only machinist around who could fix it.

From that moment, the dream of a mass-produced watch faded to give way to the dream of a practical car.

It took ten years to make it to the primitive engine clamped to his wife's drain board, while he earned a living as a Westinghouse repairman and part-time farm machinist and helper. And it took another ten years of rebuilding, experimenting, and trials with his two racing cars — the Arrow and the 999 — while other cars, the Oldsmobile among them, were coming on the market, before the nine original investors in Ford pooled their money and took their great gamble.

By coincidence, it was in that same year, 1903, that the Wright Brothers took their first flight. ◆

CHEVROLET

L et the record show that Louis Chevrolet was so unhappy with the car he designed and built that he walked away from it after less than four years.

It was in 1911 that he teamed up with that incredible wheeler-dealer, William Crapo Durant, to form the Chevrolet Motor Company and became its chief engineer. They spent two years fiddling with five experimental models, but when they finally settled on the famous Classic Six, it was not to Chevrolet's liking at all. He wanted his name on a high-class, quality car, while Durant wanted to squeeze Ford's Model T in the low-cost market.

Although the sixteen thousand cars they sold in the next twenty months earned a profit of $1.3 million, these two headstrong geniuses collided head-on over policy. In December 1913, Chevrolet picked up his marbles and went home. He had not realized, however, that he no longer had legal title to his own name, so the Chevrolet, revved up by Durant, went on to become the Chevy — everybody's set of wheels.

Frankly, the Chevy was not Louis Chevrolet's kind of car, and he must have hated driving from behind a desk. For more than ten years, he had been making his reputation as a racing driver, often in competition with one-time cycle racer Berna Eli Oldfield, better known as Barney, who became a legend overnight when in June 1903, hand-picked to test-drive Henry Ford's new racing car, the 999, he covered five miles in five minutes and twenty-two seconds.

Chevrolet and Oldfield, both speed freaks, competed many times. On May 20, 1905, Chevrolet nosed out Oldfield by pushing a Fiat over a measured mile in 52.8 seconds, or 68 mph, a new world's record. In 1917, he won the 100-mile auto derby in Chicago at 106.5 mph; and in 1918, the year Oldfield retired from racing, Chevrolet topped 111 mph in the 100-mile futurity at Sheepshead Bay, New York.

Chevrolet must have been an impressive figure. Weighing more than two hundred pounds and standing over six feet, he sported a flowing moustache very much in the French style. He spoke with colorful phrases and drove with reckless flair.

Chevrolet's one personal boast was that only once had he been beaten by Barney Oldfield, "and that," he recalled, "was because my machine broke down."

In fact, Chevrolet was for a decade the world's leading racing driver, piling up one world record after another on every important track in the

Louis Chevrolet

The Chevy was not Louis Chevrolet's kind of car.

Women everywhere helped design the NEW CHEVROLET SIX

A CAR FOR HER, TOO

CHEVROLET

The Greatest
CHEVROLET
in Chevrolet History

Women everywhere helped design the new Chevrolet Six—with its beautiful new bodies by Fisher. Their letters have come from all over America—now with a suggestion, now with a request, now praising this or that feature.

And every one of these letters was carefully considered by Chevrolet and Fisher designers. The steering wheel should be set lower . . . the brakes should be easier to apply . . . the gasoline gauge should be on the dash . . . seats should be made deeper.

Others asked that certain features be retained—the adjustable driver's seat

. . . the smooth clutch action . . . the easy steering . . . the harmonious design of the fittings . . . the comfortable and stylish interiors.

Every worthwhile suggestion was adopted. For women are using Chevrolet cars more widely every day—and their tastes, their desires, their suggestions are entitled to the utmost consideration.

Chevrolet and Fisher believe you'll like the Greatest Chevrolet in Chevrolet History. Its design, in every particular, is meant to be better suited to a woman's taste and needs.

Chevrolet Motor Company, Detroit, Michigan
Division of General Motors Corporation

A   SIX   IN   THE   PRICE   RANGE   OF   THE   FOUR

Top left: Louis Chevrolet poses with his experimental 1911 car, which went into production in 1912. Bottom left: The 1957 Chevy Bel Air two-door hardtop has become one of the most sought-after Chevrolets of all time. Right: This appeal to women buyers appeared in McCall's *and* Household *magazines in March 1930.*

United States.

He was not, however, an American by birth. He was born on Christmas Day, 1878 (the same year as Oldfield), at La Chaux de Fonds, one of Switzerland's most important watchmaking centers. His watchmaker father, Joseph Félicien Chevrolet, moved to Beaune in the Burgundy region of France six years later, where Louis as a teenage schoolboy running his own bicycle repair shop invented a new kind of wine-barrel pump.

At twenty, following his mechanical interests, Louis Chevrolet began to work in a Beaune auto plant. Then, two years later, in 1900 he moved to the States as technical advisor to the U.S. branch of French automaker De Dion Bouton in Brooklyn, New York.

These were only the opening moves in a restless working life. Within the next eight years, he had jobs with De Dion, Walter Auto in New York, the Winton Company of Cleveland, A.G. Southworth of Toledo (who made the Rambler and the Pope-Toledo), Fiat of Poughkeepsie, the Bliss Company of Brooklyn, the Autocar Company of Pennsylvania, and the Mattheson Company of Wilkes-Barre, Pennsylvania.

It was not a pensionable job he was looking for. All Chevrolet wanted was to drive fast cars faster and develop new ones. In 1907, while he was with Autocar, William C. Durant offered him a place on the Buick racing team.

Durant was a genius at merging both people and businesses. He became owner of Buick simply by buying the Flint (Michigan) Wagon Works, which owned the rights to the gasoline motor car designed by David Buick. When he had built the newly named Buick Motor Car Company into the world's biggest automaker in only three years, he used it as the base for General Motors.

This time, Durant bit off more than he could chew. After mergers with Albert Champion's AC Spark Plug and the Olds, Oakland, and Cadillac cars, Durant tried to gobble up Ford, but failed because Henry Ford, offered payment in stock, wanted hard cash. Durant was so far out on a limb financially that he gave up control of General Motors to the banks holding huge loans.

It was then he turned to Louis Chevrolet to help him get back into the market by designing a new automobile. In only fourteen months, Durant was back in business with the Chevrolet Classic Six, a touring car that sold for $2,150. Powered by the largest Chevy engine built until the 1959 V-8, it was driven out of the shops in November 1911, with his son Clifford at the wheel and Louis Chevrolet's wife in the passenger seat.

It was a touching symbol of the Durant-Chevrolet collaboration, but the corporation marriage went on the rocks by 1914.

Louis Chevrolet, only thirty-six, went back to racing cars and his restless life of constant motion. He designed a radically new racing car called the Monroe-Frontenac, which incorporated four-wheel brakes for the first time. He also invented the flexible steering wheel and helped to develop the valve-in-head engine. With his brother Gaston at the wheel, his Frontenac won the 1920 Indianapolis speed race, and a redesigned Frontenac repeated the feat the following year. That made Chevrolet the only man ever to design two successive Indy winners.

Louis Chevrolet sits at the wheel of one of his early racers, accompanied by a riding mechanic.

Later he spent two years as consulting engineer with a small Indianapolis repair company, then turned to speed-boat racing and won the Miami Regatta the first time he entered. For a while he operated a plant that made cylinder heads for Ford racing cars, jumped from that to a mechanic's job with Stutz, and from there to aircraft design with the Glenn Martin Aircraft Company.

Even after retirement, he put in ten months working on the production line making axles, and guess where: in the Chevrolet division of General Motors!

He died almost exactly thirty years after the birth of the Classic Six. ◆

CHRYSLER

Walter Percy Chrysler

It was love at first sight of a brand new Locomobile.

What would make a man of thirty-five decide to turn his back on a lifetime of railroading, the backbone of North American transportation at the turn of the century, and fall in love with the newfangled gas buggy?

For Walter Percy Chrysler in 1908, it was the sight of a brand new Locomobile in the automobile show in Chicago. It was love at first sight.

"I saw this Locomobile touring car," he reminisced in his 1937 autobiography, *The Life of an American Workman.* "It was painted ivory-white and the cushions and trim were red. The top was khaki, supported by wood bows, and on the running board there was a handsome toolbox that my fingers itched to open. Beside it was the tank of gas to feed the front headlights. Just behind the hood on either side of the cowling was an oil lamp shaped like those on horse-drawn carriages. I spent four days hanging around the show, held by that automobile as by a siren's song."

At that time, Chrysler was a worker at the Union Pacific shops in Olwin, Iowa. Later he joined the American Locomotive Company in Pittsburgh as works manager. He had worked his way to the top since the day when as a teenager he got a job as flue cleaner and sweeper in the locomotive sheds of the Union Pacific, where his father was a railroad engineer.

The elder Chrysler was born in Chatham, Ontario, but before the boy was born, the family had moved into the States to a county where it was common enough for settlers to be killed by Cheyennes protecting their land. The Chryslers often had to live on buffalo meat and buffalo soup, and they sometimes had to burn buffalo dung when they could not buy coal.

The family lived by railroading, and it became young Walter's life, too. He was proud of being a mechanic, and even after he got behind a desk, he said, "I could put the center valves on the ranges and get them right, and not many mechanics can do that single-handed." That was one reason he itched to get inside that toolbox on the running board of the five-thousand-dollar Locomobile. He had saved seven hundred dollars, so he borrowed the rest, ran the car back home, and for three months never drove it again, just took it apart and put it together, over and over again.

Three years later, in 1911, the year Charles F. Kettering put the first self-starter in a Cadillac, Chrysler resigned his twelve-thousand-dollar-a-year railroading job to become works manager at Buick for half the salary.

At that time, Buick was turning out forty-five cars a day and Ford one thousand. Within three years, Chrysler had boosted production to 560 a day.

They go well together...
orchids and the Chrysler
Town and Country...perfect
background for those to whom
distinction comes naturally.

There's an air about this glorious
convertible...a whisper of country clubs
and moonlight rides...There's poise
in every dashing line...a car
that's at ease in any company.

the beautiful Chrysler

Town and Country

WITH CHRYSLER HYDRAULICALLY OPERATED
TRANSMISSION AND *gyrol* FLUID DRIVE

NEW CHRYSLER "52"

*Still Higher Quality—
Yet Lower Prices*

$725
TO $835 F.O.B. DETROIT

- 52 miles per hour
- 5 to 25 miles in 8 seconds
- Full-sized Bodies for
  adult passengers

New Chrysler "Red-Head"
Now Available for New "52"

Left: *As America moved to the suburbs
in the post-World War II period,
Chrysler offered the Town and
Country model. This advertisement
ran from 1946 to 1948.* Above: *The
1928 4-cycle Chrysler "52" was
replaced by the first Plymouth in July
of that year.*

He was made executive vice president, demanding and getting twenty-five thousand dollars a year.

For a long time he dreamed of designing his own car. In those days, the market offered cars with names like Durant (Chrysler called William C. Durant "the great genius of cars"), Flint (where Durant was once an insurance agent), Star (built to compete with the Ford line), and, of course, Maxwell and Willys Overland, manufactured by the company that Walter Chrysler took over in 1920.

With a few trusted associates, Chrysler began to put together at great cost a custom-built test car from components taken from other makes. It was a designer's nightmare on the outside, but under the hood, Chrysler had hidden a new high-compression engine. He said it was great fun to take this shabby vehicle out on the streets among the large, sleek cars with their chauffeurs and

Left: *Assembling the frame at the Chrysler plant. The frame started at the chassis assembly conveyor upside-down and, while in this position, the front wheel suspension and springs, the rear axle and springs, and those parts that are underneath the car were mounted. Then the frame was turned over and placed on the overhead monorail conveyor for further assembly. Right: An advertisement for the 1927 Chrysler "Finer 70." This car was produced from September 1926 to October 1927.*

surge away from the traffic light while they were still moving sedately into second gear.

He stole a march on his marketing rivals, too. When they organized to refuse the new product entry into the automobile show of 1924 in New York City, Chrysler simply hired the entire main lobby of the Commodore Hotel, which just happened to be the favorite rendezvous of the big men of the automobile world.

Chrysler was soon being described as a "colossus" of that world and one of "the big three" — and with reason. He sold $5 million worth of Chryslers in the first year. By 1926, there were four models, including the Imperial 80, and when he bought Dodge from the widows of John and Horace Dodge, there was no stopping him.

That was more than half a century ago, and still the name Chrysler is attracting sensational publicity. There cannot be many shareholders still around from the incredible year 1933, when the company outproduced Ford for the first time and the stock values multiplied seven times within that twelve-month period.

Besides the name, there is also one other monument to his genius. In the 1930s, he organized, financed, and built the Chrysler Building, second only in size to the Empire State Building. ◆

VI

HUCKSTERS, TRADERS, AND MERCHANTS

TIFFANY

Charles Lewis Tiffany

Charles Lewis Tiffany was the only Tiffany ever to run Tiffany's of New York.

Let us not confuse the store with the lamp.

Tiffany's of New York is not the creator of Tiffany lamps and Tiffany glass. Those revolutionary art nouveau designs and others originated in the colorful imagination of Louis Comfort Tiffany. As the son of Charles Lewis Tiffany, the store's founder, he was on the board for several years, and worked briefly as director of design.

Tiffany, the son, had gone his own way early in life, and began to make his own reputation as a design artist in 1878, by which time Tiffany's store was already a romantic legend.

The son's independence in following his own bent was a replay of the way Charles Lewis Tiffany himself had struck out against the wishes of his own father, Comfort Tiffany, owner of a small manufacturing company in Killingly, Connecticut, who had in fact done much the same thing with *his* father. Comfort Tiffany was born on the family farm, but when he decided to work in textiles, he simply turned his back on his father's business.

As for Charles Lewis, he showed a head for merchandising at such an early age that his father opened a general store and gave it to him to run before he had turned fifteen. He worked behind the counter, kept the books, and went on buying trips. Apparently he was a merchandising genius, for by the time he had turned sixteen, he was paying a man to run the store while he went back to school.

He knew exactly what he wanted to do. When he came of age, his father offered him a partnership in the mill, but he turned it down and instead headed for New York in 1837 with John P. Young, his future brother-in-law.

It was not the best time. New York was reeling under a crushing depression. Banks were collapsing; interest rates hit 3 percent per month; and inflation attacked rents, food, and fuel. The price of flour rose 50 percent, and cabbages, usually given away, cost thirty cents a head. As three hundred businesses closed their doors within two months, shouting mobs began to crowd around City Hall, crying for relief.

Charles Tiffany's father warned him, "Don't go. Stay in Killingly where you have a secure future." But listening to fathers was not, it seems, in the Tiffany tradition.

The young man was influenced by John Young, who had spent a few months as a clerk in a New York store selling fancy goods, which meant everything from stationery to cheap jewelry.

With capital of only one thousand dollars, the pair decided to open a store

but could not afford to rent in the fashionable part of downtown. Since no lady of quality would shop uptown, north of Canal Street, Tiffany and Young finally decided to open on Broadway next door to Stewart's. A.T. Stewart was the Irish-born colonel who opened America's first department store in 1823, and Tiffany hoped to pick up some of Stewart's customer traffic. They rented half a building, with fifteen feet of valuable frontage on Broadway, midway between Stewart's and a fashionable milliner, just across from City Hall Park.

On opening day, September 21, 1837, they had assembled a stock of the usual fancy wares: stationery, playing cards, cutlery, walking sticks, and various chinoiserie, from fans to brass gongs. When they put up the shutters that night, their total sales amounted to $4.98.

On Day 2, sales plummeted to $2.77. But on Day 3, with a dramatic turnaround to $24.81, the Tiffany fortunes began a continuous spiral upward as the store moved from one location to another, to come to rest finally on Fifth Avenue at 57th Street.

They also moved from "fancy goods" into luxury items. In 1848, a year of political unrest in Europe, Tiffany bought up diamonds and jewelry from bankrupt merchants, which encouraged them to open a Paris office to keep their New York store supplied with imported valuables. In 1859, they opened a branch to sell their items to Parisians.

Even after Tiffany set up his own silversmithy and began acquiring historic gems — including relics of noble houses, the crown jewels of the Empress Eugénie, the Esterhazy collection, and the huge "Tiffany diamond" — Charles Tiffany never lost his country business sense. In 1858, he bought what was leftover after the laying of the Atlantic cable, cut it into short pieces, and offered them as souvenirs. The crowds were so huge the police had to be called to clear the street.

After John Young died in 1853, the store remained the sole property of Charles Lewis Tiffany until his death in 1902.

He was the only Tiffany ever to run Tiffany's of New York.   ◆

PABST

Frederick Pabst

When Admiral Robert E. Peary reached the North Pole on April 6, 1909, he found a bottle of Pabst Blue Ribbon beer, ready chilled in polar ice.

That curious fact is found in a scholarly history, published in 1948, of the city of Milwaukee, which as every drinker knows was made famous by beer.

How the beer got to the North Pole nobody knows. But if it was a promotional stunt, it was a natural coming from somebody like Frederick Pabst, a man with champagne tastes who was able to satisfy them on a beer income.

Pabst has left behind him, as his ostentatious memorial, an ornate mansion on Wisconsin Avenue, Milwaukee, which cost $250,000 in 1890 money. It took three years to finish and more than thirty servants to run. Among the typical Pabst touches are a chandelier whose design imitates candles, oil or kerosene lamps, and electric light; paneling imported from Bavaria; German sayings inscribed around the walls; and masses of carved ornamentation based on the grape, the vine, and the hop. Today, both the mansion and the Pabst brewery are tourist attractions, open to the public.

Tacked onto the main stone building is the brewery pavilion from the 1893 World's Columbian Exposition, where Pabst beer won its first blue ribbon; and the house still holds the furniture with nautical motifs and the steamship decor, installed to remind the capricious owner of his early days as a ship's captain.

Frederick Pabst was born in Nicholausreich, Germany, in 1836. When he came to the United States at the age of eleven, he had no education and had to settle for a job as a waiter in Chicago hotels. Within three years, he left dry land to become a cabin boy on one of the steamers owned by Sam Ward that plied the western lakes. He was Captain Fred Pabst before he was twenty-one.

It was the most natural thing in the world for him to be attracted to Milwaukee, a mere ninety miles north of Chicago, for it was on his regular routes. Founded the year before he was born, Milwaukee had just been incorporated as a city, and in every real sense it was a German city. "It is the only place in America," one settler wrote, "where Americans learn German, and where you will find beer cellars and German beer."

Ironically, the first Milwaukee brewery was established in 1840 by a Welshman; but more important to Pabst was the arrival of one Jacob Best in 1844, who brought with him across the Atlantic from the Rheinland his entire brewing business and his four sons to help him run it.

Then both Jacob Best and his eldest son retired, and two other sons withdrew to establish their own brewery. It was left to Phillip Best, then about thirty-six, to manage the brewery and build it into the largest in Milwaukee by 1860.

In the meantime, he acquired an energetic son-in-law named Frederick Pabst, who married his daughter Maria. Pabst said goodbye forever to the lake boats and joined the brewing company, but that did not mean he became next in line to inherit the brewery. To complicate matters, in 1866 Best's other daughter, Lizette, married Emil Schandein, a brewer who had come to Milwaukee from Bavaria by way of a fifteen-year detour in Philadelphia as a bookkeeper and traveling salesman.

These two sons-in-law — Pabst and Schandein — ran the company with great success. Phillip Best, very active in the various military organizations in Milwaukee and at one time a major general in the state militia, grew older and ailing until eventually the company was incorporated, still under the Best name, in 1865, with Pabst as president. His influence dates from that year.

In an attempt to restore his health, Best made a trip to Bavaria in 1869 in company with Schandein, but he died there, leaving the company virtually under the control of Frederick Pabst.

The name remained Best for another twenty years as the company gradually grew to become the most extensive in the country.

Then Emil Schandein also died. He had been his father-in-law's companion during his long illness, while also taking important posts in Milwaukee brewing associations as vice-president of the Phillip Best Brewing Company. When he collapsed and died in 1888 on a visit to Bremen, he was replaced as vice president by his wife.

Within six months the corporate name was changed to the Pabst Brewing Company, which, with capital stock valued at more than $4 million, was poised to take part in the great expansion of the 1890s.

Above: *The Phillip Best Brewing Co. was the forerunner of the Pabst Brewing Company. This early logo shows the four beers that the Best Company produced. The third bottle from the left was produced with high-quality ingredients, which resulted in a consistently high-quality brew. To distinguish this "Select" beer, the company came up with the idea of hand-tying a bit of blue silk around the neck of every bottle of Select beer in 1882. Enthusiastic beer drinkers kept calling for more bottles of "Blue Ribbon" and the name caught on. In 1895, the words "Blue Ribbon" were added to the label of Select beer.*
Bottom left: *The sight of scores of dray-drawn beer wagons was a daily event in the shipping yard of Pabst's Milwaukee brewery at the corner of Tenth and Juneau streets. The strength and courage of the drivers were legendary.*

Sports advertising played an important role in Pabst's promotions. The advertisement on the left ran in 1950, the one on the right ran in 1946.

Captain Pabst was recognized as "a man of liberal impulses." For example, when the Grand Army of the Republic met for its annual meeting in Milwaukee in 1899, Pabst supplied all the grandstand seating for hundreds of visitors, as well as for the citizens of Milwaukee, on "a floating palace erected on Lake Michigan."

When the Captain bestowed his own name on the brewery, he made one punning tribute to his late father-in-law by adding to the Pabst label a sentence that read, "He drinks Best who drinks Pabst."

He was, however, forced in 1898 to give up using the other slogan he invented, which read, "Milwaukee's beer is famous — Pabst made it so," when Schlitz charged that it was too similar to their own slogan, "The beer that made Milwaukee famous," which they had bought for five thousand dollars several years earlier from a small brewing house.

Pabst was a tireless promoter. He added the name Blue Ribbon to his trademark, opened fashionable drinking places in other cities, built the Pabst Hotel in New York, Pabst's Loop on Coney Island, and the Pabst Harlem restaurant on Eighth Avenue.

Anybody who can do all that, and hire movie stars to drink to his health publicly with Pabst beer, is man enough to put a bottle on ice at the North Pole. ◆

SAKS

What did President Calvin Coolidge of 1600 Pennsylvania Avenue, Washington, D.C., have in common with Mrs. E.T. Scott of 127 West Eighty-Second Street, New York City, on September 15, 1924?

Simple: They were the first customers of Saks Fifth Avenue on its opening day. Mrs. Scott was the first to enter the store for personal shopping, and the president was the first to take delivery at home of one of the store's expensive items.

It is not recorded what Mrs. Scott bought, if anything, but the president took possession of a top hat in a leather box. "It fitted him well," said the report, "and it is quite becoming."

The hat was conveyed to him, accompanied by a personal note from the Saks vice president, by a uniformed aide, who made the trip to Washington by train.

Fronting Fifth Avenue between Forty-Ninth and Fiftieth Streets, the new building rose twelve stories high, seven of which were for buyers of expensive wearing apparel for men, women, children, presidents, and princes. Saks was said to be the largest single store in the world devoted to fine wearing apparel, leather goods, jewelry, and toilet articles.

Hundreds of window-shoppers crowded the streets and rushed the doors when they were finally opened. There was a stampede in the men's department on the sixth floor of such dimensions that the elevators were jammed for more than an hour on the mistaken rumor that the Prince of Wales was to join the official party for lunch with the mayor of New York, Jack Dempsey, and Horace A. Saks, vice president.

The prince did not show, but then neither did Bernard Gimbel, one of the proprietors of Gimbel Brothers, the famous low-cost, cut-price competitor of Macy's. That is not as irrelevant as it sounds, for Saks Fifth Avenue, where the elite meet to greet, was in fact owned by Gimbel Brothers, inventors of the bargain basement.

Without an $8 million leg up from the well-heeled Gimbel Brothers, Saks might never have made it to Fifth Avenue. Saks grew from a small clothing store established by Andrew Saks in Washington, D.C., just after the Civil War. Saks, born in Baltimore, made his way in life at first by selling newspapers on Philadelphia streets, then as an itinerant peddler in Washington, scrimping and saving until he had enough money to set himself up in a small clothing business on Pennsylvania Avenue. This store did so well that soon he was able to expand and open other stores in Richmond (Virginia) and in

Horace A. Saks

"To present to New York a specialty store in a scale never before attempted."

I'm on My Way to
SAKS·FIFTH·AVENUE

To the Extraordinary Sale of
Saks·Fifth·Avenue Fenton Footwear
at 5.95

5000 Pairs of Shoes for Afternoon Wear and all Daytime Occasions. All made to sell at very much higher prices in regular stock.

This advertisement ran in the New York Herald Tribune *on Saturday, March 11, 1933.*

Indianapolis.

He also managed to pay for the education of his son Horace Andrew Saks, born in 1882, at private schools in New York and Princeton. The younger Saks had not quite finished the university when his father decided to take a crack at the New York shopping scene. Horace Saks promptly set down his books and joined the family firm.

When they opened in their new location on Thirty-Second Street near Herald Square, the firm also included Horace's brother William and his uncle Isadore.

Eight years later, Gimbel Brothers, originally an Indian trading post dating from 1842 in Vincennes, Indiana, which had set up stores in Milwaukee in 1887 and Philadelphia in 1894, opened a store just a block away and began their famous running battle with Macy's, right on Herald Square.

These three merchandising neighbors went their own way until the early 1920s, when Horace Andrew Saks, president since his father's death in 1912, realized that the trend in New York was uptown and began looking around for a better location for his special clientele. Though he found the ideal site quickly enough, one big obstacle was the clubhouse of the National Democratic Club standing right in the middle, which his company could not afford to buy.

It was Bernard Gimbel, grandson of the founder of Gimbel Brothers, who suggested a merger, which — like many another corporate marriage — was at first coolly denied by the principals and by the "marriage brokers."

The first hint of the merger had come more than eighteen months earlier, when the clubhouse of the National Democratic Club, founded in 1844 and famous as the heart of Tammany, was bought by a real estate developer named Frederick Brown. The club had bought the property in 1890 for $175,000; they sold it to Brown late in 1922 for just over a million.

Brown disclaimed any intention of turning the building over to be torn down for a department store. But a few weeks later, that is exactly what Horace Saks announced, and for an encore he announced a Saks and Gimbel merger.

"The magnitude of the merger," commented *The New York Times*, "is indicated by the latest reports of annual sales of the two firms . . . . The combined reported sales for the two organizations for their last fiscal year was very close to $88 million."

When news of the sale first got out, Gimbels did not do anything to quiet the rumor that the new building was to be simply an annex to their downtown store; but at last it was admitted that under the new merger, Saks would operate under its own name.

The merged company was to operate five stores. Gimbels would take over Saks premises near Herald Square, and Saks would occupy the grand new emporium, which the world would then know as Saks Fifth Avenue and which — according to the joint announcement — was to "present to New York

...but at least their clothes are well-mannered;
they come from SAKS FIFTH AVENUE

SAKS FIFTH AVENUE, AT ROCKEFELLER CENTER, NEW YORK • CHICAGO • BEVERLY HILLS • DETROIT

Left: *This advertisement appeared in*
The New Yorker *on August 30, 1947.*
Right: *Saks Fifth Avenue in a
photograph taken in the 1920s.*

a specialty store in a scale never before attempted in the selling of wearing apparel of the finer grade."

The final act of the merger took place in 1926, only three years later, after Horace Andrew Saks's early death at forty-four. Adam Gimbel became president of Saks Fifth Avenue and headed it until 1969. Today, both Gimbels and Saks are under new corporate ownership. ◆

REYNOLDS

Richard Joshua Reynolds

"I'd walk a mile for a Camel."

Where there's smoke there's fire, but there is also money and lots of it, when the smoke curls up from a slim cylinder of paper wrapped around a few cured strands of *Nicotiana tabacum*.

Take just one brand out of the thousands that have been packaged in the last hundred years or so. In 1913 in Cleveland, Ohio, a new blend of fine cured sweet burley tobacco, mixed with a little Turkish, was launched onto the national scene at ten cents for a packet of twenty by R.J. Reynolds of North Carolina. To compete with at least fifty others being offered at the same time, all with exotic names like Omar, Zubelka, Mogul, Fatima, Cairo, and Oasis, this one also took its name from the Arabian desert.

It was called Camel, and the packet was illustrated with an actual shot of an actual camel, which in real life was the dromedary Old Joe, then on display at the Barnum & Bailey Circus.

Only two years later, in 1915, 2.3 billion Camel cigarettes had been sold and 6.5 billion were sold the next year. The 1913 advertising claim — "Tomorrow there'll be more Camels in this town than in all Asia and Africa combined" — had been proved right.

The creator of the Camel cigarette was Richard Joshua Reynolds, one of several tobacco merchants hungry for money and power. Once the Camel showed its hump, the American Tobacco Company struck back with Lucky Strike ("It's Toasted."), Liggett & Myers repackaged their Chesterfields ("They Satisfy."), and Reynolds Tobacco streamlined its slogan to read "I'd walk a mile for a Camel."

That battle of the brands is long over, but the tobacco giants of the day — notably R.J. Reynolds and Buckingham (Buck) Duke — had been at one another's throats for decades, as they launched smoking on its merry commercial way from its humble beginnings in North Carolina.

Durham County, North Carolina, in the mid-1860s was the locale of a small factory owned by J.R. Green, who produced a brand he called "Best Flavored Spanish Smoking Tobacco," which became a great favorite with both Confederate and Union troops. They began calling this tobacco Bull Durham, the name that started to make North Carolina famous for tobacco.

There were already more than one hundred small tobacco enterprises in the state, which produced in total just over a million dollar's worth for local markets. But the Civil War helped to create the habit of smoking, and this more than anything else created what one historian called "the private initiative and ruthless competitive power" of the tobacco pioneers in the United

States.

Buck Duke was the son of Washington Duke, who started curing tobacco on a small farm in Durham County in 1865 and whose three sons — Brodie, Buckingham, and Benjamin — peddled their Pro Bono Publico pipe tobacco from wagons up and down country roads. They all became multimillionaires within thirty years; but the most famous, or notorious, was Buck Duke, who in 1890 created the American Tobacco Company, one of the most powerful trusts in the world.

R.J. Reynolds came on the scene when he was about twenty-five years old, investing twenty-four hundred dollars in a small factory, only thirty-six by sixty feet, in the town of Winston, which was amalgamated with its neighbor to form Winston-Salem in 1913.

Originally, Reynolds came from Virginia, another tobacco-famous state, where he was born in 1850, the son of Hardin W. Reynolds, a merchant and trader in raw tobacco. Hardin Reynolds was also one of the largest slave owners in the Old Dominion of Virginia, in Critz, Patrick County. The son divided his early years between school (including studies in business at Emory Henry College) and hard work, both on the homestead farm and in his father's tobacco factory. Like the Duke brothers, he and his brothers peddled tobacco by wagon throughout neighboring states.

When he finally did settle in Winston, later to be immortalized in the cigarette that "tastes good like a cigarette should," he had behind him not only selling experience but practical experience in production, gained from nearly six years as superintendent of his father's factory.

Reynolds and Duke became instant competitors, if not enemies, though in the broadest sense they were working opposite sides of the street. Reynolds in those early years concentrated on chewing tobacco, including plug and twist, while Duke was turning out cigars (5 billion by 1890) and was among the first to go into cigarette production.

Cigarettes, a Spanish invention originally called *apeletes*, were taken up by an Englishman in 1856, then imitated a few years later by a London merchant named Philip Morris, whose name, in the cry of the radio bellhop —

Above: *Stud was a trademark first used by Allen Washington Turner of Macon, Georgia, as early as 1884. Reynolds purchased it in 1909. He had a great love of horses, and probably liked the virility suggested in the Stud name. The brand was advertised with very vivid counter displays and window posters in the early 1900s.*
Bottom left: *A 1920 poster for Camels. According to company legend, the slogan came about when a foursome of golfers ran out of cigarettes. Among them was Martin Reddington, who handled R. J. Reynolds's outdoor ads. While the group waited for a caddy to deliver some cigarettes, one golfer said, "I'd walk a mile for a Camel." Reddington liked the slogan and worked it into a poster.*

Above: R. J. Reynolds plug box labels. Their brands reflected such themes as southern womanhood, horsemanship, American Indians, and famous Americans. The label on the right features R. J. himself.

Chief Joseph of the Nez Percé tribe was featured in many advertising pieces from 1913–1914.

"Call for Philip Morris!" — became one of the most famous in the world.

Buck was the first in the United States to mechanize cigarette making when he bought patent rights to the machine invented by a Virginia tobacco farmer named James Bonsack in the early 1880s. The British rights were bought by W.D. & H.O. Wills.

Buck's tobacco enterprises became so huge that he began his campaign of amalgamating other makers into a great trust. Meanwhile, Reynolds was making his own way at his own pace, building up his business until in 1890, with his brothers William and Walter, he incorporated as R.J. Reynolds Tobacco Company.

All this time he went around snarling, "If Buck Duke tries to swallow me, he'll get the bellyache of his life," (quoted in *Tobacco Tycoon*, John K. Winkler's story of James Buchanan Duke) but he too caved in. Though he joined the American Tobacco Company, he was relieved to get out when the United States antitrust laws forced its breakup on May 29, 1911.

The split created new independent companies: Liggett & Myers, P. Lorillard, United Cigar, and Reynolds Tobacco. Reynolds crowed, "Now watch me give Buck Duke hell!"

Reynolds was riding on profits from Prince Albert Tobacco. In all of 1908, it sold 250,000 pounds, but by 1917, it was selling that much every four days. The "Prince Albert Special," thirty-five freight cars long, puffed out of the Winston railway station every day.

Today, R. J. Reynolds is a diversified conglomerate, branching into other products and brands such as Nabisco and Del Monte. But all that happened long after the founder's death in Winston-Salem in 1918.

Old Buck Duke outlived him by nearly ten years. ◆

SPALDING

Guess who didn't get elected to the National Baseball Hall of Fame when it was dedicated in Cooperstown, New York, in June 1939?

Would you believe Abner Doubleday, the man who was hailed in December 1907 as the game's inventor by the special commission set up by the major leagues to investigate its origins?

They confirmed him as the originator of baseball on the basis of a letter written by an old friend of his, claiming that he had been on the spot in Cooperstown back in 1839 when Doubleday, a twenty-year-old raw recruit in the U.S. military, who later gained fame as a Civil War general, had his incredible inspiration.

Nowadays, however, one biography refers to Doubleday as "the man who 'invented' baseball" and another as the "alleged inventor," and you cannot get more dubious than that.

You could argue that Doubleday did not get elected to the Hall of Fame because he did not play the required ten years in the major leagues. But then, neither did Albert Goodwill Spalding, whose name is in there with Honus Wagner, Lou Gehrig, and Babe Ruth. They were all in the Hall of Fame when it opened in 1939, but not Doubleday. So why Spalding?

In this modern age, the name Spalding is known mainly because it appears not only on baseballs and bats, but also on family games, sportswear, school supplies, and even backpacks and auto tires, all manufactured by the diversified Spalding Corporation, which is an outgrowth of A.G. Spalding and Brother founded in 1876.

That all goes back to the day, long before the major leagues took over baseball, when Albert Spalding was one of the greats of the game. After his death in 1916 at the age of sixty-five, the sportswriter of the New York *Sun* brought back "the picture of a clean, lithe, and sinewy youth standing as the central figure in a deployed field force of red-stockinged hireling heroes, and delivering across the home plate ball after ball of amazing swiftness and curiously perplexing simplicity of propulsion."

In other, simpler words, Spalding was a hot-shot pitcher.

That was his reputation, but he made it into professional sport only after he stopped listening to his mother, who told him she didn't raise her boy to be a baseball player.

As for Albert Spalding's father, a struggling farmer of Byron, Illinois, descendant of an English parson who came to the American colonies in 1630, he probably never even heard of the game. He worked too hard to have time

Albert G. Spalding

♦

Long before the major leagues took over baseball, Albert Spalding was one of the greats of the game.

♦

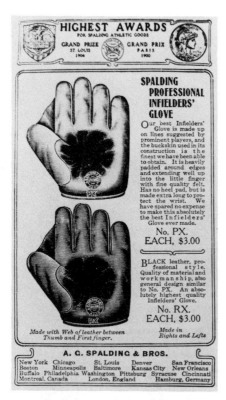

Above: *An advertisement from the early 1900s.* Bottom right: *The champion Boston Red Stockings of 1874. Spalding stands second from the left, with ball in hand.*

for sports, and anyway he died in 1859 when Albert was only nine.

After a few years of common schooling, ending at the commercial school in Rockford, young Albert became a grocery clerk at seventeen. Then by turns over the next few years, he was a bookkeeper in a Chicago wholesale house and a publisher's cashier. In his spare time, he played the new game of baseball, which, like cricket, evolved out of the old English game of rounders.

American settlers brought rounders over with them and played it from around 1700. Sometime during the 1830s, they made it a rule that runners were out when tagged. In rounders, the runner had to be "plugged" (hit by a thrown ball), and that was the main difference between rounders and early American baseball.

The "father of organized baseball" is Alexander Cartwright, who organized the Knickerbocker Base Ball Club of New York in 1845, the first of its kind; and it was Cartwright who laid down baseball's first set of rules, including tagging.

Albert Spalding took to the game like a duck to water when it was introduced into Rockford by a soldier invalided out of the Civil War. While still a grocery clerk, Spalding was one of the strongest players, both at the plate and on the pitcher's mound, with the Forest City Club of Rockford, which in 1867 defeated the National Club of Washington, then renowned as the best in the whole U.S.A.

Spalding immediately got offers from clubs in Cleveland and New York to play for fabulous salaries ranging up to twenty-five hundred dollars a year, ten times his earnings as a clerk. He would have gone like a shot, but the prospect scared both his widowed mother and his sister, who persuaded him to turn down all the offers and take a safe job in a Chicago wholesale grocery store.

Sometimes mothers can be wrong, and this time Mrs. James Lawrence Spalding was dead wrong. The grocery firm folded, Spalding lost his next job with an insurance company, his next with a newspaper, and his next as a bookkeeper for another insurance agent.

All told, Spalding struck out with seven different firms before he stopped taking his mother's advice. In 1871 he signed on with the Boston team as a pitcher-outfielder and led the team to victory in the pennant races of the National Professional Association from 1872 to 1875.

Spalding was so famous he was sent to England in 1874 by the Boston and Philadelphia clubs to arrange a transatlantic match. In 1875 he was appointed manager of the Chicago club.

The following year, he pitched every one of the club's games, winning fifty-two out of sixty-six in the 1876 season. That same year, the National League was formed with eight competing teams to become the first major league, and Albert Spalding retired from baseball.

At twenty-five, he was neither worn out nor disillusioned. For years, he and other players had put up with equipment not specially designed for the game, and Spalding decided to do something about it. Some of the games in the early 1870s were played with a ball Spalding had made himself in his experiments with equipment, so it was only logical to bring into play his specially made ball when the first major league game was played in 1876.

It was in February of that year that he and his brother Walter each put up four hundred dollars to open a sporting goods store in Chicago, under the name A.W. and J.W. Spalding. The sign over the door proudly announced, "Spalding has gone into the baseball business."

Though it is not proven, Spalding may have been the first to put a label on a baseball bat to show the run of the grain, for one of the batter's earliest warnings was to "keep the Spalding up!"

Albert Spalding was baseball's first ambassador. As long ago as 1888, while president of the National League's Chicago club, he took the Chicago and All-American teams on a tour of the world to introduce baseball to less fortunate nations. They even played one exhibition game on the sands in front of the Egyptian pyramids, presumably with the sphinx as umpire.

Spalding's last tribute to the game he loved was a book titled *America's National Game*, a history of baseball published in 1911, four years before he died.

The press in turn paid him their tributes. The St. Louis *Post-Dispatch* said that "as a maker and vendor of the requisites of the game" his name was "as well known as that of the President's." And the New York *Press* declared that he "came into the baseball field when it was reeking with all that hurts sportsmanship . . . and left it notches higher as an outdoor amusement and helped to make it America's foremost sport." ◆

When Spalding was president of the National League's Chicago club, he took the Chicago and All-American teams on a tour of the world, which included an exhibition game in front of some Egyptian pyramids. This photograph was taken February 9, 1899. Spalding, wearing a pith helmet, stands alongside his mother in the middle of the picture.

J. WALTER THOMPSON

James Walter Thompson

♦
*A go-getter working
for a dreamer.*
♦

It was on a Monday morning, December 5, 1864, that Captain William James Carlton wrote in his diary, "Commenced to canvas for advertisements this morning for several papers."

There's nothing in that diary entry to suggest that the J. Walter Thompson advertising agency had just been born. But that is the date picked by company historians to mark the beginning of the JWT group of eight associated advertising businesses, the second biggest group in the world.

In 1864, the year of General Sherman's march to the sea in the closing months of the Civil War, James Walter Thompson, age seventeen, was on duty somewhere at sea in the U.S. Marines. If you believe the company records, he signed on board the U.S.S. *Shenandoah*, but the *National Cyclopedia of American Biography*, which carries a picture of the man late in life in the uniform of a commodore, as a member of the New York Yacht Club, says that he served aboard the U.S.S. *Saratoga*.

Wherever he was, he was certainly not working for Carlton & Smith, Advertising Agents, of 171 Broadway, New York City. You can ignore Edmund A. Smith, who walked away from the business after only a couple of years, leaving his partner to carry on as William J. Carlton Company.

To quote the December 7, 1964, issue of *Advertising Age*, which marked the JWT centenary, "Carlton, a youth of twenty-seven, just being mustered out as a captain in the Union army was a quiet, studious, book-loving man" who went into advertising because his stepfather happened to be the senior agent of the Methodist Book Concern and treasurer of the Missionary Society of the Methodist Episcopal Church.

That may not be the best training for the life of an ad man, but was James Walter Thompson getting any better? Had he done anything in his life to fit him for the advertising world?

Thompson was born on October 28, 1847, in Pittsfield, Massachusetts, son of a builder named Alonzo Decalvis Thompson and his wife Cornelia, one of the Roosevelts. Company records say that J. W. Thompson was a fourth cousin of Theodore Roosevelt (Theodore was born eight years later).

The father's business took him to Fremont, Ohio, where the elder Thompson built a bridge over the Sandusky River and where at the age of eight James learned to sail. Sailing became his lifelong passion.

For almost the rest of his life (he died in 1928) James W. Thompson was never without a boat. According to Charles E. Raymond, who opened JWT's Chicago office in 1891, Thompson was the twenty-eighth person to join the

New York Yacht Club when it was founded; and at some period in his life, he even bought a line of canal boats, which he ran under the name Owl Transportation Company.

There is nothing in all that to suggest an advertising vocation. Indeed, when he left the Marines in 1868 and turned up in New York looking for a job, he was rejected at the first agency he tried because he seemed "too easily discouraged" for the life of hard sell.

It was then that William J. Carlton hired twenty-year-old James Walter Thompson as general clerk and bookkeeper, with a sideline in soliciting customers for various religious publications.

The early American advertising agent did not have a stable of clients but tried to corner magazines covering roughly the same field. Carlton specialized in the potentially rich field of religious publications, as there were then about four hundred religious weeklies looking for advertisers. Francis Wayland Ayer, founder of N.W. Ayer & Son in 1869, who was the first to act as agent for the advertiser rather than for the publisher, specialized in newspapers; Lord & Thomas specialized in agricultural periodicals.

It was the yacht-loving, easily discouraged ex-Marine James Walter Thompson who brashly stirred up this cozy arrangement. But it took time.

When he joined Carlton, the agency was billing about fifty thousand dollars a year, mostly, as a contemporary put it, "through the influence of Carlton's father."

As Thompson served his months of clerking and soliciting at fifteen dollars a week — a large sum in those days — Carlton became more and more the bookworm. One of his friends, the one who had refused to hire Thompson, recalled in a 1905 memoir that Carlton would rather "spend six hours

This is the letterhead used by J. Walter Thompson in 1893.

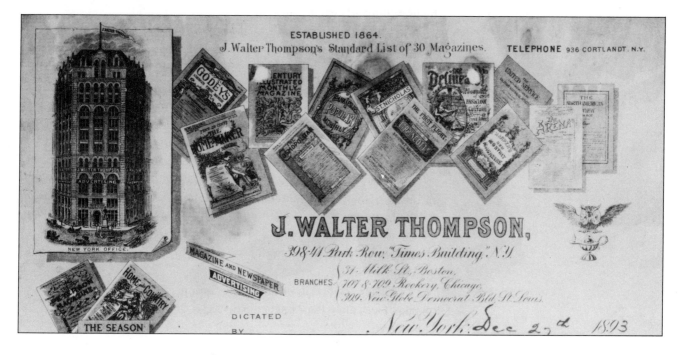

A 1902 advertisement for J. Walter Thompson's advertising company.

trying to resurrect for a friend some scarce volume worth possibly twenty cents than devote half that time securing an advertising order that might produce a profit of $100."

James Thompson, a go-getter working for a dreamer, sensed that there was a whole world of print out there beyond the religious field, including the new world of magazines for women. He may not have been the first to realize that it is women who spend most of a family's income, but he was certainly the first advertising man to put the idea to work.

The day that idea struck him is the day JWT was founded. He first aimed at *Godey's Lady's Book* and *Peterson's Magazine*, both published in Philadelphia and both living off their wide circulations. They thought ads would lower the tone of their tasteful pages, but Thompson got his foot in the door with one ad each and used that ad to sell other reluctant publishers. The editor of *Harper's* threatened to resign when he heard that Mr. Harper had agreed to accept advertising revenue, saying that he did not want to edit a magazine as if it were "a cheap circus magazine." And when in 1878 Thompson sent *Peterson's Magazine* twenty-five pages of ads for a single issue, the editor said he would not dare send out a magazine "with so much advertising in it."

That was the year James Walter Thompson took over from William James Carlton. A few months before his thirty-first birthday, Thompson bought out his boss for five hundred dollars, plus eight hundred dollars for the furniture in the third floor office of the old Time Building at 30 Park Row. He named his agency J. Walter Thompson because he did not want to be confused with the other twenty J.W. Thompsons with accounts at his bank.

George Rowell wrote, "Carlton became a bookseller and the firm of J. Walter Thompson became, in an almost incredibly short time, a greater house than Carlton had ever dreamed of."

For that matter, J. Walter Thompson has become a greater house than James Walter Thompson ever dreamed of.

He ran the business for thirty-eight years, working with names such as Pond's, Prudential, Crisco, Yuban, Mennen, and Jergens, until in October 1916, at the age of sixty-nine, he sold out to Stanley Resor, who had joined the agency in 1908, and a group of associates. The price was five hundred thousand dollars, one thousand times the price Thompson had paid in 1878. No figure was put on the furniture.

Company legend says he was old and tired, and anyway he thought that the business, then billing more than $3 million annually, had gone about as far as it could go.

He was wrong, and Resor and associates, including James Webb Young, who were dubbed "the young tigers from Cincinnati," obviously thought differently.

When Resor, who ran the agency for another thirty-eight years, sold out, the billing was more than $200 million. Today, it is more than $2 billion. ◆

WOOLWORTH

What was the most unusual feature of the Woolworth Building when it was formally opened in New York in 1913?

That it was the tallest building in the world at that time, rising to sixty stories and providing thirty acres of floor space? That its Gothic design was inspired by the Houses of Parliament in London, England? That it was described as a "beautiful house of commerce"? That its elevators, the first to be equipped with telephones, were operated by an electric dispatcher? Or that it was the first to have its own electrical generator?

None of the above. Its most unusual feature was that it carried no mortgage, no interest-bearing bonds, no long-term loan. Frank Winfield Woolworth made just one cash payment of $13.5 million, plunked down for the head office of the world's first five-and-ten-cent stores.

Today, the merchandise at Woolworth's has no price limit. The ceiling was removed in 1935 by the board of directors, who had clung to the five-and-ten limit for thirteen years after the founder's death in 1919. It had been a Woolworth policy for more than fifty years.

In *Skyline Queen and the Merchant Prince*, John P. Nichols plots Woolworth's determined progress from one small store to his great skyscraper head office. He had his master plan and his vision, and his views on American merchandising were continuously tempered by frequent trips to Europe. He made forty-four transatlantic crossings in his lifetime, the first of which, in 1890, lasted eighty-eight exhausting days through four countries.

Storekeeping must have been in Frank Woolworth's blood, for he apparently never had any other ambition but to work in a store and one day to own one.

Like many other American entrepreneurs, Woolworth came from a long line with roots in the settlement surge to New England in the seventeenth century. The name, originally Wooley, got misspelled in the early records.

Frank was born in 1852 on a farm at Rodman, Jefferson County, New York, but when he was seven, his parents moved to another farm at Grand Bend, where he went to the district school. He and his younger brother Charles Sumner Woolworth (who became company president after Frank died) used to play store after their farm chores were done, selling to nonexistent customers items from a display set up on the dining table.

Frank even prepared for his future by taking a course in store management in his spare time at a business college in Watertown, but in his teens he was turned down by one storekeeper after another for being "too green."

Frank Winfield Woolworth

In one year he sold 318 tons of hairpins.

*Two early photographs of Woolworth's
5 and 10 Cent stores.*

"His business career," to quote the *National Cyclopedia of American Biography,* "began in the village store when farm duties permitted, and in 1873 [he would then be 21] he obtained a position as clerk with the firm of Augsbury & Moore, later Moore & Smith, merchants, working three months without pay to gain experience." Altogether, he worked on and off at Moore & Smith for six years.

It is a nice touch that forty years later, when sixty-one-year-old Frank Woolworth presided over the opening of his new head office, at the head table were William Harvey Moore and Perry H. Smith, the two men who had given him his chance in 1873.

More than that, it was at Moore & Smith that he was allowed to try out his idea of opening up a special counter on which nothing would cost more than a nickel.

Woolworth was not the inventor of the "five-cent counter." The idea had already been tried out elsewhere, but it was he who saw its immense possibilities. He persuaded Moore & Smith to order one hundred dollars' worth of "Yankee notions" — buttonhooks, red napkins, basins, tinware, dippers — and mix them with hard-to-sell items such as gaudy cravats and end-of-line ribbons. To everybody's surprise, an eager public swept the counter clean in a matter of hours and did the same at the next sale and the next.

When Frank Woolworth saw the five-cent counter emptying as if by magic, he could hardly wait to open a store of his own. Again Moore & Smith gave him a leg up by guaranteeing him a five-hundred-dollar line of credit to stock his venture. After all, his chosen locale, Utica, New York, was well out of competition range.

But this great Woolworth venture, the world's first "Great 5¢ Store," as he called it, sank without trace within four months, mainly because the store was on a side street, off the shoppers' beaten track.

Frank Winfield Woolworth's reaction was characteristic. He identified the reason for the failure and tried again. Instead of retiring defeated, he took his little remaining cash, moved his entire operation to a different city, and opened again in Lancaster, Pennsylvania, on June 21, 1879. There on the main street, he opened his "mother store," the first of hundreds of red and white store fronts, identified by the diamond W trademark.

Success was immediate. Woolworth turned over his stock of five-cent items three times in three weeks and soon had to scramble to buy enough stock to keep up with the demand and stay in business.

It was when he found it hard to find enough five-cent items that he made his second great marketing decision. He opened up a "10¢ counter."

Within a year of leaving Moore & Smith, he announced that F.W. Woolworth had become "the world's first 5-to-10 cent store." No fewer than six chains of five-and-ten-cent stores sprang up in imitation, while Woolworth began an intense plan of expansion. Not only did he add to his stores — there were more than one thousand when he died — but he also added to his stock by including toys, stationery, toilet items, and hardware. In one year he sold 318 tons of hairpins! He also revolutionized Christmas by opening up a counter for five-and-ten-cent ornaments, mostly imported from Germany. When World War I cut off his sources, he encouraged U.S. manufacturers to establish a new Christmas ornament industry.

In 1912 Woolworth swallowed up five chains of competing stores and thus became the largest merchandiser in the world. The following year, he paid out $13.5 million in cash for a suitable head office.

When he died — he worked at his desk almost until his last day — the New York *Sun* wrote, "He won a fortune not in showing how little could be sold for much, but how much could be sold for little." ◆

An early photograph of the Woolworth Building in New York City.

SEARS

Richard W. Sears

By his innovative
"Send No Money"
policy, he made an
instant impact on
the mail-order
business.

Wanted: Watchmaker with reference who can furnish tools. State age, experience, and salary required.

It was that ad in the *Chicago Daily News* of April 1, 1887, that brought together Alvah Curtis Roebuck, a young beanpole of a man who dressed in undertaker's black, and Richard Warren Sears, a handsome young fellow — later he sported a flowing moustache — with a taste for flashy clothes.

The company born of this partnership, later known as Sears Roebuck, has lasted to this day, but Roebuck himself sold his interest for twenty-five thousand dollars only eight years later. If he had retained even a minor stake, he would have become several times a millionaire, but he just couldn't take the heat in the Sears kitchen.

When Roebuck first saw the ad, he was living quietly as a watch repairman in Hammond, Indiana, little realizing that he was about to have his life turned upside-down by one of the great American hucksters.

Why did Richard Warren Sears need a watchmaker anyway? The answer is a key to his whole life and personality.

Sears was born in 1863 in Stewartville, Minnesota, into the family of a wealthy wagonmaker who lost everything in a crazy stock farm speculation. He lived to see his son a successful businessman. Young Sears, who was not yet fifteen, became head of the family, which included his mother and sisters. He learned wireless telegraphy and worked his way up to become freight agent of the Minneapolis and St. Louis Railway located at North Redwood, Minnesota.

He liked living in a small town, for there were all sorts of ways he could add to his weekly pay of six dollars. He sold coal and lumber and bought blueberries and venison from the Indians for resale to city buyers. But that was nothing compared to the killing he made in the summer of 1886, when a shipment of half a dozen gold-filled watches, refused by a local jeweler because he said he had not ordered them, was left abandoned in the freight shed.

Sears bought them on credit for twelve dollars each and sold them at fourteen dollars each to station agents along the line, who unloaded them "retail" at sixteen dollars. Clear profit at no risk, and it worked so smoothly that Sears bought up other abandoned shipments of watches, recruited more agent-salesmen, and pocketed nearly five thousand dollars in profits after only a few months.

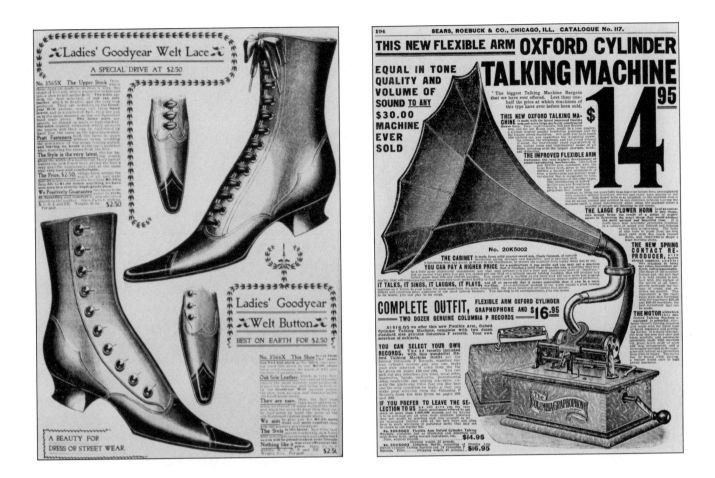

He quit his job, moved to Minneapolis, and printed a letterhead reading R.W. Sears Watch Company. Before the end of that year, business was so brisk that he moved to Chicago and ran that fateful ad in the *Daily News*. He had decided not to go on selling other people's watches but to buy movements and cases and have somebody else assemble them.

Roebuck really looked the part. He was neither a salesman nor a promoter like Sears; he was just a small-town craftsman who liked to fix watches. Apparently his main contribution to the Sears business was to create a cost-cutting assembly line as production increased.

It was not yet a Sears Roebuck partnership in those early months. Sears sold, while Roebuck toiled. Then suddenly one day two years later, Roebuck looked up from his worktable, removed the loupe from his eye, and learned that Sears had not only sold the company out from under him, but had actually disposed of Roebuck himself, as if he were part of the furniture. Roebuck went along with it.

After a brief period dabbling in farm mortgages, Sears got back into the mail-order business through the back door. Prevented by the terms of the sale agreement from using his own name in business for three years, he set himself up as the Warren Company, using his middle name.

Left: *Described as "the very latest style," these shoes featured in the 1897 Sears, Roebuck & Co. catalog boasted toes no wider across than a half-dollar.* Right: *From the 1908 Sears, Roebuck & Co. catalog, the Oxford Cylinder Talking Machine had a large flower horn whose "design was the result of a series of experiments to determine the exact shape that would produce the most natural and beautiful tone."*

Sears, Roebuck and Co., Chicago

Spring and Summer 1927

Index and Information Pages 459 to 485

He then brought to bear his personal magnetism — or maybe he used hypnotism — on his former employee and watch assembly man. He persuaded Roebuck to buy the Warren Company, to rename it A.C. Roebuck Inc. in 1891, sell back to Sears a half interest, and appoint him president. Roebuck went along with it all.

Two years later, with the name restriction removed, there was one last reorganization. The company was miraculously reborn as Sears, Roebuck and Company with Sears himself holding two-thirds of the stock.

He was entitled, for without Sears, Roebuck might just as well have gone back home to Hammond, Indiana. Sears did not invent the mail-order business, but by his innovative "Send No Money" policy, he made an instant impact on a business that had been dominated by Montgomery Ward, a firm that resented what they called the "risk, trouble, and annoyance" of a purchaser wanting to examine the goods before accepting them.

Sears changed all that and used advertising more widely than any other businessman of his day. He ran ads in everything that would take ink and supplemented them with his catalogues, most of which he wrote himself. They offered not only watches, jewelry, clothing, musical instruments, and farm machinery, but also maternity clothes, trousseaux, and gravestones.

Buy, buy, buy, but "Send No Money!" It worked like a charm. Within three years sales topped four hundred thousand dollars, and two years later sales were nearly twice that, while the catalogues had tripled in size.

What a time for Alvah Curtis Roebuck to think of pulling out. He admired the Sears drive and financial honesty, but he did not care for some of the sales copy, which was not always truthful and not always backed up by stock in the warehouse. Besides, he could not keep up physically with the eighty-four-hour work week that Sears imposed on himself.

Roebuck sold his one-third interest in 1895 and so cleared the way for the arrival of Julius Rosenwald, who, more than even Sears himself, engineered the ballooning expansion of Sears Roebuck from about $1 million in annual sales when he took over as vice president in 1896 to $443 million in 1929, just before he died.

Sears himself gave way to Rosenwald, when in 1908 they disagreed on fundamental policy. Rosenwald advised restraint; Sears, always the huckster, argued for still wider advertising. When the board supported Rosenwald's conservatism, Sears stepped down and retired to his farm with a personal fortune of about $45 million. When he died in 1914, he was only fifty. ◆

Above: *A view of watchmaking in the jewelry department of Sears, Roebuck & Co. Sears took credit for compelling "manufacturers and dealers generally to modify their selling plans, so that today it is possible for men and women to secure watches and rings and other articles of this character at a lower price than ever before."*

Opposite page: *The cover of the 1927 Sears, Roebuck mail-order catalog.*

DOW JONES

Charles Henry Dow

Edward C. Jones

Against one wall in a small room at the rear of a soda fountain on Broadway in New York City stood a Heath Robinson contraption in a wooden box several feet high. A crank at one side could be turned to raise a ninety-six-pound weight to the top, and as it slowly fell — like the weights of a grandfather clock — it generated enough current to send out signals over wires to a score of business offices in and around Wall Street.

The time was the early 1890s. The device was the world's first wire service, an invention of Charles Henry Dow, financial journalist, founder and first editor of *The Wall Street Journal*, senior partner of Dow Jones & Company, and creator of the Dow Jones Industrial Average, the world's most closely watched statistic.

Vermont Royster of *The Wall Street Journal* wrote that Dow "was the first to attempt a statistical measure of the New York stock market, evolving the theory "that the market tended to move in broad patterns, like the waves of the ocean." In time, this became known as "the Dow theory," as others elaborated its details.

As a person, Charlie Dow was by no means a mere statistic, though he must have been more colorful in his early years. He was only fifty-one when he died in 1902, but he was always remembered as being a soberly dressed, rather portly gentleman, with "the grave air and the measured speech of a university professor."

Oliver Gingold, who worked under Dow as a young reporter, said, "I never recollected his smiling, and he did not talk much to anybody." Once, at *The Wall Street Journal* which Dow and his partner Jones founded on July 8, 1889, a few people were talking about the kinds of work they had done as young men. Dow quietly took a pencil and began writing. Then, without a word, he handed over a list of more than fifty different occupations. What they were has been lost. Nobody kept the list, but at least the first must have been farm boy.

Dow was born in 1851 on the old family homestead in Sterling, Connecticut, first taken up by the Dows around 1790. Since his father died when he was six, and two older brothers died while still children, Charles Henry was the last of a line of Dows that first settled in this country in 1637.

Farm boy he may have been, but he never became a farmer. He must have had his eyes fixed on journalism early, since the first documentary record of Dow's professional life lists him as assistant editor, at the age of twenty-one, on the Springfield, Massachusetts, *Daily Republican*, which at that time was published by Samuel Bowles III, one of the great American newspapermen and grandson of the paper's founder.

It was Bowles who set down for all time the reporter's first commandment: "Put it all in the first sentence."

Waldo Cook, a later editor of *The Springfield Republican*, recalled that Dow was one of the paper's "notable graduates." In a letter to Bishop he wrote, "Not infrequently I heard my elders mention Charlie Dow and his success in financial journalism."

After three years at the *Daily Republican*, Dow — by then a fully trained editor and newspaperman — moved to Providence, Rhode Island, partly because he wanted to get out from under the shadow of Samuel Bowles, partly because he wanted to live closer to his hometown, just across the Rhode Island–Connecticut state line.

It was a historic move, for not only did Dow come into contact with the world of finance and stock promotion for the first time, he also made the acquaintance of Edward C. Jones, who became the other half of Dow Jones.

The forgotten third partner was Charles M. Bergstresser, another Kiernan employee. In *Charles H. Dow and the Dow Theory*, George W. Bishop notes that Jones was desk editor, "dictating to the clerks through a walrus moustache," while Dow and Bergstresser gathered news on the streets. Bergstresser was made a partner because he refused to be a mere employee, but he agreed to the crisper Dow Jones & Company as a firm name instead of the long-winded Dow, Jones & Bergstresser.

In 1877, the town of Leadville, Colorado, hit the headlines with news of a silver strike so rich that the town's population soared in two years from one to twenty thousand. A few lucky prospectors became millionaires, including "Silver Dollar Tabor," whose widow later died in poverty, huddled in a shack beside her late husband's Matchless Mine.

Charlie Dow, assigned to the story in 1878, filed reams of profitable copy and filled his notebooks with the names of mining experts, eastern financiers, businessmen, and bankers, whom he met in the private railroad cars shuttling between Leadville and New York City. Dow estimated the total wealth in the group in one opulent car at more than $90 million. By the time the story fell off the front pages, Dow had moved to New York, followed by Edward Jones, both to become involved in financial journalism.

Jones, five years younger than Dow, had dropped out of college to go into the newspaper business, first as reporter, then as editor of the *Providence Star* and later the *Providence Sunday Dispatch*. Both Dow and Jones got jobs separately with the Kiernan News Agency, but left together to form Dow Jones & Company in 1882.

Like Kiernan, they were in business to collect news from brokers and financial houses, then circulate the items by means of "flimsies" copied in longhand by a battery of scribes and delivered by a squad of "lively boys"

The front page of the very first issue of
The Wall Street Journal.

who were sometimes alert enough to pick up news on the run. One boy brought back a scoop: the collapse of the Wall Street Bank in 1884.

Dow devised a primitive mimeograph to duplicate the flimsies mechanically. When he converted his *Customers' Afternoon Letter* into *The Wall Street Journal,* he invented the boxlike wire service apparatus.

He did not live to see his ripple, wave, tide theory of stock movement become almost a religion, complete (in some analysts' language) with old and new testaments. To put it in Dow Jones language, he died about six months before the end of the bull market of 1900–1902, a few weeks after selling *The Wall Street Journal* to his Boston correspondent, Clarence Barron, on a day when the Dow Jones index stood at 70.

Did he ever dream the index would one day rise above 2,000?   ◆

WRIGLEY

A t last, an answer to the question, "Who was William Wrigley, Sr.?" No, not the present William Wrigley, Sr., current president of the well-known makers of chewing gum. We're talking about the original of that name.

Everybody knows his son, William Wrigley, Jr., who got an entire nation chewing gum.

In baseball, he was known as the owner of the Chicago Cubs, in which he first took an interest in 1924, pouring $5 million into the team as he built it up.

In the high-rise world, he was known as the builder of the white terra cotta Wrigley Building, the first large office building erected north of the Chicago River outside the Loop.

In land development, he was known as the owner of twenty-one-mile-long Catalina Island, twenty-six miles off the coast of Southern California, which he bought in 1919 and converted into a pleasure resort.

In hotels, he became owner in 1931 of the magnificent Arizona Biltmore, a winter resort just outside Phoenix. Only a year later, he died at the age of 70, to quote *The New York Times*, "of acute indigestion, complicated by apoplexy and heart disease" in La Colina Solana, the winter home he had built nearby.

In mining, he was known as the owner of silver, copper, and zinc mines, one of the unexpected riches on Catalina, from which he also mined thousands of tons of rock and clay for building projects throughout California.

In swimming, he was known as the sponsor of the Wrigley Ocean Marathon of January 1927, which challenged athletes to swim between Catalina Island and the mainland.

In the Great Depression, he was known as the man who gave one of his buildings, furnished with light and heat, to the Salvation Army to house and feed five hundred unemployed men a day.

And in business, he was known as the world's leading manufacturer of chewing gum, consumed so internationally that the Wrigley gum wrappers were printed in dozens of languages.

Everybody knows William Wrigley, Jr., but who was his father?

William Wrigley, Sr., was not a nobody, by any means, and he actually had an indirect connection with chewing gum, though it was his son who made the millions out of it.

The Wrigley family is traced back to Edmund Wrigley of Saddleworth, a woolen manufacturing town in the north of England county of Yorkshire. His son Edward emigrated to the United States and opened a woolen mill in

William Wrigley, Jr.

"People chaw harder when they're sad."

---

209 ♦

Wrigley's Scouring Soap

Above: *A selection of Wrigley's gums, circa 1900–1914.* Right: *An advertisement for Wrigley's Spearmint gum in Spanish from the 1930s.*

Philadelphia. Edward Wrigley's son — William Wrigley, Sr. — decided to go into the soap business, which in the 1860s was becoming what we would call "consumer-oriented." In Philadelphia in 1870, he founded the Wrigley Manufacturing Company which made Wrigley's Scouring Soap.

The young William, then nine, could hardly wait to plunge into the adult world. When he was only thirteen, he left school to work in his father's factory, learned the business, and then became the Wrigley traveling salesman in the eastern states. In 1891, at age twenty-nine with a wife and daughter, he set up in Chicago as his father's distributor for the growing Midwest market.

It was a one-man operation. William Junior was sales manager, salesman, bookkeeper, packer, and, above all, promoter. It was his own idea to offer a premium for every box of soap a retailer bought. One of his early premiums, the newfangled packaged baking powder, was in such demand that the following year he switched from selling soap to baking powder.

That left him without a premium to offer. It so happened that society was becoming slightly more genteel, and though hotels did not throw out their brass spittoons for years, the chawing of tobacco and spitting in public were no longer considered gentlemanly. One tobacco substitute was a primitive chewing gum made from spruce gum and paraffin, which permitted chewing but required no spitting. Wrigley decided to offer this socially beneficial commodity as a premium to his baking powder retailers in 1892.

Lucky William Wrigley! He hit on the chewing gum idea at the very time when chicle, the resinous latex produced from the Central American sapodilla [plum] tree, was being imported for use in the growing rubber industry.

Chicle, unlike gums from spruce or tamarack, was so naturally sweet that it had to be processed to make it tolerable. Gathered from trees tapped in the spring by natives hired by Wrigley's agents, the sap was dried and then boiled in large vats. Wrigley was no chemist, but he guessed and guessed right that a

chewing gum with chicle as the main ingredient would hit a sweet tooth the world did not even know it had.

By then, his premiums, which had been used to sweeten his sales of baking powder and soap, included not only chewing gum but showcases, toilet articles, knives, cutlery, and guns and fishing tackle. But chewing gum was the winner, and here he was giving the stuff away!

He soon changed that by going into business as a manufacturer of chewing gum. He turned the United States into a nation of chompers with Wrigley's Vassar and Lotta, then Spearmint with the familiar broad arrow, and the seductive Juicy Fruit. Double Mint was introduced in 1914.

Success came slowly until 1907, which ironically was a depression year. It may have been the $250,000 that he poured into his ad campaigns that year, but Wrigley himself credited bad times. "People chaw harder when they're sad," he said, salting away his vast profits.

His obituary in *The New York Times* on January 26, 1932, recorded what the paper called his simple philosophy and outlook. "What I have accomplished has been done because the work has kept me happy. And I've enjoyed every moment of the battle. I'm not much more successful than the average person. I have more money, but I've only three suits of clothes, a place to sleep, three square meals a day and a bathtub. Maybe it's a little better bathtub." ♦

Left: *A 1927 advertisement for Wrigley's Double Mint.* Right: *A 1918 advertisement for Wrigley's gums that appeared in* The Saturday Evening Post.

FULLER

Alfred Carl Fuller

"I had no qualifications, but I could sell brushes."

Radio comic Fred Allen put it this way: "Edison gave us the electric light, Marconi gave us the wireless, and Fuller gave us the brush."

That's only partly true. The only brush Fuller ever gave away was the Handy Brush, customarily handed out at the door as a gift. Everything else had its selling price.

In the years between 1906 and 1968, when he sold the company, Alfred Carl Fuller manufactured and sold more than 125 different kinds of brushes, as well as waxes, soap, and personal cosmetics, all of which were carried around door to door by his army of salesmen (first dubbed Fuller Brush Men in a 1922 article in the *Saturday Evening Post*) and saleswomen (who first came on the scene in 1948 and were promptly dubbed Fuller's Fillies by *Time* magazine).

Fuller's career in brushes began on January 7, 1905, when he got a job as salesman with the Somerville Brush and Mop Company of Somerville, Massachusetts. He was just six days short of his twentieth birthday, and the folks back home must have been wondering when if ever he was going to settle down and make something of his life.

He was born the eleventh of the twelve children of Leander and Phebe Fuller, whose family had been farming the same one-hundred-acre tract of land in King's County, Nova Scotia, for more than a century. The Fullers had originally come to the New World on the *Mayflower* to settle in the Connecticut Valley, and it was Alfred Carl Fuller's great-great-great-grandfather who took up the Nova Scotia crown grant in 1761. In those days, it was simply a move from one part of the British colonies to another.

By the time young Fuller decided to try his luck across the border, he was a fifth-generation Canadian and a raw gangling farm boy, well over six feet tall and powerful. His education, however, had stopped well short of the seventh grade. He picked Boston because two of his brothers had also made the break, and he had two married sisters living there.

Fuller got fired from his first job as a streetcar conductor because he had passed himself off as twenty-one. He got fired from his second job as a groom because he forgot to currycomb the owner's favorite mount. He got fired from his third job because he found it boring to drive a delivery wagon.

In desperation, he managed to get a selling job with the Somerville Brush and Mop Company, but only because one of his brothers had started the firm, then moved west and recommended him to the new owner.

"I took the sample case," Fuller recalled in the *New Yorker* in 1950, "with

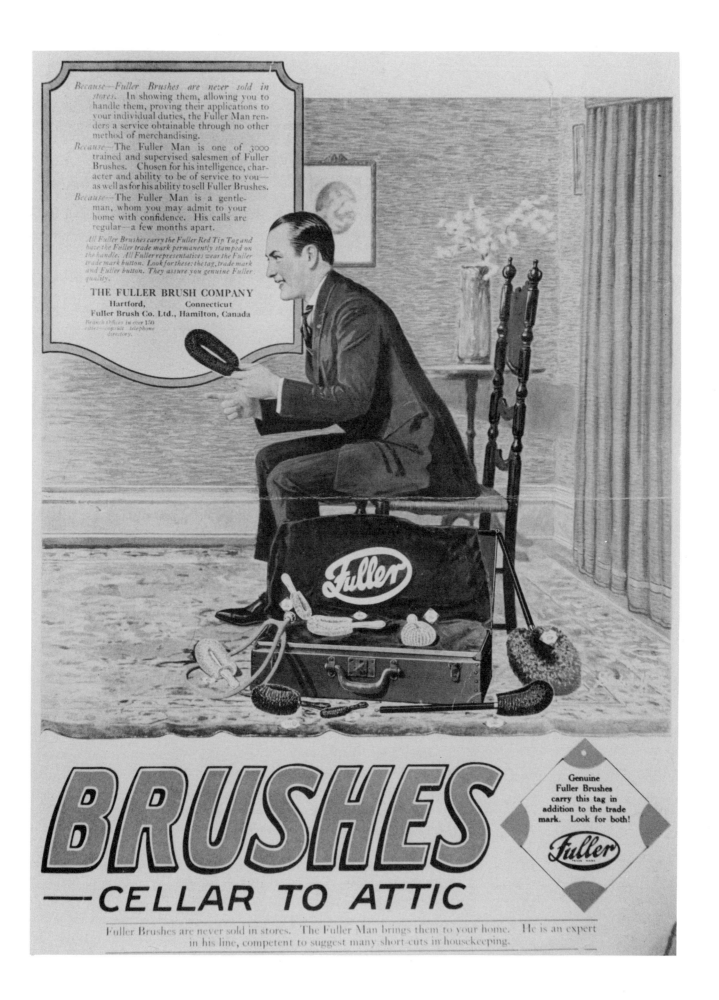

brushes in it, and made a sale on my second call. I even sold a brush without knowing what it was for. I told the woman it was our radiator brush, and she right away went over to the radiator and started brushing between the flanges." Fuller did not invent the radiator brush, he just invented the name in order to clinch the sale.

He put it this way, "I had no qualifications, but I could sell brushes." In fact, he could sell brushes that did not even exist, as he found out when people started asking him for brushes for certain purposes. He brought all these ideas back to Somerville, but the boss would not listen.

So one day, while Fuller was going over the items in his sample case, he took a closer look at them and came to the conclusion that "any product that can be made as cheaply as those wire-twisted brushes, and can be sold that easily, must be a pretty good thing."

Already he had saved up $375. Ignoring his brother's advice not to risk his own money, he left his job at Somerville, put out $80 on materials, and set up business in the basement of his sister's house. The workshop was a twelve-foot bench stretching between the furnace and the coal bin, equipped with a hand-operated wire-twisting machine he had made himself. His materials were spools of soft galvanized wire, imported hog bristles, horsehair, and hanks of "istle," a durable fiber from Tapico, Mexico.

He turned out his brushes at night, limiting himself to a range of seven types: scrub, bottle, clothes, bath, hand, and floor. Oh yes, and radiator. But he never made more than enough to fill the orders he took in during his door-to-door selling in the daytime.

As his brushes caught on, he added a radically new curved handle to the bath brush and designed a hook-shaped brush for cleaning spittoons, a clothes whisk with two backs to give double the life, a sweeper with non-scratching ends, and a nail brush that could fit into the palm of the hand.

He soon outgrew his sister's basement. For the first few months he did most of his selling in Boston. Then one day he took the train to Hartford, Connecticut, and liked the place so much he rented a shed for eleven dollars a month and moved all his equipment there.

There is a tattered bankbook still in existence showing the Fuller balance on October 10, 1908, at $74.79. By July 1909, the balance was $532.76. On the strength of that, Fuller got married, hired a helper, and went on making brushes, selling door to door in the mornings, working at the bench in the afternoons.

Though all the brushes were made by Fuller, they were not yet Fuller brushes. He called his new company the Capital Brush Company, but he had not been operating under that name for more than a year when he heard that there was already a Capital Brush Company in the country, and it was making threatening legal noises.

Fuller simply turned to the name he liked best anyway and in 1910 formed the Fuller Brush Company. By then, he was employing twenty-five salesmen and six brushmakers, and he was selling twenty thousand dollars' worth of brushes a year.

The trick that turned Fuller from a small-scale brush manufacturer into a national institution was a simple ad in the *Syracuse Post-Standard* in 1911: *Agents wanted for new line of brushes covering all household needs.*

"I'd forgotten about the ad," Fuller recalled late in life, "until I started getting replies." There were so many hundreds that he had to hire a secretary to answer them all. (That secretary stayed on to become assistant treasurer by 1948.)

"That little ad," he said, when he was selling to more than 20 million families on the continent, "changed the whole thing from a one-man effort to a company operating nationwide."

In 1918, Fuller became an American citizen.

He gave his customers the brush all right, but he always admitted that the tidal wave of jokes about the Fuller Brush Man was worth a million dollars in free advertising. By the time he retired as president in 1943, his company was the biggest of its kind in the world.

Before he bowed out, he wrote and published his own book on salesmanship. Typically, it was titled *A Foot in the Door.* ◆

Fuller sold his wares door to door in the morning and made brushes in the afternoon.

ELIZABETH ARDEN

Elizabeth Arden

◆

*"A little paint,
discreetly applied,
could enhance a
lady's appearance."*

◆

Elizabeth Arden was and is a work of romantic fiction. It is a name that has meant escape, if not escapism, into a dreamworld of feminine beauty.

A typical day in the Arden salon included massage, exercise, steam bath, shampoo and set, restyling, manicure, pedicure, facial, make-up, and lunch — all in an eighteenth-century French or Regency setting, dominated by the famous Elizabeth Arden pink. She wore pink, tinted her hair pink, and had her Fifth Avenue apartment, where she lived for the last thirty years of her life, decorated in shades of pink.

Yet the name itself, perfect though it sounds for the purpose, was not the outcome of any brainstorming session by corporate image makers. It was one woman's instant decision, based not on any magic in the syllables, but on simple shortage of ready cash.

The woman was Florence Nightingale Graham, whose father raised vegetables on a two-hundred-acre farm he leased just outside Woodbridge, Ontario, about twenty miles northwest of Toronto. William Graham, a Scot, who had met his wife, Susan Todd, in Cornwall, eloped with her to Canada and set himself up sometime in the 1880s as a farmer and breeder of horses. Susan Graham died soon after presenting her husband with the last of five children, and Florence at five years old was left with her three sisters and brother in a condition of near poverty. She did, however, later recall that her father clung to his horses and remembered that he used to harness his aging thoroughbreds to the wagon that carried his produce to market.

Florence Graham did her share, first on the farm, then at various jobs. While still in her teens, she drifted from one job to another: apprentice nurse, bank clerk, pieceworker in a truss factory, part-time in a real estate office and for a dentist. Finally in 1908 she turned up in New York, where her brother William found her a place as a stenographer and bookkeeper. Her birthdate is said to be December 31, 1884, so she was not yet 24.

She worked diligently for her new employer for all of ten days before she discovered her own escape into the world of beauty by taking a clerking job at a salon on Fifth Avenue, the New York branch of a London, England, cosmetics firm owned by Eleanor Adair, a pioneer in modern cosmetics.

She was just in time to meet the future head-on.

In those days, no respectable woman would be seen using rouge or lipstick, which were the mark of women of easy virtue. The respectable did their alluring best with a puff of talcum powder, the scent of rose water, a touch of lightly colored glycerin. But women were also beginning to sniff the new liberating air, and they wanted to ride bicycles, smoke, and find daring new ways to adorn themselves.

The Eleanor Adair salons were among the first to give facials and massage and to experiment with new formulas for face creams and lotions.

By her early thirties, Florence Graham had knocked around the world enough to know that the way to wealth was to work for yourself, not for a wage. So after less than two years at Adair's, she went into business in 1909 with an established beautician, Elizabeth Hubbard, in a salon at 506 Fifth Avenue. The note in *Vogue* read, "Mrs. Hubbard has opened a beautifully appointed salon, serving women socially prominent in the Metropolis and outskirts, offering Grecian preparations, Daphne skin tonic and muscle oils, at $2.00 per treatment."

A year later they parted company, or rather Mrs. Hubbard moved to larger premises, leaving Florence Graham with two small rooms on the second floor and a sign in the window that read Elizabeth Hubbard.

After paying the seventy dollars for a month's rent, Florence Graham had only a few dollars left, but she was determined to make her own way. Most of the money went for yards and yards of pink ribbon and bows, her first trademark, with which she festooned the entire salon. Then came the choice of name. With little ready cash to pay a sign painter, she decided to leave the name Elizabeth and replace only the Hubbard.

Since her own name, Graham, she thought too ordinary for her image, she borrowed part of the title of Tennyson's "Enoch Arden," which was not only a favorite poem of hers, but also a popular success. So Elizabeth Arden she became.

For a while she was almost a split personality. She was known as "Mrs." Graham, since business people tended to place more reliance in a married woman than a single woman; but when clients came in asking for "Miss Arden," she usually told them that "Miss Arden" was away on business.

Her salon was a success almost from the start, partly because she made an ingenious deal with the seven Ogilvie sisters who ran a millinery shop in association with a scalp treatment salon. Soon Ogilvie clients were being referred to Miss Arden's fashionable salon, while Miss Arden's clients were being confidentially told of the exciting hats and millinery to be found at the Ogilvie's.

At the same time, Florence Graham plunged into a study of creams and lotions, since fashion was always changing. In 1912, *Vogue* suggested that "a little paint, discreetly applied, could enhance a lady's appearance," and Florence wanted to be ready with her own palette of colors. In January 1915, after a wartime trip to Europe, where she explored all the salons and picked up samples of mascara, eye shadow, perfumes, and new creams, she made an agreement with A. Fabian Swanson, a partner in Stillwell & Gladding, analytical chemists, to synthesize creams and perfumes for her.

"The strain of social life is enormous; its call upon the vital energies severe." The Elizabeth Arden Treatment, offered in this 1922 advertisement, was "the much-needed antidote."

Left: *Elizabeth Arden's leg make-up was promoted in this 1946 advertisement.* Right: *Pink violet was the color to wear according to this 1958 advertisement, which appeared in* Harper's Bazaar.

That year, she married Thomas Jenkins Lewis, a silk wholesaler and merchandising genius, who managed the mercantile side of her empire until their divorce, when he promptly went to work for her greatest rival, Helena Rubinstein.

By then, business had soared from $20,000 a year in 1920 to $4 million in 1930, and the Elizabeth Arden name was found on salons wherever society congregated, whether in North America or Europe. When she died in 1966, she was the sole owner of a company with annual sales of $60 million. Not even her husband had been allowed to buy a single share of stock.

As Mrs. Elizabeth N. Graham, she became one of America's leading racehorse owners. In 1947 her Maine Chance Stables won more races than any other in the United States, and when she made the cover of *Time* magazine in 1946, it was as a horsewoman, not as a cosmetician.

Still, people used to say she treated her women clients like horses and her horses like women, even to massage and conditioning. On both, she kept a very tight rein. ◆

KRESGE

As an individual, Sebastian Spering Kresge was a tightwad. But as a public figure, he gave away millions of dollars.

He wore his shoes until the soles got so thin he had to line them with cardboard. He wore cheap, plain suits and only threw them out when they were threadbare.

Once in the mid-1920s, this multimillionaire owner of a company capitalized at $100 million, living in a two-floor apartment on New York's Park Avenue, noticed that his valet pressed his suits after every wearing.

"Don't press them so often," he ordered, "and they'll last longer."

He neither drank nor smoked, because it wasted money, and he never played cards because it wasted time. In his mid-fifties, friends persuaded him to take up golf, but he wasted so much time chasing lost balls "because they cost so much," that nobody would play with him after the first three rounds.

Yet at that same time, he was establishing the Kresge Foundation, with an initial grant of $1.5 million, and by the time of his death in 1966 at the age of ninety-nine, he had given away a total of $63 million, which had appreciated to $170 million. The income went to building facilities at dozens of universities and colleges, children's homes, churches, and temperance organizations such as the Anti-Saloon League.

He always swore he would never give a dollar to a church whose pastor either smoked or drank, but probably he had no way of monitoring the habits of university professors and presidents.

He was clearly a moralistic old skinflint.

But S.S. Kresge saw it differently. "I think I was successful," he once said, "because I saved and worked hard. When you start at the bottom, and work hard eighteen hours a day, and learn how to scrape, everything becomes easy."

For him, that was the truth. He worked like a dog from his earliest years and only began to ease off when he was well into his eighties.

Kresge was the great-great-grandson of a Swiss farmer who immigrated to the United States in 1740 to begin homesteading not far from Scranton, Pennsylvania, on a farm that remained in the Kresge family for four generations. Sebastian Spering Kresge was born there in 1867 and began pitching in with the farm chores at the age of five, attending rural schools in his spare time. When he was in his teens, with his mind set on taking a business course at the Eastman Business College, he struck an unusual bargain with his father.

"Pay for my way through business college," he said, "and I'll give you all

Sebastian Spering Kresge

He liked the idea of the cash transaction because "it encouraged thrift."

---

my earnings until I'm twenty-one."

The earnings he was referring to came from the twenty-two dollars a month he made partly from teaching at a local school and partly from his job as deliveryman and clerk in a Scranton grocery store. His own pocket money he made from beekeeping, a hobby he maintained all his life.

"Bees," he used to say, "always remind me that hard work, thrift, sobriety, and an earnest struggle to live an upright Christian life, are the first rungs on the ladder of success."

Ridiculous sentiment? Perhaps, but Kresge, for all his miserliness, lived by that creed as he amassed a nickel-and-dime fortune.

The way led from that Scranton grocery store to bookkeeping in a Scranton hardware store, to a five-year stint as traveling salesman for a Wilkes-Barre tinware manufacturer. He got that job, by the way, because the owner happened to hear that young Kresge had bought up a number of rusted cast-iron stoves, repaired and polished them, and sold them at a handsome profit.

In his commercial travels through New England and the north-central states, Kresge one day made a sales pitch to none other than Frank W. Woolworth, the new dime-store merchandising phenomenon, and was stunned to get an order for nineteen gross of articles, one gross for each of Woolworth's

These two advertisements both appeared in December 1920 in The Saturday Evening Post.

nineteen stores.

It was the biggest order Kresge had ever seen, and he was impressed by the possibilities in the chain-store industry, then an American novelty. He liked the idea because it was based on the cash transaction and "it encouraged thrift." In his clerking days, he had noticed that customers tended to buy more than they could afford, simply because the merchant gave credit at no interest, often being forced to borrow to pay his own suppliers' bills.

That gave him his direction. Since penny-pinching was second nature to him, Kresge by 1897 had saved eight thousand dollars. With that money he joined with John G. McCrory, owner of a tiny chain of six bazaar stores and two five-and-ten-cent stores, to set up two new stores in Memphis and Detroit.

Kresge became the sole owner of the Detroit store in 1899, which is the year usually given as the start of the Kresge chain.

There was, however, a brief corporate detour. In 1900 Kresge joined with his brother-in-law, Charles J. Wilson, to form Kresge & Wilson, which operated stores in Detroit and Port Huron, Michigan. Within seven years, business was so good that Kresge was able to buy out Wilson's half interest.

In 1907 he launched his own chain, with the name S.S. Kresge for the first time proudly displayed over the red-front stores in Toledo, Pittsburgh, Cleveland, Columbus, Indianapolis, and Chicago. That was the real beginning of the Kresge nickel-and-dime empire, which he headed — either as president or as chairman of the board — until a few months before his death.

He was less successful with his chain of wives. His *New York Times* obituary, which ran on the front page and continued for three full columns inside the paper, said: "A pinch-purse attitude was a part in the breakup of two of his marriages." His first wife, to whom he was married for more than twenty-five years, complained of his stinginess in personal matters. His second wife, after less than four years of marriage, "divorced him in 1928 after a series of charges and countercharges that made Mr. Kresge's name a headline word in New York."

It was she who insisted that he move from Detroit to the New York apartment and tried to interest him in opera, ballet, and society. His third and final marriage was more tranquil.

"Paradoxically," said the *Times*, "Mr. Kresge was open handed in his divorce settlements . . . . A generous spirit also marked Mr. Kresge's dealings with his associates and employees."

Yet he never, as the *Times* so nicely phrased it, "attained proficiency in the art of spending money on himself."

"If we could only get along," he once said, "without useless things." He doubtless forgot that he was one of the most energetic suppliers of modern consumerism. ◆

This store in Hazleton, Pennsylvania, was number 143 in the Kresge chain. The photograph was taken January 31, 1936.

Index

Photo Credits

Part I: Branding the American Home

Baker: courtesy General Foods Archives, 11, 12, 14 right; Hard Times Collectibles, Box 5222, Santa Cruz, CA 95062, 13, 14 left.

Colgate: courtesy The Colgate Palmolive Company, 15, 16 bottom, 17 left; Hard Times Collectibles, Box 5222, Santa Cruz, CA 95062, 16 top, 17 right.

Harper: courtesy Harper and Row Publishers, Inc., 18, 19 right, 20; Hard Times Collectibles, Box 5222, Santa Cruz, CA 95062, 19 left.

Levi Strauss: courtesy Levi Strauss and Company, 21–25.

Singer: courtesy The Singer Company, 26–28.

Borden: courtesy Borden, Inc., 29, 31, 32; Hard Times Collectibles, Box 5222, Santa Cruz, CA 95062, 30.

Steinway: courtesy Steinway and Sons, 33, 34 bottom, 35, 36; Hard Times Collectibles, Box 5222, Santa Cruz, CA 95062, 34 top.

Butterick: courtesy The Butterick Company, Inc., 37–39.

Campbell: courtesy The Campbell Soup Company, 40–42.

Horlick: courtesy The Racine County Historical Society and Museum, Inc., 43, 45; Hard Times Collectibles, Box 5222, Santa Cruz, CA 95062, 44, 46.

Swift: Hard Times Collectibles, Box 5222, Santa Cruz, CA 95062, 48; The Chicago Historical Society, (negative number IChi-142-50) 49.

Heinz: courtesy H.J. Heinz Company, 50, 51 bottom, 52, 53 bottom; Hard Times Collectibles, Box 5222, Santa Cruz, CA 95062, 51 top, 53 top.

Bissell: courtesy Bissell, Inc., 54, 55, 56 top right; Hard Times Collectibles, Box 5222, Santa Cruz, CA 95062, 56.

Hires: courtesy The Proctor and Gamble Company, 57–59; Hard Times Collectibles, Box 5222, Santa Cruz, CA 95062, 60.

Gillette: courtesy The Gillette Company, 61, 62, 63 bottom; Hard Times Collectibles, Box 5222, Santa Cruz, CA 95062, 63 top.

Kraft: courtesy Kraft, Inc., 64–67.

Maytag: courtesy The Maytag Company, 67–70.

Schick: Wide World Photos, 71; courtesy The D'Arcy Collection of the Communications Library of the University of Illinois at Urbana-Champaign, 72–74.

Part II: The Young Scientists

Bausch & Lomb: courtesy Bausch & Lomb, 76–78.

Westinghouse: courtesy The Westinghouse Electric Corporation, 79, 80, 82 right; Hard Times Collectibles, Box 5222, Santa Cruz, CA 95062, 81, 82 left.

Libbey-Owens-Ford: courtesy Libbey-Owens-Ford Company, 83, 84, 85, 87, 88 left, 89; Hard Times Collectibles, Box 5222, Santa Cruz, CA 95062, 86, 88 right.

Johnson & Johnson: courtesy Johnson & Johnson, 90, 91, 93, Hard Times Collectibles, Box 5222, Santa Cruz, CA 95062, 92.

Dow: courtesy The Dow Chemical Company, 94–96.

Eastman: Culver Pictures, 97, 100; Hard Times Collectibles, Box 5222, Santa Cruz, CA 95062, 98, 99.

Ferris: courtesy the collection of Richard Flint, Baltimore, MD, 102 left, 103; The Chicago Historical Society, 102 right.

Part III: Machinists and Tinkerers

McCormick: courtesy Navistar International Corporation, 106, 107.

Deere: courtesy Deere and Company, 108–111.

Bigelow: courtesy Bigelow-Sanford, Inc., 113, 114 left; Hard Times Collectibles, Box 5222, Santa Cruz, CA 95062, 114 right.

Yale: courtesy Scovill/Yale Security Group, 116, 117.

Otis: courtesy The Otis Elevator Company, 118–120.

Crane: courtesy The Crane Company, 121–123.

Armstrong: courtesy Armstrong World Industries, Inc., 124–126, 127 left; Hard Times Collectibles, Box 5222, Santa Cruz, CA 95062, 127 right.

Remington and Underwood: Hard Times Collectibles, Box 5222, Santa Cruz, CA 95062, 130; courtesy The D'Arcy Collection of the Communications Library of the University of Illinois at Urbana-Champaign, 131, 132.

Pitney-Bowes: courtesy Pitney-Bowes, 133–135.

Part IV: Gunsmiths

Remington: courtesy The Remington Arms Company, Inc., 137, 138; Hard Times Collectibles, Box 5222, Santa Cruz, CA 95062, 139.

Colt: bequest of Elizabeth Hart Jarvis Colt, The Wadsworth Atheneum, Hartford, CT, 140; courtesy The Connecticut State Library, 141 top, 142 right; Kansas State Historical Society, Topeka, KS, 141 middle; Hard Times Collectibles, Box 5222, Santa Cruz, CA 95062, 141 bottom; from *COLT, An American Legend*, by R.L. Wilson (New York: Abbeville Press), 142 left.

Smith & Wesson: courtesy the collection of Roy Jinks, 143–146.

Winchester: courtesy The Buffalo Bill Historical Center-Winchester Arms Museum, 147, 148 top and bottom left, 149 top; Hard Times Collectibles, Box 5222, Santa Cruz, CA 95062, 148 bottom right, 149 bottom.

Part V: Auto Mechanics and Expressmen

Goodyear to Seiberling: courtesy The Goodyear Tire and Rubber Company, 152, 153, 154 top, 155, 156; Hard Times Collectibles, Box 5222, Santa Cruz, CA 95062, 154 bottom.

Studebaker: courtesy Studebaker National Museum, Inc., 157–159.

Pullman: courtesy Pullman Research Group, 160–162.

Buick: courtesy Buick Motor Division, General Motors Corporation, 163–165.

Olds: courtesy the R.E. Olds Museum Association, Inc., 166, 167; Hard Times Collectibles, Box 5222, Santa Cruz, CA 95062, 168.

Packard: The National Automotive History Collection, Detroit Public Library, 169, 171 top; courtesy Dragonwyck Publishing, Contoocook, NH, 170 bottom right; Hard Times Collectibles, Box 5222, Santa Cruz, CA 95062, 170; courtesy The Henry Ford Museum, (negative number B-1865) 171 bottom.

Ford: from the collections of The Henry Ford Museum and Greenfield Village, (photograph by Bachrach, negative number 84429) 172, (negative number 987) 173 top, (negative number 5252) 173 middle, (negative number D-750) 174; Hard Times Collectibles, Box 5222, Santa Cruz, CA 95062, 173 bottom.

Chevrolet: courtesy Chevrolet Motor Division, General Motors Corporation, 175–177.

Chrysler: courtesy The Chrysler Historical Collection, 178–180.

Part VI: Hucksters, Traders, and Merchants

Tiffany: courtesy Tiffany and Company, 182, 183 right; Culver Pictures, 183 left.

Pabst: The Milwaukee County Historical Society, (negative number 6001) 184, (negative number 9730) 185 top, (negative number 1548) 185 bottom; Hard Times Collectibles, Box 5222, Santa Cruz, CA 95062, 186.

Saks: New York Times Pictures, 187; courtesy The D'Arcy Collection of the Communications Library of the University of Illinois at Urbana-Champaign, 188, 189 left; courtesy Saks Fifth Avenue, 189 right.

Reynolds: courtesy R.J. Reynolds Tobacco Company, 190–192.

Spalding: The National Baseball Library, Cooperstown, NY, 193–195.

J. Walter Thompson: courtesy J. Walter Thompson Company, 196–198.

Woolworth: courtesy F.W. Woolworth Company, 199–201.

Sears: courtesy Sears, Roebuck and Company, 202–205.

Dow Jones: courtesy Dow Jones and Company, Inc., 206, 208.

Wrigley: courtesy The William Wrigley, Jr., Company, 209–211.

Fuller: courtesy The Fuller Brush Company, 212–215.

Elizabeth Arden: courtesy Elizabeth Arden, 216; courtesy The D'Arcy Collection of the Communications Library of the University of Illinois at Urbana-Champaign, 217, 218.

Kresge: courtesy K-Mart Corporation, 219, 221; courtesy The D'Arcy Collection of the Communications Library of the University of Illinois at Urbana-Champaign, 220.